LISTEN UP
OR **LOSE OUT**

Robert Bolton and
Dorothy Grover Bolton

LISTEN UP OR LOSE OUT

How to Avoid Miscommunication,
Improve Relationships, and
Get More Done Faster

⁴AMACOM
AMERICAN MANAGEMENT ASSOCIATION
New York • Atlanta • Brussels • Chicago • Mexico City • San Francisco
Shanghai • Tokyo • Toronto • Washington, D.C.

Bulk discounts available. For details visit:
www.amacombooks.org/go/specialsales
Or contact special sales:
Phone: 800-250-5308
E-mail: specialsls@amanet.org
View all the AMACOM titles at: www.amacombooks.org
American Management Association: www.amanet.org

This publication is designed to provide accurate and authoritative information in regard to the subject matter covered. It is sold with the understanding that the publisher is not engaged in rendering legal, accounting, or other professional service. If legal advice or other expert assistance is required, the services of a competent professional person should be sought.

Library of Congress Cataloging-in-Publication Data

Names: Bolton, Robert, 1929- author. | Bolton, Dorothy Grover, author.
Title: Listen up or lose out : how to avoid miscommunication, improve
    relationships, and get more done faster / by Robert Bolton and Dorothy
    Grover Bolton.
Description: New York : AMACOM, [2018] | Includes index.
Identifiers: LCCN 2017030627 (print) | LCCN 2017040987 (ebook) | ISBN
    9780814432020 (ebook) | ISBN 9780814432013 (pbk.)
Subjects: LCSH: Communication in management. | Business communication. |
    Interpersonal communication. | Listening.
Classification: LCC HD30.3 (ebook) | LCC HD30.3 .B656 2018 (print) | DDC
    658.4/5--dc23
LC record available at https://lccn.loc.gov/2017030627

ABOUT AMA
American Management Association (www.amanet.org) is a world leader in talent development, advancing the skills of individuals to drive business success. Our mission is to support the goals of individuals and organizations through a complete range of products and services, including classroom and virtual seminars, webcasts, webinars, podcasts, conferences, corporate and government solutions, business books, and research. AMA's approach to improving performance combines experiential learning—learning through doing—with opportunities for ongoing professional growth at every step of one's career journey.

10 9 8 7 6 5 4 3 2 1

To Our Children

William Gabor

Robert Gabor

Hallie Hawkins

James Bolton

Betsy Bolton

Douglas Bolton

Kristin Bolton

A good listener is not only popular everywhere,
but after a while he knows something.
—WILSON MIZNER

CONTENTS

INTRODUCTION

What This Book Will Do for You

> Listening is not only the skill that lets you into the other person's world; it is also the single most powerful move you can make to keep the conversation constructive.
>
> −DOUGLAS STONE, BRUCE PATTON, AND SHEILA HEEN

L IKE MOST PEOPLE at work and in their personal lives, you probably spend many hours a day conversing with others informally or in meetings, face-to-face interactions, telephone calls, and so forth. These conversations can either strengthen or weaken work and other interpersonal relationships, including ties to friends and loved ones. As consultant Susan Scott notes, "[O]ur work, our relationships, our very lives succeed or fail . . . one conversation at a time."[1]

When people converse, they generally underestimate the importance of listening. They tend to be more concerned about talking than about how well they listen. As they anticipate significant conversations, they worry about what they're going to say, not whether they'll get what the other person is communicating.

Unquestionably, the ability to speak effectively is a key asset. But the undramatic skill of listening is no less important.[2] As Thoreau pointed out, "It takes two to speak the truth—one to speak and the other to hear."[3]

Listening lies at the heart of just about everything we do with people. The average person spends about 50 percent more time listening than speaking.[4] In fact, the typical person listens about a book's worth a day.[5] Regrettably, as you'll see in Chapter 3, the typical listener actually misses more of a message than she takes in.

When listening is ineffective, meaningful conversation is unlikely. And poor listening can be costly. It's frustrating to think of the information that went in one ear and out the other, the opportunities that were lost, and the relationships that were strained or broken because we missed the message.

Research-Based Listening Skills

Fortunately, social scientists have discovered methods that greatly improve listening, as well as the kinds of behaviors that militate against it. Rather than spinning ivory tower theories, they observed people's conversations to learn which listening behaviors are effective and which ones are detrimental. Initially, they studied interactions between therapists and patients. Soon they turned the research spotlight on conversations between teachers and students, husbands and wives, parents and children. Some investigators found ways to observe how people listen in the course of business meetings, sales transactions, and the like. Newly invented recording devices secured an accurate account of every word in a conversation.[6]

Here's how psychologist Carl Rogers, one of the preeminent pioneers in researching listening, described some of those moments:

> I cannot exaggerate the excitement of our learnings as we clustered about the machine that enabled us to listen to ourselves, playing over and over some puzzling point at which the interview clearly went wrong, or those moments in which the client moved significantly forward. . . . We discovered that we could pinpoint which response of the therapist caused a fruitful flow of significant expression to become superficial and unprofitable. Likewise we were able to spot the remark that turned a client's dull and desultory talk into a focused exploration.[7]

Researchers repeatedly listened to their recordings. They pored over transcripts of the interactions. When motion picture and video technology became available, the investigators were able to document changes in a speaker's posture, gestures, facial expression, and eye contact in response to the way their conversational partner was listening. Some of the analyses were incredibly thorough—one description of a five-minute transaction filled an entire book.[8] Another researcher spent *four to five hours a day for a year and a half* studying a very brief filmed segment of a family's dinnertime conversation, *wearing out 130 tapes of the recorded sequence.*[9]

These kinds of painstaking research revealed ways of listening that encourage speakers to open up and talk frankly. Behavioral scientists found that those same ways of tuning in to others enhanced the listener's ability to understand and retain what was said. Furthermore, good listening was found to improve the speaker's fluency. Thus, good listening often initiates a virtuous cycle of greatly enhanced communication. Equally important, these improved ways of listening increase rapport between the listener and the speaker. We refer to this research-based listening as "skilled listening."

The researchers also identified a set of widely used dysfunctional "listening" habits that are likely to trigger defensiveness in the speaker, who then tends to become more guarded and to withhold useful information. (In this book, quotation marks around the word, "listener" or "listening" indicates that the person is using nonlistening behavior when it would be appropriate for her to be listening.) These listening missteps not only inhibit frank communication; they also chip away at the "listener's" relationships.

Listening had never been studied so thoroughly or so scientifically. The most significant outcome of this research was an integrated set of best listening practices that you'll learn as you read this book. Although the discoveries are several decades old, they've not been disseminated widely. And in the ensuing years, enhancements in skilled listening have made it even more effective. So, for most readers, the methods taught in this book will provide a new and much more effective way of listening. I think you'll be amazed at how this better way of listening will contribute to virtually every facet of your life. These skills will enable you to capitalize on opportunities that a poor listener would likely miss. They will reduce communication glitches, diminish the likelihood that the speaker will become defensive, get problems into the open, calm tense situations, and ultimately improve your relationships as you listen better to colleagues, customers, family, friends, and others.

Who Are We to Teach You How to Listen Better?

Robert (Bob): His ability to teach others how to listen better is enhanced by the fact that he's traveled every step of the pathway from being a poor listener to becoming a competent one. For the first three and a half decades of his life, he was shy, self-conscious about expressing himself, and a poor listener. Then, in his late thirties, a colleague recommended that he attend an interpersonal relationships course led by two social scientists. Participation in that workshop and further training equipped him to relate better to others and greatly increased his effectiveness at work. Impressed by the usefulness of the abilities he learned, he read widely in the field of interpersonal communication and earned a Ph.D. in the applied behavioral sciences.

Dorothy (Dot): Her experience was a different story. From her early years, she naturally gravitated toward people. She was president of her class throughout her secondary education, the leader of the marching band in high school, and, when she attended Syracuse University, International Sweetheart of Sigma Chi and waterski doubles champion in the Canadian Open. She also toured the United States, Europe, and North Africa as a performer. A few years later, she earned an Ed.M. and served as a school psychologist for several years while raising three children.

After our marriage, we jointly acquired intensive training in psychology and interpersonal communication, and founded Ridge Training, where we developed a network of forty-five to fifty trainers to teach communication skills for graduate credit in numerous locations in New York State (College of St. Rose), Pennsylvania (Marywood College), and Connecticut (University of Bridgeport).

A few years later, most of our clientele were Fortune 500 companies, such as Apple (vice presidents to first-line supervisors), Citibank, Goodyear, IBM (USA), IBM (Australia), JP Morgan, PepsiCo International, and many others. There were other types of clients too, such as the Japan Management Institute and Sisters of Charity, Halifax, and Nova Scotia. Soon we again had a cadre of forty-five to fifty trainers leading our various interpersonal skills workshops.

A number of clients relied on Dot's one-to-one Personalized Executive Development practice for their fast-track managers whose people skills were inadequate for success as they moved higher in the corporation.

The Importance of Listening

We've long believed that listening is the "first among equals" of what we think of as the five basic interpersonal communication skills:

1. Listening
2. Talking
3. Influencing
4. Solving problems cooperatively
5. Resolving Conflict

Robust listening is an essential part of conflict resolution and cooperative problem-solving methods. And when it comes to talking and influencing, what you learn from listening to your conversational partner can help you tailor your message to that person, so she's more interested in and more open to what you say. So when you listen well in a conversation, you position yourself to be more effective in using each of the four other major oral communication skills. Consequently, skillful listening can enhance every significant interpersonal situation you find yourself in.

Overview of the Book

Listen Up or Lose Out has five parts and one appendix. Part I contains four chapters focused on the importance of listening in the workplace and in personal life. Parts II, III, 1V, and V teach the skills of listening with applications both in one's personal life and at work.

PART I: WHY IMPROVE YOUR LISTENING?

- *Chapter 1: Quality Listening Enhances Work Relationships.* This chapter documents the importance of quality relationships in virtually all facets of our lives, with an emphasis on work life. Quality listening helps people develop and maintain relationships.
- *Chapter 2: Listening Well Is Good Business.* After noting the importance successful corporate leaders place on listening and the huge amounts of time that many of them devote to it, this chapter documents the fact that the average person in the workplace is a poor listener and is unaware of how deficient her listening is.
- *Chapter 3: A Good Listener Is a Rare Find.* Listening has become an essential skill as jobs have moved rapidly from requiring little to no interaction among the workers to regular and important interactions with coworkers.
- *Chapter 4: Quality Listening Strengthens Personal Relationships.* This chapter discusses the importance of three types of personal relationships: friendship, marriage, and parent–child. The contribution that empathic listening makes to strengthening and enhancing these crucial ties is stressed.

PART II: DO'S AND DON'TS OF GREAT LISTENING

- *Chapter 5: Trouble Spots in the Talking–Listening Process.* Trouble spots in the talking–listening process make it vulnerable to miscommunication. Language is imprecise. Talking conveys only an approximation of what we mean. Listening is educated guesswork. And we're seldom aware that miscommunication has occurred until faced with the resulting damage.

- *Chapter 6: Identifying Your Listening Missteps.* People often turn what should be a listening situation into a speaking situation. And when they reply instead of listening, they often use one of the communication missteps explained in this chapter.

- *Chapter 7: Reducing Major Missteps.* This chapter describes how to identify and decrease your reliance on missteps that have been damaging your listening effectiveness. You'll learn a four step process for greatly reducing your use of your most serious missteps — one misstep at a time.

- *Chapter 8: Skill-Based Listening.* This chapter describes how ordinary listening is developed and provides an overview of what great listeners do. It teaches the skill to replace run-of-the-mill listening with skills that proficient listeners use.

- *Chapter 9: Whose Turn Is It?* Knowing when to listen and when to speak is central to making your interactions more focused and productive. Here you'll learn *the communication skill selection question,* which you can use to guide you into making good decisions about *when to listen* and *when to speak.*

- *Chapter 10: Focus Your Attention.* This chapter teaches attending and the companion skill of encouraging. Here you'll learn how to employ the body language of good listening, which is a vital part of listening in all conversations of importance to one or both people.

- *Chapter 11: Be a Great Asker.* Asking well-targeted questions can be immensely important in one's business as well as personal life. This chapter gives you five guidelines for the process of asking questions productively.

- *Chapter 12: Creating and Sequencing Productive Questions.* This chapter shows how to create effective questions and sequence them productively. How you phrase a question can have a significant impact on the usefulness of the responses you get.

PART III: REFLECTING CONTENT

- *Chapter 13: Reflective Listening: Antidote to Miscommunication.* This chapter describes what reflections are and when they're useful. It explains the inner process of reflecting and the four types of reflections.

- *Chapter 14: Paraphrase What's Important.* This chapter explains what paraphrasing is and how to do it. It describes the many benefits of using this skill.
- *Chapter 15: Listen Through the Pauses.* Here you'll find six important but little known facts about pauses. The chapter then stresses the importance of listening through the pauses and offers tips on how to learn more by listening through the pauses.

PART IV: READING AND REFLECTING OTHER PEOPLE'S FEELINGS

- *Chapter 16: Why Listen to People's Feelings?* Feelings permeate our lives to a far greater degree than many of us realize. This chapter discusses the impact of feelings, for better or worse, on our performance and satisfaction in seven important realms of our lives.
- *Chapter 17: "Read" People's Feelings.* The ability to understand the feelings of others is a key listening skill and a strong contributor to a good life. Here, you'll find ways to help you read people's feelings.
- *Chapter 18: Reflect Feelings and Meanings.* You'll learn how to put into one reflection the feelings and the content of the speaker's message. Now that you've learned the basic how-to's of listening, it's time to loosen up a bit by seeing how you can move into a more conversational mode of reflecting, one that allows your personality to shine through.

PART V: THINGS TO KEEP IN MIND

- *Chapter 19: Wrap It Up with a Summary Reflection.* The focus of this chapter is on summary reflections; the best way to assure that everyone is on the same page during and at the end of a conversation or a meeting.
- *Chapter 20: Results-Focused Listening.* This chapter provides a process for the listener to use to move the speaker through stages of exploring the problem under discussion to a transition that leads into the resolution of the problem.
- *Chapter 21: The Listening Spirit.* Undergirding all the skills taught in this book is what we call the *Spirit of Listening*. If the

skills are learned to manipulate and judge people, they will fall flat. If they're used in the spirit of trying to understand others as you treat them with respect, they will help you do your best work.

- *Chapter 22: Make Great Listening Part of Your Everyday Life.* Now that you've developed the basic knowledge and skills of great listening, the seven ideas in this chapter will help you integrate great listening into your daily life.

This book is based on intensive scientific research into the most productive ways of listening and on the forty-plus years of experience that we and our colleagues have had in using and teaching this exceedingly effective way of listening. We encourage you to develop these skills that can enhance your communication, improve your relationships, and make your daily life more productive and pleasurable. For as Plutarch noted twenty centuries ago, "Right listening is the beginning of right living."[10]

> The famous bank robber Willie Sutton was once asked why he robbed banks. He replied, "That's where the money is." The Endnotes following the Appendix note some of the sources we "looted" when writing this book.

LISTEN UP
OR **LOSE OUT**

PART I

WHY IMPROVE YOUR LISTENING?

Of all the communication skills,
listening is the earliest learned and the most frequently used.

Yet it is the least taught and the least mastered.
Although we spend more than one-half
of our communication time listening,
much of it is wasted because we listen so poorly.

—EASTWOOD ATWATER[1]

1

Quality Listening Enhances Work Relationships

Few people are successful unless a lot of other people want them to be.

—CHARLES BROWDER

L IFE IS LARGELY a matter of relating to other people. As far back as 328 BCE, Aristotle wrote, "Man is by nature a social animal." Centuries later, in 1624, English poet John Donne coined the phrase, "No man is an island"—a metaphor so telling that it reverberated through the centuries and is widely known today by schoolchildren and literature-loving adults alike. Those were more elegant ways of saying what contemporary medical and social science research has confirmed: Quality relationships are crucial to human well-being.

This chapter discusses the importance of quality relationships to one's success at work. Here we note that:

- Work organizations are clusters of collaborative relationships.
- The quality of relationships in an organization greatly impacts the organization's success.
- The quality of one's relationships affects customer retention.
- Poor work relationships can be disastrous to one's career.
- Strong work relationships boost one's career.
- Quality work relationships increase your access to useful information.

- The quality of your relationships influences the amount and value of the cooperation you receive.
- Weak ties can be unexpectedly beneficial.
- Evolution equipped the human brain to pay special attention to managing our relationships.
- Digital device overuse erodes empathy, shallows relationships, hinders learning, and hampers productivity.
- Empathic listening builds connections and enhances relationships.

Work Organizations Are Clusters of Collaborative Relationships

Most full-time employees spend a majority of their waking hours at work. The quality of their work relationships significantly impacts their sense of personal fulfillment, as well as their on-the-job effectiveness and satisfaction with their employment. These relationships are also crucial to long-term success at work. However, it's not unusual for highly task-oriented employees who've been sent to an interpersonal skills workshop or executive development program to express puzzlement or annoyance over the assumption that it's important for them to relate effectively to others at work. They're convinced that in today's streamlined organizations, it's difficult to find enough time to devote to their all-important task responsibilities. Spending time maintaining and improving work relationships seems unrealistic. One manager expressed the sentiments of many when he said, "I get paid for results, and I focus on achieving those results without worrying about the state of my relationships with coworkers. They should get it; this is a business, not a social club."

The problem with that line of thinking is that people are people—not robots. And organizations are not impersonal entities but are clusters of collaborative relationships. In fact, the word "company" derives from the French *compain*, which originally meant "*companions.*"[1] Work organizations have always been networks of relationships, and in our increasingly interconnected world, they've become much more interactive. Not long ago, 30 percent of work was collaborative and 70 percent the result of individual contribution. That figure soon reversed: 70 percent of all work became collaborative while only 30 percent (now probably less) is done individually.[2]

Good relationships improve one's performance. Researchers observed two types of groups performing motor-skill and decision-making tasks:

1. Groups of *friends*
2. Groups of *acquaintances*—people who only knew each other casually

The results were clear: On average, the groups of friends completed more than three times as many projects as the groups comprised of mere acquaintances. In decision-making tasks, groups of friends were more than 20 percent more effective than groups of acquaintances.[3] These studies parallel other research demonstrating that when it comes to decision making and productivity, good relationships make a powerful contribution.

To be successful in virtually any position in today's highly interactive organizations, one must obtain cooperation from other people and work effectively with them. So being relationally adept is an important qualification for virtually every position. And one's competence at building and maintaining mutually supportive relationships becomes even more important as one's career progresses.

The Quality of Relationships in an Organization Greatly Impacts the Organization's Success

Good relationships are a lubricant that makes the operations of an organization run smoothly. As University of Michigan professor of business administration and psychology Jane Dutton says:

> Abundant research suggests that a fundamental key to increasing energy in the workplace, and thereby increasing the effectiveness of both individuals and organizations, is the building of high-quality connections—ties between people marked by mutual regard, trust, and active engagement. A focus on high-quality connections and their energy-generating capabilities . . . can transform the energy possibilities in both people.[4]

Cathy Carmody, a change agent at Monsanto, says of former CEO Bob Shapiro that he "believes that the company's competitive advantage is how we relate to each other." And Samuel Culbert, professor of management at UCLA's Anderson Graduate School of Management, says, "No more effective management tool exists than a trusting relationship."[5]

Strong social networks facilitate learning by conveying information and knowledge, and transmitting the organization's culture. Thus, as one might expect, researchers found that high-caliber work relationships were associated with more innovative output and the likelihood that people's work will be satisfying to them. Researchers also found that when employees interact well with one another, productivity and profits increase, while absenteeism and job discontent decrease.[6] Robust interpersonal networks also reduce turnover rates, decreasing severance costs and hiring and training expenses. MIT Professor of social studies of science and technology Sherry Turkle highlights the business impact of time spent in conversation: "Studies show a link between sociability and employee productivity."[7] Good relationships also enhance creativity.[8]

For years, the employees of Radnor Partners, a large high-tech consulting firm, worked mainly from their homes, and they loved it. Then in 2004 a new CEO, who was not a fan of telecommuting, headed the company. Shelly Browning, the vice president in charge of human resources, summarized the CEO's message to the troops:

> He said, "We're a growing company. Change only happens when people collaborate. You can't collaborate as effectively at home, where you don't run into someone in the cafeteria. You don't bring them up to speed on that thing; you forget to tell them the nine other things. It slows down the rate of change. . . ." So, he said, "All our leaders are going to be in offices. . . . Your job is in an office because that's where we collaborate."

Grudgingly, people came to work in offices. Over time, however, attitudes changed. Browning says, "But over eight years [the CEO] has changed every one of our minds." The result? When everyone worked in the same location where they experienced face-to-face relationships daily, the company began to grow at five times its previous rate![9]

In the book, *Good to Great,* Jim Collins emphasizes that companies that excelled consistently were noted for having collegial relationships so strong that many lasted a lifetime. As Dick Appert of Kimberly-Clark told Collins, "I never had anyone at Kimberly-Clark in all my forty-one years say anything unkind to me. I thank God the day I was hired because I've been associated with wonderful people. Good people who respected and admired one another."[10] Here's Collins's summary of his research on high-performing companies:

> The people we interviewed from the good-to-great companies clearly loved what they did largely because they loved who they did it with.[11]

Low-quality work relationships, on the other hand, have been found to impede the transfer of knowledge, decrease employee motivation, and in numerous other ways reduce personal motivation, job satisfaction, and organizational effectiveness. Mediator Daniel Dana, writes:

> It has been estimated that over 65% of performance problems result from strained relationships between employees—not from deficits in individual employees' skill or motivation.[12]

When you couple the benefits of good work relationships with the detrimental effects of poor work relationships, the implications are dramatic. So it's not surprising that in *Businessweek's* annual survey of business schools, a major reason that Duke University's Fuqua School of Business received top ranking was that "Fuqua students are exceptionally good at collaborating." As Bill Boulding, the school's dean, put it, "To be a great leader you need to be great in a team setting, and I think that's where we get credit from employers."[13]

This is not to suggest that you should be buddy-buddy with everyone at work. But you do need to build sufficient rapport with people both inside and outside the organization to accomplish tasks effectively.

The Quality of One's Relationships Affects Customer Retention

The strength of one's relationships is also a primary determinant of customer retention. One of the nation's large service firms surveyed its customers and found to its surprise that, while technical competence was necessary, it was not the most important factor in customer retention. Clients expected the expertise: The empathy and personal concern they experienced are what made them stay.[14]

Poor Work Relationships Can Be Disastrous to One's Career

Talent that's not supported by collaboration ultimately produces limited or negative results. Researchers found that, when people are fired, it's usually because they are inept at creating and maintaining productive relationships. Researchers at the Center for Creative Leadership found that when successful executives derail their careers, it's usually due to interpersonal insensitivity rather than a lack of task competence. A Carnegie Foundation study discovered that 80 percent of workers who lost their jobs were terminated because of their inability to communicate effectively. When a person is released because of "communication problems," it's usually due to poor interpersonal relationships that have been created because of their lack of communication skills. In fact, a study of executive terminations found that only "16 percent of the discharged executives were fired because of their failure to achieve overall results." Most were terminated because they had trouble getting along with other people in the organization.[15]

Strong Work Relationships Boost One's Career

The seventy-five-year-long (and still continuing) Grant Study of 268 Harvard College men found that, above a certain level, financial success (and presumably career achievement) depends on warm relationships rather than on intelligence.

The fifty-eight men with the best scores for warm relationships were three times more likely to be in *Who's Who*. Their maximum income in 2009 dollars was an average of $243,000 a year.

By contrast, the thirty-one men with the worst scores for relationships earned considerably less than half as much—a maximum average income of $102,000 a year.

Furthermore, George Vaillant, who directed the study for more than three decades, said that the main conclusion of the research was that "warmth of relationships throughout life has the greatest positive impact on 'life satisfaction.'"

Here are three of the many ways that quality *relationships can enhance your career.*

Quality Work Relationships Increase
Your Access to Useful Information

As Woodrow Wilson wisely said, "We should not only use all the brains we have, but all that we can borrow." Extensive organizational research supports the common-sense notion that good relationships enhance the flow of accurate and useful information. Positive relationships create a climate of psychological safety in which people are more likely to open up and say what they really think.

When relationships are strained, however, communication is inhibited. People avoid one another as much as possible, and the stream of communication dwindles to a trickle. When circumstances require adversaries to interact, their communication tends to be hostile or guarded or both. When they interact with each other, the conversation usually is underproductive or counterproductive.

The Quality of Your Relationships Influences the Amount and Value of Cooperation You Receive

In terms of the internal work of organizations, relationships impact the degree of support and cooperation you get. In today's highly interdependent organizations, that can be crucial to your success. Let's say that a project you're heading requires assistance from someone in another department. If you've allowed that relationship to deteriorate, that person may understand your need for assistance perfectly well but, out of resentment, may make excuses to avoid fulfilling the request. Or, with "malicious obedience," he may find creative ways to execute your request in an unsatisfactory manner. On the other hand, when a positive relationship is in place, cooperation is the normal outcome.

Weak Ties Can Be Unexpectedly Beneficial

Relationships you have with people you don't know very well—have weak ties with—can be surprisingly beneficial. Stanford sociologist Mark Granovetter was instrumental in showing the importance of weak ties. He surveyed a number of managerial, professional, and technical workers who recently used a personal contact to obtain a job and asked:

Prior to switching employers, how often did you see the person who helped you get the new job?

- 17% replied, "Often."
- 55% replied, "Occasionally."
- 28% replied, "Rarely."

So 83 percent of the job seekers in the survey got a job based on input from people with whom they seldom or rarely interacted. Granovetter also found that:

> Usually such ties had not even been very strong when first formed. . . . Chance meetings or mutual friends operated to reactivate such ties. It is remarkable that people receive crucial information from individuals whose very existence they have forgotten.[16]

Many people don't realize how pleasant it is to treat every person along the way with interest and respect in order to build a positive relationship, however fleeting. In addition to expressing common courtesy, there may be times, as Granovetter points out, when you will benefit significantly from having extended these little civilities.

Evolution Equipped the Human Brain to Pay Special Attention to Managing Our Relationships

The eighteenth-century Irish philosopher and statesman Edmund Burke believed the human instinct for sociability is as fundamental as the instinct for self-presentation. That reality has gained increased emphasis in the scientific community in recent years. Renowned child psychiatrist Bruce Perry and award-winning science journalist Maia Szalavitz assert, "Humans evolved to be especially sensitive to social cues. In fact, the complexity in dealing with group social life is believed to be one of the key reasons our brains became so big."[17] And Matthew D. Lieberman, recipient of the American Psychological Association Distinguished Scientific Award for Early Career Contribution to Psychology, points out that evolution outfitted Homo sapiens with a *default network*—certain regions of the brain that are automatically activated when the mind is not working on something else. *The regions of the brain that are stimulated at such times are the ones that deal with managing our relationships. So, as soon as your brain has concluded the task at hand, instead of becoming idle, it works at helping you make sense of other people and yourself.* For example, Lieberman says that, when you are in a PET scanner, after performing a cognitive task, when the word "Rest" appears, you are aware that you have a bit of "idle time" before you have to engage in the boring task again. Lieberman then explains that during the so-called idle time your mind certainly wasn't doing nothing:

Instead of being at rest, your mind was highly active. If you are like most people, you thought about other people, yourself, or both. . . . In other words, *the default network supports social cognition—making sense of other people and ourselves.*

To the extent that we can characterize evolution as designing our modern brains, this is what our brains were wired for: reaching out to and interacting with others. . . . These social adaptions are central to making us the most successful species on earth. [Emphasis is ours.]

. . . . While we tend to think it is our capacity for abstract reasoning that is responsible for Homo sapiens' dominating the planet, there is increasing evidence that our dominance as a species may be attributable to our ability to think socially.

The bottom line of Lieberman's argument is that evolution:

figuratively speaking, made a big bet on the importance of developing and using our social intelligence for the overall success of the species by focusing our spare time on it.[18]

Digital Device Overuse Erodes Empathy, Shallows Relationships, Hinders Learning, and Hampers Productivity

Face-to-face conversation is increasingly being replaced by electronic communication. MIT's Sherry Turkle is probably the world's leading expert on the social and psychological impact of personal communication technology. She's very savvy about the positive uses of digital devices. As she put it, "I am not anti-technology, I am pro-conversation." However, after more than a decade of interviewing teens and college students, as well as some parents, she's very concerned about the way social media has changed the way people, especially young people, connect to one another. For example, many prefer texting to talking. Some spend most of their waking hours in virtual places. But research shows that overuse of iPhones and tablets leads to the atrophying of empathy, the erosion of relationships, and a decrease in learning, self-reflection, creativity, and productivity.

"Face-to-face communication," Turkle says, "is the most humanizing thing that we do; it's where we learn to put ourselves in the place of the other." She's convinced that much of what constitutes our humanity is threatened when we replace face-to-face conversation with electronic communication.

In a TED Talk, "Connected but alone," Turkle outlined her concern over the misuse of iPhones and tablets:

1. The communication technologies not only change what people do; they change who they are.
2. People are developing problems in relating to each other, relating to themselves, and their capacity for self-reflection.
3. People using these devices excessively "expect more from technology and less from each other" as the subtitle of one of her books put it.
4. The capacity for being alone is not being cultivated.
5. Traditional conversation has given way to mediated connection leading to the loss of valuable interpersonal skills.

Empathic Listening Builds Connections and Enhances Relationships

Few things enhance relationships more than quality listening. It is a major resource for establishing, maintaining, monitoring, and adjusting our relationships. Psychiatrist Karl Menninger, cofounder with his father of the famed Menninger Clinic and later the founder of the Winter Veterans Administration Hospital, which became the largest psychiatric training center in the world, marveled at the power of quality listening:

> Listening is a creative and magnetic thing, a creative force. The friends who listen to us are the ones we move toward, and we want to sit in their radius. When we are listened to, it creates us, makes us unfold and expand.

The quality of one's listening strongly influences how a relationship gets started, the amount of conversational chemistry that develops, and how vital the relationship becomes. When you listen attentively to another person you strengthen your ties with that person for, as John Powell wrote:

It is impossible to overemphasize the immense need humans have to be really listened to, to be taken seriously, to be understood.[19]

On the other hand, a person's inability or unwillingness to listen effectively can do untold damage to her relationships. In her decades of doing executive coaching and counseling for leaders in Fortune 500 corporations, one of the authors found that the inability or unwillingness to listen open-mindedly to other people's thoughts and feelings was usually a major issue and often was the chief complaint to be addressed by the coaching and counseling. The late best-selling business author Stephen Covey emphasized that:

The root cause of almost all people problems is the basic communication problem—people do not listen with empathy.[20]

The chapters in Parts II–VI of this book will help you enhance your relationships as you learn how to develop and use the skills of empathic listening.

Today nobody succeeds alone. If you don't have the

skills to build relationships,

you'd better win the lotto, because you'll never

thrive in any organization.

−J. TAMM AND R. LUYET[21]

2

Listening Well *Is* Good Business

No one ever listened himself out of a job.

—CALVIN COOLIDGE

ONE OF THE authors spent years doing a one-to-one program called Personalized Executive Development (PED). The program was designed for individuals who excelled at their work, were of great value to the company, and at one time were expected to be promoted well beyond their current level in the organization. However, their lack of people skills was about to bring their advancement within the company to a screeching halt.

The first step in the PED program is to gather feedback on the participant's strengths and development areas. What follows is a representative sample of development feedback given on perceived deficits in answer to the question, "If you were the coach, what would you work on to improve his/her performance?"

This guy is the world's worst listener. That's the first thing I'd work on, listening.

Peter disrupts meetings with his monopolizing. He seems not to hear what others contribute and yet feels free to jump in at any time with irrelevant input and takes much too long to say it.

You've heard the expression, 'In one ear and out the other.' Lorene is a great example of that.

I've given up trying to get through to Manoj. It's clear that he lives in his own little world to which no one has access.

I know that Joanne isn't deaf, but she sure gives a good imitation of someone who is.

Hearing what others have to say seems to be way down in Bill's priority. I avoid him whenever possible.

If you could teach Ken how to listen, it would be a gift to all of us. If not, I don't see a future for him here.

Certainly other deficits were reported in the feedback. However, we believe that it's fair to say that for every one of the participants in PED, whether man or woman, person of color or white, whether immigrants or born in the United States, an inability to listen to others was pointed out in the feedback as a major weakness that was interfering with success.

In this chapter, you'll see that:

- Listening is a more important skill than is generally realized.
- Listening has become increasingly important in the workplace.
- Quality listening is a key factor in career success.

Listening Is More Important Than Is Generally Realized

In a typical day, most people spend more time communicating with one another than in any other activity except sleeping. However, miscommunication is appallingly common. As a former head of Los Alamos National Labs once said, "Miscommunication is the sand in the gears of modern technology."[1]

One of the best ways to minimize miscommunication is to improve your listening ability. It's been estimated that of the time we spend communicating with one another:

- 45 percent is spent listening.
- 30 percent speaking.
- 15 percent reading.
- 10 percent writing.

So listening occupies nearly half of the average person's communication time. As one communication expert put it, the average person listens a book a day.[2]

Of course, the percentage of time that's devoted to each of the four aspects of communication will vary from person to person, and with a given person it will fluctuate from day to day. But even when these variations are considered, the average person does an enormous amount of listening in a typical day. When we spend a major amount of our time doing any activity, it makes sense to learn how to do it well. Regrettably, as you'll see in Chapter 3, researchers discovered that people are typically unskilled listeners who generally miss more of a message than they take in.

Not only do we spend a major amount of our lifetime listening to others, quality listening is a significant contributor to performance effectiveness. Communications experts Douglas Stone, Bruce Patton, and Sheila Heen argue that:

> Listening is not only the skill that lets you into the other person's world; it is also the single most powerful move you can make to keep the conversation constructive.[3]

And social psychologist Daniel Goleman reports:

> Listening well has been found to distinguish the best managers, teachers, and leaders.[4]

Listening Has Become Increasingly Important in the Workplace

Early in the twentieth century, most nonagricultural workers labored in noisy factories where it was difficult to hear one another above the clatter of machinery, so not much talking or listening went on. However, that lack didn't affect productivity much because most people worked at simple, repetitive tasks for which there was relatively little need to communicate with coworkers or even supervisors. Consequently, being a poor listener seldom was a workplace problem.

Over time, however, jobs became more complex, changed more rapidly, and required more interaction with other people—all of which greatly increased the importance of effective listening. In recent decades, galloping technological advances, coupled with greatly intensified global competition and the increased need for cooperation, spurred the development of communication-intensive organizations, further increasing the importance of listening at work.

Then too, ineffective listening in the workplace causes lower morale, increased absenteeism, decreased productivity, and obviously less effective communication—with all the implications for reduced organizational performance.

Effective listening is crucial to business success. Nearly all significant work situations are handled more effectively by a person who is listening well than by someone whose listening is below par. Bernard Ferrari, dean and professor at Johns Hopkins Carey Business School, who consults with CEOs of several of the world's largest corporations, says effective listening is "the most critical business skill of all."[5] Sam Walton founded what is now known as Walmart in 1962 (Wal-Mart Discount City) and by 2010 had developed it into the world's largest corporation. As "Mister Sam," traveled from store to store, he told employees, "The secret to success is to get out into the store and listen to what the associates say." Jeffrey Immelt, chairman of the board and CEO of General Electric and in 2009 one of *Time* magazine's one hundred most influential people in the world, agrees:

> When I catalogue the traits and practices that I want to emphasize in General Electric, and that I strive to improve in myself, the first item on my list is to become a better listener. . . . Listening isn't some natural gift like athletic ability or an ear for music. It is a skill that demands constant attention and constant practice, because *only through good listening can any of us gather the information we need to do our jobs well.*[6]

The link between good listening and effective job performance has undoubtedly been a major motivator for many other busy executives to make ample room in their crowded schedules for listening. Take Thomas Watson, Jr., who headed IBM for twenty of the corporation's highest-performing years. Under his leadership, IBM revolutionized the computer industry, put its logo on 70 percent of the world's computers, tripled its revenue in six years, and maintained a 30 percent growth rate. In recognition of his accomplishments, President Lyndon Johnson awarded Watson the Medal of Freedom, the highest award a U.S. president can bestow on a civilian. *Fortune* magazine celebrated Watson on its cover as "the greatest capitalist in history." *Time* magazine named him one of the hundred most influential men of the twentieth century.

Year in and year out, despite all his other responsibilities, this very busy and famous man made room in his crowded schedule to carve out 25 percent of his time for listening to and following up on conversations with people at the lower levels of the corporation.

Here's an example of how Watson's listening and consequent follow-up contributed to IBM's bottom line. An entry-level worker had several compensation discussions with his supervisors that, from the employee's point of view, were very unsatisfactory. Using IBM's open-door policy, this entry-level employee ultimately obtained an appointment with the CEO.

"Mr. Watson," he said, "your people are not treating me fair . . . . I make more pieces per hour than anyone in that shop, and I get the lowest pay."

Watson was skeptical but called the plant and asked, "Does he make the most pieces and get the lowest pay?"

"Yes," came the reluctant answer, along with a number of "reasons" for the low compensation — "reasons" that did not affect the employee's performance and that Watson thought were none of the company's business and therefore should not affect the man's pay.

Watson saw to it that henceforth the employee's compensation would be based on his productivity. Additionally, after listening to that disgruntled employee, Watson realized that IBM's compensation practices were not linked sufficiently to productivity. So he took a step that gave IBM a huge payoff from his investment in listening. "That [incident]," he said, "caused us to go through every plant in America and relate pay to [performance]."[7]

Years after Watson retired, the giant corporation was again floundering. Louis Gerstner, an executive from outside with no experience in the computer industry, was brought in to break up the giant corporation. But before doing so, he and his top leaders traveled to key customers in various parts of the world and listened to their needs and concerns. What they learned from their listening and relationship-building mission changed the focus of the corporation, which in turn led to its recovery and ultimately to IBM again becoming one of the most valuable corporations in the world.

Like Watson and Gerstner, John Elter, the former vice president and chief engineer of Xerox, was a remarkably successful businessman, having developed programs that brought in $40 billion of revenue. When asked what role listening played in the nuts-and-bolts creativity of new product development, he replied:

It is everything. The challenges of product development are not about products. They are about interpersonal relations: power, trust, alignment. My team worked hard to learn how to listen, without judging, to what the other person was trying to say—really to be there.[8]

Communication scholars Andrew Wolvin and Carolyn Coakley summarized the many contributions that listening well makes to organizational performance:

> Businesses with effective listeners are rewarded not only with increased sales and more satisfied customers but also with *increased employee satisfaction* and *increased productivity*, both of which often lead to increased profits. Through effective listening, we gain more information, upgrade decision making, make fewer mistakes, spend more time productively (in conducting meetings, performing job tasks that are more clearly understood, avoiding misunderstandings, etc.), share more viewpoints, and improve management/employee relationships.[9] (Emphasis in the original.)

In 2000, A. G. Lafley became CEO of Procter & Gamble, a traditional top-down organization. In addition to his strong organizational skills, Lafley is considered an intrepid listener who believes that "good leadership *is* good listening."[10] Under his listening-oriented guidance, the company became much more collaborative and innovative. After eight years with him at the helm, revenues had doubled.

Quality Listening Is a Key Factor in Career Success

Since effective listening boosts performance significantly and incompetent listening diminishes productivity, it's not surprising that inept listening is likely to damage one's career. People come in all shapes and sizes, and the way to work effectively with them is to listen to them. Researchers at the Center for Creative Leadership analyzed why some managers made it to the top of their organization while others were given their walking papers. Twenty successful executives were compared with twenty-one who derailed. The successful executives had a pattern of continued career progress; those who derailed had been fired or forced into early retirement. The study found that listening, the "ability—or inability—to understand other people's perspectives," was the most glaring difference between those who succeeded and those who derailed. Turns out, there's much truth to the saying, "Listen up or lose out."

In this chapter, we saw that listening is an ability that's more important than is commonly realized. It's a capability that has become increasingly important in the workplace. And it's an important contributor to a person's success. Unfortunately, as you'll see in the next chapter, few people are good listeners.

3

A Good Listener Is a Rare Find

Most people spend far more time learning to hit a
ball or dance or swim than they do learning how to
avoid getting their lives fouled up through discom-
munication.

—PHILIP LESLY

I N THE LAST hundred years, the importance of listening in most jobs
soared from relatively insignificant to indispensable. As explained in
Chapter 2, early in the twentieth century, most nonagricultural workers
labored in noisy factories where it was difficult to communicate above the
clatter of machinery. However, due to the simple, repetitive nature of the
tasks, there was little need to communicate, so being a poor listener seldom was a problem.

Over time, jobs became more complex, changed more rapidly, and
required more interaction with others, which called for better listening
and other interpersonal skills. In spite of these changes in the workplace,
some people with exceptional technical competence often succeeded despite being inept listeners and ineffective collaborators.

In the waning decades of the twentieth century, though, enormous
changes occurred in the nature of work, which continue unabated today.
Incessant technological advances, coupled with greatly intensified competition, spurred the development of today's communication-intensive
organizations. Today's workplace requires more and better listening by
virtually every employee.

In this chapter, you'll see:

- That the average person is a mediocre listener.
- The cost of mediocre listening in the workplace.
- Employers increasingly expect quality listening.
- Mediocre listening endangers one's career.
- Bush-league listening undermines close relationships.
- Quality work relationships enrich one's personal life.
- Why so many people are mediocre listeners.
- The essential elements of a better way of listening.

The chapter concludes with an overview of the essential elements of a better way of listening.

The Average Person Is a Mediocre Listener

Since listening has become so central to our work and personal lives, one would think that most people would be fairly good at it. In fact, the opposite is true. Centuries ago, the psalmist complained, "They have ears to hear but they hear not."[1] That complaint would not be off the mark today. Dr. Lyman Steil, a founder and past president of the International Listening Association, asked thousands of managers and executives to assess their competence in listening. Eighty-five percent rated themselves average or lower.[2] But how good is average? Obviously, being average is nothing to crow about, but one would assume that being an "average listener" would at least be adequate. Not so. As you'll see in a moment, the caliber of listening in our society is so poor that a merely average listener is an inept one. Check your own experience. How often do the people you work with give you their full attention, carefully follow what you are saying, make sure they've gotten your point, and refrain from chiming in with their ideas until they've heard you out?

Difficult as it is to imagine, listeners often miss more of a message than they take in. Researchers at American University in Washington, D.C., found that the average television viewer got only one-third of the points covered in a given newscast.[3] The succinct presentations were prepared by trained writers, delivered by professional speakers, and supported by top-notch visuals. Those outstanding conditions aren't present in our everyday conversations, so it's not surprising that people are apt to misunderstand, distort, ignore, or soon forget what they are told.[4] Dr. Steil and his collaborators concluded that "it can be stated with virtually no qualification that by any standard set, people in general do not know how to listen."[5] It's frustrating to think of the information that was missed, the opportunities that were lost, and the relationships that deteriorated because we weren't listening well.

Though few people think of themselves as great listeners, they rarely consider themselves as deficient at listening as the research suggests. That's because *we are seldom aware of what we miss in a conversation.* When leading a workshop, trainers sometimes begin by asking participants to introduce themselves briefly to the other members of the group. After the introductions, the trainer says, "Now, at the outset of the workshop, we'll establish a baseline by testing your current listening ability. Please write down what was said by the person who preceded you in the introductions." This statement is usually met by a long, palpable silence, followed by a roar of laughter as people realize that just about everyone in the room has drawn a blank on what his or her neighbor said. *Yet, until they were asked to write it down, they were unaware that the message had gone in one ear and out the other.* When the activity is debriefed, someone typically explains, "I didn't get what was said because I was thinking of what I would say." Most of the others nod their head in agreement. Of course. That's what happens in our everyday conversations: We miss much of what we're told because we're thinking of what *we* will say as soon as there's an opening. And we seldom realize what we're missing.

The Cost of Mediocre Listening in the Workplace

Deficient listening at work squanders time, causes unnecessary mistakes, alienates coworkers, and results in lost opportunities and missed sales—all of which translate into decreased effectiveness and diminished profits. Admittedly, the consequences of a typical listening lapse often are undramatic. People must be recontacted, shipments returned, schedules revised, and so forth. Taken individually, these mistakes due to faulty listening may seem insignificant. But when you think of each employee having numerous interactions daily and multiply that number by the total of employees where you work, it's easy to see how defective listening could cost your organization serious money. Some years ago, executives at one division of a telephone company discovered that inaccurate listening held up about 20 percent of its operator-assisted calls. The average delay was only fifteen seconds. But when the expense of all those fifteen-second mistakes was totaled, the operators' listening errors cost the division an average of $874,800 per year.[6] (Subsequent training in better listening eliminated about $500,000 of that annual loss.) In company after company, the cumulative cost of many seemingly minor listening errors adds up to big bucks.

There are times, of course, when a single listening mistake has disastrous consequences. NASA studied the causes of commercial airline accidents and found that a staggering 60 percent were the result of faulty talking and listening. One of the worst disasters in aviation history occurred when two passenger planes collided at a fogged-in airport in the Canary Islands. The official investigation determined that inept listening caused the disaster, which tragically took 581 lives. The dreadful loss of life dwarfs the economic impact of the crash. But the financial toll can't be ignored—$500 million in lawsuits plus $63 million to replace the aircraft.[7]

Unfortunately, some people of unusual intelligence, remarkable talent, and/or extraordinary charisma are able to climb to the highest rungs of the organizational ladder despite their inability or unwillingness to listen to other points of view. However, when a key executive can't or won't listen effectively, it's often a prelude to disaster. Sydney Finkelstein, professor of management at Dartmouth's Tuck School of Business, headed a six-year study of executive failure—the most extensive investigation of the subject ever made. It focused on CEOs and top executives "whose failures were breathtakingly gigantic, who have taken huge, world renowned business operations and made them almost worthless." Individually, these executives were responsible for the destruction of hundreds of millions and, in several cases, billions of dollars' worth of value.[8] Several of the corporations they led were forced into bankruptcy. In one case after another, a persistent "refusal to listen" to advisors, employees, and customers was a major factor in the disastrous failures.[9]

Employers Increasingly Expect Quality Listening

Ironically, even in corporations where top executives don't listen well, others in the organization are expected to be competent at this critical workplace tool. In one study, 80 percent of the executives responding to the survey rated listening as the most important workplace skill.[10] Mark McCormack, entrepreneur and author of *What They Don't Teach You at Harvard Business School,* says one can probably develop no greater business asset than the ability to listen well. The "bottom line is that almost any business situation will be handled differently, with different results, by someone who is listening and someone who isn't."[11]

A survey cited by *Training and Development* magazine found that more than a quarter of the responding executives believe that *listening is the skill most lacking in the workforce.*[12] The organizational world has changed, but the average employee's listening has not kept up. So it's not surprising that approximately 70 percent of Fortune 500 companies conduct training designed to enhance the caliber of their employees' listening.[13]

Mediocre Listening Endangers One's Career

Inept listening is often a barrier to promotion or a cause for dismissal. Recall from Chapter 2 that researchers at the Center for Creative Leadership analyzed why some managers made it to the top of their organization—and some did not. The study found that listening, the "ability—or inability—to understand other people's perspectives," was the most glaring difference between those who were on track and those who derailed.[14] Once again, "Listen up or lose out."

Bush-League Listening Undermines Close Relationships

When you don't tune in to what loved ones say, they feel unappreciated, devalued—unloved. Two marriage counselors asked people what they wanted most from marriage. The resounding answer was "a friend." When asked what they meant by friendship, people typically spoke about "a relationship with someone who will listen to them without judging them," someone who will be "empathic."[15]

It's certainly not unreasonable for friends and family members to expect that you will listen attentively to them. Yet the lonely reality is that *the state of listening in our homes is even worse than it is at work.* Dr. Steil's questionnaire, referred to earlier, asked people to rate how they thought their best friend, manager, business colleague, job subordinate, and spouse would rate them as listeners. *After reviewing thousands of these self-reports, Steil found that most people thought their domestic partner would rate their listening ability even lower than their friends and business colleagues would.* Many reported that their partner was equally ineffective in listening to them.[16] Incredibly, listening is at its lowest ebb in what should be the closest relationship of all. Worse yet, Steil found that the longer people had been married, the lower they rated the quality of listening in their marriage.

Most of us want more than the domestic loneliness portrayed by T. S. Eliot:

> Two people who know they do not understand each other,
> Breeding children whom they do not understand
> And who will never understand them.[17]

Readers of the *Ladies Home Journal* were asked, "If you could improve one thing about your husbands what would it be?" The number one response by far was for the husband to be a better listener. Surprisingly, 57 percent wished her husband was a better listener compared to 46 percent who wanted him to help more around the house and 40 percent who wished he brought in more money.[18]

Why So Many People Are Mediocre Listeners

When you stop to think about it, it's not surprising that good listeners are the exception rather than the rule. Listening is an ability that must be learned. So how do people learn to listen? It is mostly by example, and, where listening is concerned, there are lots of bad examples.

The foundation of one's listening ability is laid in the home. Children observe the way their parents communicate and absorb many of their behaviors. Psychologists discovered through unobtrusive tape-recording of normal family conversations that few parents are good listeners. The recordings revealed that parents generally talk far more than they listen. They seldom pay attention when others, especially children, are talking. They interrupt frequently, often disagreeing with or criticizing what was said without hearing the other person out. One study found that when parents interact with their children, the parents are responsible for 89 percent of the interruptions.[19]

When people grow to adulthood and become parents themselves, they often do the kind of listening that their parents did. Families get caught in a generational chain reaction where the communication faults of parents are visited on their children who, in turn, pass those shortcomings on to their children. This book can help you put an end to that dismal chain of miscommunication.

Schooling provides another negative influence on our development as listeners. Educational researchers recorded thousands of hours of classroom instruction by elementary and secondary school teachers. In the analysis of the recordings, it was discovered that in most classrooms, faulty listening is modeled all day long to such a degree that learning is seriously impaired.[20] Teachers tend to further erode children's ability to listen by talking nonstop for longer periods than pupils can concentrate. A leading educational researcher concluded, "In most classrooms children are seen and not heard."[21] Influenced by factors like these, students' listening ability plummets throughout their school years. In one study, teachers were asked to stop in the middle of what they were saying and ask, "What was I talking about?" In the first grade, 90 percent of the pupils could answer the question. In the second grade, 80 percent answered correctly. By the time children were in middle school, fewer than half (43.7 percent) could respond accurately. In high school, all but 28 percent were clueless about what the teacher had said.[22]

The average person's listening ability is not the result of training; rather it stems from a lack of training and faulty modeling during their preschool and school years. When you combine the widespread modeling of ineffective ways of listening with the absence of training, it's easy to see why a good listener is a rare find.

Essential Elements of a Better Way of Listening

Dwelling on the prevalence of poor listening can be discouraging. Fortunately, a better way of listening has been identified that's much more productive than the inadequate ways that are in general use. Anyone of normal intelligence can master it. The basic skills of this improved way of listening have been known for years. But they've not been disseminated effectively. So, for most readers, the skills taught in Parts II–V of this book will describe a new and a much better way of listening. As noted in the preface, the skills of listening taught here stem primarily from extensive research by Carl Rogers, Ph.D., into what listening behaviors and attitudes increase communication effectiveness and heighten rapport. (Rogers is considered second only to Sigmund Freud as the most eminent psychological clinician of the twentieth century.[23])

Later, numerous researchers delved into how this set of listening skills actually perform in all sorts of real-world environments. The results were impressive. In all types of work situations—management, assembly, teaching, engineering, customer relations, sales, accounting, service, health care, maintenance, purchasing, and so on—this way of listening proved much more effective than the types of listening that one generally encounters in our society. It greatly increased communication accuracy. At the same time, it helped build more productive relationships and enhanced teamwork. This way of listening was found to have a similarly powerful impact on family relationships—with one's partner, with children of all ages, and with elderly parents. Bonds with friends were strengthened as people experienced more attentiveness and less stress in their interactions.

People who learn this improved way of listening are amazed at the way it reduces communication glitches, keeps others off the defensive, gets problems out into the open, helps calm tense situations, and improves relationships.

This book was written to help you equip yourself with the skills of better listening. You'll learn the skills shortly, but first, it's important to understand why the typical ways of listening tend to be so ineffective compared to the level of effectiveness that you'll soon learn to achieve.

4

Quality Listening Strengthens Personal Relationships

The first duty of love is to listen.

–PAUL TILLICH

H AVING TALKED AT some length about the importance of *work rela-tionships* and the role listening plays in keeping them vital, in this chapter we discuss the *importance of three types of personal relationships*: friendship, marriage, and relationships with one's children. And we'll note the contribution that empathic listening makes to maintaining and enhancing these crucial ties.

Friendship

Although we humans are social animals and most of us wish for a strong and rich social life, at any given time, the typical person in our culture has few and sometimes no long-term friendships. British novelist and medie-valist C. S. Lewis wrote:

> To the Ancients, Friendship seemed the happiest and most hu-man of all loves; the crown of life and the school of virtue. The modern world, in comparison, ignores it.

Take a moment to come up with the number of *close friendships* you have had in your life so far. Is it four or five, three or two, or one? Henry Adams wrote:

> One friend in a lifetime is much; two are many; three are hardly possible.

At any given period, the typical person has few or perhaps no long-term-frequent-face-to-face-contact friendships—the kind that tends to be much richer and deeper than "friendship-lite" which is so common today. Why is it so difficult to have more than a handful of really engaging friendships in a lifetime? The mobility of our society is a major hindrance to maintaining long-term friendships. But much of the answer to that question may be found by looking at what it takes to make and maintain a rich, long-term friendship. Among other things, it involves:

- An investment of time.
- Good chemistry.
- Self-disclosure.
- Managing relationship white water.
- Skilled listening is a key ability for enriching friendships.

AN INVESTMENT OF TIME

Good friendships take time. But these days many people find that time is in short supply. The forty-hour workweek is a myth for many. A few years ago, a Gallup Poll report on the workweek noted that it had climbed to an average of 46.7 hours. When you add the commute time and extra time working evenings and weekends that employees often put in, for many, work-related activities occupy a huge chunk of their week. Then, too, many people spend an hour or more a day surfing the Internet. While that's an optional activity, for many it's a time-consuming part of their typical day. So nowadays, far more than in recent decades, in order to enjoy a few rich friendships, you must discipline yourself to carve out time for face-to-face connections.

Good friendships do take time: time to build, time to maintain, and time to enjoy. Famed biographer James Boswell noted that there is something mysteriously wonderful about the forming of a close friendship as it develops progressively over time:

We cannot tell the precise moment when friendship is formed. As in filling a vessel drop by drop, there is at last a drop which makes it run over: so in a series of kindnesses there is at last one which makes the heart run over.

That's the moment when a developing relationship blossoms into a rich friendship.

Notice the phrase "drop by drop" in the Boswell quote. Few friendships are created without a significant investment of time in the relationship—time for listening to each other, for getting to know and understand each other, time to grow in respect for each other, time for shared experiences, and time to laugh together. It's no wonder that our friendships are so few in number since a sizable quantity of quality time is essential in developing and nurturing close relationships. And, as mentioned, time is a scarce element in our fast-paced lives.

GOOD CHEMISTRY

Good chemistry is another requirement for the development of a friendship. *Webster's II New College Dictionary*, after giving the scientific meanings of chemistry, states that "chemistry" can also refer to "mutual attraction or sympathy; rapport." Having chemistry with another person involves having a special combination of similarities and differences. But to say, "We had the right chemistry from the start" or "The chemistry just wasn't there" sounds so ethereal. Well, it is very special.

SELF-DISCLOSURE

Friendships may start with discussions about the weather, the big game, or the latest headline, but over time the acquaintances open the door, however gingerly, into the world of what they truly care about. They develop a balance between disclosing their thoughts, interests, concerns, and values with listening to their friend's thoughts and feelings.

Balance is key to a satisfying friendship. When someone dominates a conversation with another person by dumping personal worries, complaints, and other challenges into the conversation without regard for the needs and interests of their friend, it can no longer be called a conversation. If sharing and disclosing are not balanced with attentive listening, the conversation has degenerated into a monologue—and few people enjoy being on the receiving end of the deluge. The ability to disclose appropriately *and* listen well is the foundation for flourishing friendships.

MANAGING RELATIONSHIP WHITE WATER

Patrick Lencioni states:

> All great relationships, the ones that last over time, require productive conflict in order to grow. This is true in marriage, parenthood, friendship, and certainly business.[1]

Even the best friendships suffer challenging times. In any close, long-term relationship, there are bound to be misunderstandings—times when one, or perhaps both of you—are not functioning at your best. There are times when the relationship is not rewarding, probably some times when it is burdensome, times, perhaps, when your friend is treating you poorly. Misunderstandings occur; trust may momentarily be shattered.

Being aware that this happens occasionally in virtually all close and long relationships makes it easier to hang in with the friendship the next time a relationship hits troubled waters. A strong sense of commitment enables you to weather sporadic moments of relationship white water.

SKILLED LISTENING IS A KEY ABILITY
FOR ENRICHING FRIENDSHIPS

Good listening has a bonding impact in friendship. Psychologist Julie Rodgers highlights the bonding effect of listening:

> The most vital activity of any friend . . . interested in building good interpersonal relationships is listening, and listening, and listening. If you want a friend for life, listen, truly listen to each other, for nothing [else] so permanently binds two people together.[2]

Marriage

A loving and lasting marriage is a wonderful thing. Although the typical person may not put it that strongly, the vast majority of us look forward to tying the knot.

MARRIAGE AND WELL-BEING

One of the most frequent findings about personal well-being is the connection between marriage and a sense of happiness and satisfaction with one's life. Survey upon survey reveals that the number one source of contentment in life is a good marriage; it ranks higher than a good job, fame, fortune, or even good health. A number of researchers found that marriage is the only important predictor of life satisfaction for both women and men. In *Grown-Up Marriage*, Judith Viorst notes that research overwhelmingly shows a strong and consistent relationship between marriage and experiencing life as being good. Even when compared with couples who live together without being married, those who are committed to a lifetime relationship fared much better.

OPPOSITES TEND TO ATTRACT ONE ANOTHER

Although people tend to marry someone of a similar background, they often marry someone whose personality is quite different from their own.[3] He's a stay-at-home; she's outgoing. He likes routine; she craves new experiences. He procrastinates; she's a do-it-now person. He's a spender; she's a saver. That tends to make their married life more interesting. But it takes more effort, more work to stay in sync with a partner whose pace and level of emotional expressivity are different from their own. Consequently, although opposites often attract, they don't always live happily ever after.

THE CHALLENGE OF MERGING TWO INDIVIDUALS INTO ONE FAMILY

Three great minds from three widely separated eras have had this to say about marriage.

Social psychologist Erich Fromm put it this way:

> There is hardly any activity, any enterprise, which is started with such tremendous hopes and expectations and yet fails as regularly, as love.

Martin Luther (1483–1546), a seminal figure in the Protestant Reformation, said:

> The first love is drunken. When the intoxication wears off, then comes real married love.[4]

Author and Buddhist teacher Jack Kornfield reminds us:

After the ecstasy, the laundry.

Unfortunately, the folklore of our society communicates the illusion that when two people fall in love and pledge themselves to each other, they will "live happily ever after." However, the fairy tale phrase "lived happily ever after" expresses a flagrant falsehood about marriage and creates unrealizable expectations for lovers at an emotionally vulnerable time. Real life is not nearly as rosy as the fairy tale cliché suggests. Shakespeare, that wise observer of human affairs, wrote:

The course of true love never did run smooth.[5]

Coming from different family backgrounds and traditions and many dissimilar personal interests and habits, a couple has to jointly make many decisions about important issues: where to live, whether to have children and if so how many, and how to raise them. Then there are the many financial decisions: whether to buy a house or rent, whether to buy a new car or a used one, how much if any money to spend on vacations, and so on and on and on. And there will be lots of smaller but not unimportant decisions about mealtimes, bedtimes, sharing of housework and yardwork, and so forth.

Furthermore, a marriage is an edifice that must be rebuilt (or at least renovated) many times as it moves through numerous stages from honeymoon, to managing a household, through the various phases of parenting, through the empty nest, and through the several periods of old age. Unless the partners creatively and energetically work at maintaining and enhancing their relationship, the joys of early love soon fade. Having started out with high hopes and goodwill but not having engaged in the maintenance work, many a couple find themselves arguing or otherwise stressed about many of the issues and decisions in their everyday lives. Over a ten-year period, Dr. R. C. Adams studied thousands of marriages and found that only 17 percent of the couples he studied could be considered truly happy.[6]

The termination of a marriage is one of the most devastating experiences a person can face. It is important for couples to squarely face and work to avert this grim threat to their marriage: More than 50 percent of all first marriages end in divorce. And, as Oscar Wilde said, remarriage often is "the triumph of hope over experience." More than 60 percent of second marriages end in divorce, and the divorce rates for third and fourth marriages are even higher. The sad prevalence of divorce is a stark reminder of how difficult married love is.

The good news, of course, is that almost half of all first marriages last. Many are very happy, although the homes of other lasting marriages are far from what many wedding ceremonies speak of as "a place of joy and a haven of peace."

Virtually 100 percent of people entering their first marriage believe it will succeed; unfortunately, half of them will be heartbrokenly wrong.

LISTEN YOUR WAY TO A MORE SUPPORTIVE AND FLOURISHING MARRIAGE

When the honeymoon fades, and life together shifts from "moonlight and roses" to "daylight and dishes," many couples continue to enjoy a great relationship and a fulfilling life together. To adjust to all of the phases of a long-lasting marriage and, for many, the challenges encountered in years of parenting, you'll do well to burnish your listening. "The road to the heart," wrote Voltaire, "is the ear." Yet, many marriage counselors say that not listening or poor listening are the primary problems in contemporary marriages.

Listening can be a powerful resource when your spouse is hurting from one of life's serious setbacks. In 1849, Nathaniel Hawthorne was sacked from his government job in the customhouse. He poured out his despair to his wife, who listened empathically to his recollection of the painful experience. When much of his despair had drained off, she brought his pen and ink, lit a fire, put her arms around him, and said, "Now you will be able to write your novel." Thus encouraged, Hawthorne set about the task. The result was his master work, *The Scarlet Letter: A Romance* published in 1850. When one faces difficult times, an empathic spouse can be a marvelous source of comfort and encouragement. Although George Bernard Shaw rightly stated, "Like fingerprints, all marriages are different," all marriages can be enriched by the use of empathic listening.

Parenting

Becoming a parent is a life changing event. As therapist Sean Grover says, "It's a learn as you go process." Most parents will agree that it's a tough job. Still it's a job with rich satisfactions and pleasures. And a big payoff comes when your children present you with grandchildren.

Listening is a skill for all seasons of parenting. It can elevate the good times, enhance the ordinary moments, and be invaluable to you during the tough times.

We'll turn to two authors living centuries apart who offered these brief thoughtful comments on child rearing. First Montaigne, one of the significant philosophers of the French Renaissance, wrote:

> There is a little less trouble in governing a private family than a whole kingdom.

And Virginia Satir, widely regarded as the Mother of Family Therapy, gives us this description of the parental role:

> Parents teach in the toughest school in the world—The School for Making People.
> You are the Board of Education, the principal, the classroom teacher, and the janitor.

Yet, virtually everyone who undertakes the demanding role of parenting is an untrained amateur.

It's unrealistic to think anyone can handle their parenting perfectly. No one gets by without their share of grim moments. As writer Peter De Vries said, "There are times when parenthood seems like nothing but feeding the hand that bites you."

Researchers found that couples with children average lower levels of happiness and life satisfaction than childless couples. A 2004 study tracked the moods and activities of 909 American working women. Taking care of kids ranked twelfth in enjoyment out of sixteen activities including cooking, eating, shopping, napping, exercising, and talking on the phone. After a particularly stressful day with her two preschool kids, one stay-at-home mom sighed, "There are an incredible number of parenting moments in a day."

Researchers found that for virtually every kind of parent—single mothers, stay-at-home fathers, British couples, spouses in Columbus, Ohio—the fewer the children, the happier the parents. Parenting can be a marvelous experience—but it's not for wimps. If you're experiencing it as a drag right now, try using some of the skills you're about to learn. They can make your parenting life less fraught with friction and more full of the good moments you yearn for. Things look even better as you contemplate the pleasures with one's grown children and the special joys of having grandchildren.

SET REALISTIC PARENTING ASPIRATIONS

As they enter parenthood, most people want to do a super job at it. They want to be *great* parents. After all, the health, happiness, and future successes of their children are at stake. According to a report by Baby-Center on modern moms, nearly 80 percent of Millennial mothers say it's important to be "the perfect mom."[7] However, when you look realistically at what's involved in raising one child (let alone one or several others at the same time), child rearing experts have found that parents with *realistic expectations* tend to achieve better results than perfectionistic parents.

Like many societies, ours does a poor job of preparing people for parenthood. Editor Malcolm Forbes said, "How children survive being Brought Up amazes me." And Samuel Butler wrote, "Parents are the last people on earth who ought to have children." After a rambunctious day with their child, many parents would agree with those statements.

GOOD ENOUGH PARENTING

Given the demands of the parental role and the long duration of it, British psychoanalyst D. W. Winnicott suggests that couples *not* aim for excellence in parenting. A better goal, he asserts, is what he calls "good enough parenting."

- Good enough parenting is less stressful for the parent.
- And, surprisingly, it's better for the child because good enough parenting gives children more room to develop on their own.

ATTENTIVE LISTENING

British psychoanalyst John Bowlby, one of the most influential thinkers in child development, observed mothers interacting directly with their children. He later followed up with those children and found that well-attuned parents (ones who pay attention, listen, and are responsive) provide a child with a "secure base"—people they can rely on when they're distraught and need comfort and love.

As children mature, parents are able to decrease their control over them. Children can have an increase in freedom, like making more decisions for themselves and taking on additional responsibilities. Obviously, as children develop, the parents' role shifts. Invaluable as the skills taught in this book are for the early years of a child's development, they're even more valuable for parenting during preteen and teen years.

Congratulations!

You've just completed Part I of this book, which provided increased understanding of how challenging interpersonal communication can be and how important a role skilled listening can play in improving its effectiveness.

PART II

DO'S AND DON'TS OF GREAT LISTENING

If I were to summarize in one sentence the single most important principle I have learned in the field of human relations it would be this: Seek first to understand, then to be understood.

—STEPHEN COVEY[1]

5

Trouble Spots in the Talking–Listening Process

No thoughts or feelings make it through someone's filters without significant disparities between what's intended and what's received.

—SAMUEL CULBERT

IN CHAPTERS 1 and 2, we saw that quality listening enhances relationships in virtually all facets of our lives. Chapter 3 noted that, although listening well is good business, few people in business or other walks of life are good listeners. Despite the impact that good listening makes to improved performance at work as well as to enhancing all relationships, Chapter 4 demonstrated that a good listener is a rare find. Although these are more than reasons enough for improving your listening ability, in this chapter you'll see that there's yet another crucial reason for becoming a better listener:

The talking-listening process is vulnerable to error. Although the process may look rather simple, speakers frequently misspeak and listeners often misunderstand what's been said. *The listening skills that you'll soon learn provide the best way of detecting inaccuracies so that they can be corrected before the resulting misunderstandings create problems.*

Many people would disagree with this somewhat negative assessment of the caliber of interpersonal communication in our society. In fact, there's a widespread tendency to believe that the talking–listening process is rather dependable. When people talk, they generally expect that the listener will understand what they've said. And when they listen, they typically assume they've grasped the speaker's meaning. After all, engaging in conversation isn't rocket science.

Although conversing with someone isn't rocket science, it's not a walk in the park either. As author and executive coach Phil Harkins wrote:

> Clear communication that moves toward results may seem easy, but it is not. In fact communication is rarely clear, consistent, and forward moving. Rather, it usually suffers the pitfalls of misinterpreted emotion and misunderstood fact. Furthermore, most communication about difficult issues is characterized by circuitous argument, uncertain outcomes, lack of clarity, conflict in personalities, and misaligned goals.[1]

This chapter discusses three crucial aspects of the vocal communication process that make it vulnerable to misunderstanding:

- Many of the things we converse about are more ambiguous than we realize.
- Shortcomings in the talking–listening process make it vulnerable to miscommunication.
- We're seldom aware that miscommunication has occurred until faced with the resulting damage.

Many of the Things We Converse About Are More Ambiguous Than We Realize

More often than we might realize, our knowledge is not as sound as we assume it to be. Many of the realities and ideas we communicate about are ambiguous—open to more than one interpretation. As Plato wrote, "Things are not always what they seem."[2] Pioneering psychiatrist Alfred Adler held that, strictly speaking, we do not *see* what's around us, we apprehend it. An apprehension is a perception with an interpretation attached to it. And Richard Feynman, recipient of the Nobel Prize and one of the most celebrated scientists of modern times, emphasized that:

Scientific knowledge is a body of statements of varying degrees of uncertainty—some most unsure, some nearly so, but none *absolutely* certain.[3]

But when we communicate with one another, we assume and speak as though the facts of the matter are more accurate and clear than they are. Behavioral scientist Caroline Webb reports:

> [T]he startling truth is that we don't experience the world as it is; we're always experiencing an edited, simplified version. Princeton Psychologist Anne Treisman discovered this selective attention feature back in 1967.[4] Even so, it's still a little hard for most of us to accept; we rather like the idea that we have a good grip on reality.[5]

Since selective attention is automatic—and therefore subconscious— it's often difficult to believe we're not experiencing an unedited version of what's actually happening.

In short, it's not uncommon for others to think they are giving you the straight scoop when they are actually passing on rumor or misinformation. And, of course, some people are not above using outright lies while swearing that they are telling the truth.

Shortcomings in the Talking–Listening Process Make It Vulnerable to Miscommunication

Another major contributor to the miscommunication that occurs when we converse with one another is a set of shortcomings in the talking– listening process that impede the accurate transmission of thoughts and feelings. Marvelous as our oral communication capability is, it is far from perfect, and we do well to be aware of and compensate for its limitations.

Adlerian psychologists Harold Mosak and Michael Maniacci relate this story about how a mother's strenuous effort to communicate was misunderstood by her youngest son:

> Two brothers, a 6-year-old and a 5-year-old, decide that today is the day they will learn how to swear. The 6-year-old says, "I'm gonna say the word 'damn,'" and the 5-year-old replies with glee, "I'll say the word 'ass,'" and they giggle and wait for their opportunity.

Mother calls for them to come down for breakfast. They run downstairs, into the kitchen, and jump on the stools. "What would you like for breakfast?" Mother asks the oldest. "Give me some cereal, damn it!" the 6-year-old replies, and without skipping a beat, Mother slaps him with the back of her hand across his face. He runs crying and embarrassed from the room. She turns to the 5-year-old and with a stern grimace says, "And what would you like?" to which he replies with a tremor in his voice, "I don't know but you can bet your ass it won't be cereal."[6]

To reduce the likelihood of miscommunication in the conversations you participate in, it's useful to be aware of and compensate for these major pitfalls that can lead to miscommunication.

LANGUAGE IS IMPRECISE

Language is a marvelous resource for the expression of ideas. It is a medium for doing many activities collaboratively—from kidding around with one another to developing the plans for and creating a spaceship to deliver humans from the earth to the moon and back. Economist and social theorist Stuart Chase wrote, "Language is perhaps the most human of all human attributes. It is what sets us off most sharply from the higher animals. It is part and parcel of our minds and of the relatively greater size of our brains."[7]

However, language, which is crucial to much of our communication and is so vital to our functioning, is also a major source of miscommunication. Linguist Deborah Tannen points out that oftentimes the "normal use of language leads to seemingly abnormal misunderstandings."[8] In the give-and-take of conversation things happen fast, and word choice often is slipshod. Additionally, conversational partners typically assume that the meaning of the words being spoken have the same connotation for the listener that they do for the speaker. Don't count on it. Words are versatile, and the meanings of most words are more elusive than you might think. As poet T. S. Eliot put it:

> Words strain,
> Crack and sometimes break, under the burden,
> Under the tension, slip, slide, perish,
> Decay with imprecision, will not stay in place,
> Will not stay still.[9]

In The Oxford Dictionary of the English Language, the 500 most frequently used words have 1,278 separate and distinct definitions.[10] That's an average of twenty-four meanings per word. Take the word "run." What a variety of meanings it has. "Beth is moving rapidly—watch her run." "In the coming election, Carmen will run for mayor." "Both believe stocks will do better than bonds in the long run." "Michelle has a run in her stocking." "The Yankees just scored another run." "Starting next month, Juan will run the accounting department." And so forth with eighteen additional meanings of the word "run" in our dictionary. It's no wonder that people don't always agree on the meaning of what's been said. Although listeners often select the appropriate meaning of the words they hear, this characteristic of language can result in misunderstandings.

Especially troublesome is the fact that each person's experience colors her interpretation of a word's meaning. What a word signifies to the speaker often differs from dictionary definitions. And the listener may attach a still different meaning to the word.[11] Two newlyweds agreed to be frugal so they can save enough to make a down payment on a house. They soon learned from their frequent arguments about finances that they had very different understandings of the word "frugal."

Since each person puts his own twist on the meanings of words, misunderstandings often bedevil our conversations. A department head was trying to get an exceptionally task-focused manager to devote more time to networking. After several fruitless conversations, an executive coach was engaged to work with them. It soon became clear that a considerable part of the snafu was due to a disconnect between what the word "networking" meant to the department head and what it signified to the manager. The department head thought of networking as building cooperative relationships with others in the company, as well as with customers and suppliers. The manager viewed networking as politicking, which, in his mind, meant getting ahead because of whom you know rather than what you achieve.

Assigning different meanings to the same word is a common occurrence. And misunderstanding happens when the *listener* assumes that the speaker attaches the same meaning to a word as *she* does. General semanticist Irving J. Lee expressed puzzlement over the fact that people "believe so surely (and wrongly) that words have meanings in themselves that they hardly ever wonder what the speaker means when he uses them."[12]

TALKING CONVEYS ONLY AN APPROXIMATION OF WHAT WE MEAN

Marvelous as our ability to talk is, it's an imperfect tool, and few people are sufficiently aware of the common impediments to quality conversational speaking. Let's take a look at each of four potential impediments to speaking clearly:

1. *People often assume they perceive a situation objectively when, in fact, they often are reacting to it and thus may misunderstand it and speak inaccurately about it.*

   Irving Lee writes:

   > A man not only sees something, he reacts to it: he has sentiments about it as well. He may like, dislike, sympathize, fear, rejoice. He may express disappointment, contempt, anger, pity, enthusiasm, indignation, cynicism, shame. He may be bored, excited, surprised, disturbed, interested. He may feel hopeful, hopeless, resentful, antagonistic. *Whatever is said in these moods often reveals little about the . . . situation. It tells more about the speakers.*[13]

   Stuart Chase highlights an even greater problem:

   > The student of semantics is embarrassed by the sheer richness of the evidence that people do not know what they are talking about.[14]

2. *To speak meaningfully to another person, you must translate your thoughts and/or feelings into words—a process called encoding.*

   Communication typically begins with the speaker formulating an idea and/or desiring to express a feeling. In order to convey his meaning, he must *encode* his thoughts and/or feelings—convert them into words. That's where miscommunication often begins since the average person is a mediocre encoder.

   Many speakers plunge into their remarks without taking into account the listener's current mindset about matters that are relevant to his topic. By contrast, effective talkers customize their message to the individual (or group) they are speaking with—an aspect of encoding that journalists refer to as *"slanting."* When you slant your message, you take into account such things as the listener's current time pressures, interests, capabilities, concerns, degree of knowledge about the present topic, and other factors and adjust the content of your talk accordingly. Effective slanting enormously improves the accuracy of communication.

3. *We ad-lib our way through most conversations, so when we talk, we're usually winging it.*

Although some important interactions are carefully planned, most of our conversations are informal and are improvised as we go along. Although this way of speaking is very casual, it's often a very comfortable and effective way of conversing. However, when we ad-lib, we sometimes inadvertently misspeak—and may be unaware that we did not convey the meaning we hoped to.

4. *The challenge of reading the speaker's nonverbals.*

The verbal message is what is said—the content of what's delivered. The nonverbal message is how the message is delivered—the gestures, movements, posture, facial expression, tone of voice, loudness, the distance between the listener and the speaker—is considered body language. (We use the terms "nonverbal" and "body language" interchangeably.)

People are constantly transmitting an abundance of nonverbal signals. Body language can often communicate more than our words do. In fact, many experts estimate that a person's nonverbals constitute the majority of the meaning in interpersonal communication. (Most estimates put it in the 50 to 80 percent range.) These nonverbal messages typically reinforce the verbal content. But sometimes they may suggest that the speaker is being less than forthcoming or is saying things that she knows are inaccurate. The listener then has to make a guesstimate as to whether to believe the verbal message or the body language. Most of the time, people give more credence to the nonverbals. As the early American essayist Ralph Waldo Emerson put it, "What you do speaks so loudly that I cannot hear what you say."

LISTENING IS EDUCATED GUESSWORK

Even when a message is not obscured by the vagaries of language or by a speaker's imprecision, there's no guarantee that it will be received as intended. The listener can still miss the point. As the saying goes, "If you explain something so clearly that no one can misunderstand it, someone undoubtedly will."

BIASED LISTENING

People sometimes take in what they want to hear rather than what was actually stated. And a message that someone is reluctant to entertain may not penetrate her defenses. Research on executive terminations found that selective deafness and wishful hearing caused most failing executives to miss the point of repeated messages that suggested that their jobs were in jeopardy.[15]

THE NECESSITY OF DECODING

Another requirement for the listener is that when she hears the words that were spoken, she has to *interpret* what the speaker meant. That's because, as mentioned, in the process of talking, the speaker must *encode* the thoughts and/or feelings she wants to communicate—translate them into words. The listener must then *decode* the message—convert the words back into what he guesses were the thoughts and/or feelings the speaker was trying to covey. In philosopher Mortimer J. Adler's words:

> [T]he mind of the receiver. . . . must somehow penetrate through the words used to the thought that lies behind them.[16]

THE PUZZLE OF FILLING IN THE BLANKS

One of the hazards of decoding is that *the speaker's message is inevitably incomplete*. Based on her extensive research on interpersonal communication, Deborah Tannen notes, "Much—even most—meaning in conversation does not reside in the words spoken at all, but is filled in by the person listening."[17] However, the listener rarely realizes that in the process of listening, she is making assumptions and "filling in the blanks" in order to make sense of the message.

Listening involves guesswork. At best, it's thoughtful guesswork. But it is guesswork nonetheless.

We're Seldom Aware That Miscommunication Has Occurred Until Faced with the Resulting Damage

We've seen that in its journey from speaker to listener, a message must survive the imprecision of language, be expressed fairly accurately despite the numerous pitfalls that confront a speaker, and survive the guesstimates involved in listening. No wonder there's considerable miscommunication in normal conversation.

However, there's significantly more miscommunication than is commonly realized. That's because, when we're speaking, we're seldom aware of any discrepancy between the intended message and what the listener received. As we've seen, the speaker typically thinks he's been perfectly clear, and the listener usually is confident of having accurately grasped what was meant—even though that's often not the case.

Communication scholars use the phrase *the illusion of understanding* to describe situations in which miscommunication occurs without either person realizing it. This happens frequently enough that playwright, critic, and Nobel laureate George Bernard Shaw asserted:

> The greatest problem of communication is the illusion that it has been accomplished.[18]

When people don't realize that they've miscommunicated, they're unaware of the potential negative consequences that could stem from their conversation. Seemingly agreed-upon actions aren't taken after a meeting. A shipment doesn't go out when it should. Follow-up with a customer doesn't happen. And so on. Other negative consequences of communication snafus include squandered time, inefficient production, misdirected plans, frustrated employees, and so forth. The combined consequences of miscommunication in most organizations are significant—lower corporate profits and customers receiving products and services of reduced quality and/or at a higher cost—factors that can ultimately lead to reduced corporate competitiveness.

Sometimes a miscommunication is merely inconvenient; at other times, it can be very costly. Several years ago, Canada's largest circulation newspaper, the highly regarded *Globe & Mail*, reported that Transit Insurance Company entered into a complicated financial agreement with a reinsurance firm. Obviously, Transit's leaders assumed they understood the terms of the contract correctly. However, the executives later learned that they had misunderstood a crucial part of the agreement. As Transit's vice president lamely explained, "What they said and what we heard wasn't the same thing." That miscommunication, coupled with the illusion of understanding, cost the company more than $5 million.[19]

Realizing that our messages are susceptible to misunderstanding, communication experts explored ways to make communication more accurate. The following chapters present well-researched solutions for coping successfully with the imperfections in the talking–listening process through better listening. Learning and employing the skills of better listening will greatly improve your interpersonal communication and thereby enhance your performance. And it will do wonders for your relationships.

In the following chapters, you'll learn how to listen in a way that enables you to successfully cope with the imperfections in the vocal communication process. Those skills will enable you to avoid most communication snafus which lead to costly mistakes and needless stress with others.

6

Identifying Your Listening Missteps

> [W]e must understand that barriers to meaningful communication are multiple, and manifest everywhere.
>
> —KENNETH KRAMER

RONICALLY, WHEN A situation calls for listening, people often respond by speaking. Organizational consultant Adam Kahane says that "our most common way of listening is not listening." And psychologist Thomas Gordon estimated that there's a 90 percent likelihood that a "*listener*" will respond with one or more ways of *speaking* when someone talks about a problem he's wrestling with.[1] And the late best-selling business author Stephen Covey argued, "Most people do not listen with the intent to understand; they listen with the intent to reply."[2]

This chapter describes the most frequently used types of speaking that people employ when they should be using their ears rather than their mouth.[3] The problem, as Toni Packer, a teacher of meditative inquiry, put it, is "How can I possibly hear you when I'm dying to say something myself?"[4]

In this chapter, we'll discuss:

- Six common dysfunctional missteps.
- Common characteristics of the listening missteps.

- Frequently used missteps.
- The missteps in action.

Six Common Dysfunctional Missteps

We call six common dysfunctional types of speaking the *missteps* of listening since they prematurely shift the listener out of the listening role and into speaking. Some of the missteps and their harmful effects on communication have been known for thousands of years, as you can see in the Old Testament Book of Job, which provides an ancient version of people's tendency to rely on missteps when listening would be a much more fitting response.[5]

When people *prematurely* shift out of listening and into speaking, they typically use one of these missteps of listening:

1. Disagreeing/agreeing
2. Criticizing
3. Questioning
4. Advising
5. Reassuring
6. Diverting

Your ability to recognize your one or two most often used listening missteps is an important first step toward eliminating those that you over-rely on and thereby greatly improving your listening.

Common Characteristics of the Listening Missteps

People generally sense that criticizing, disagreeing, and diverting can be detrimental to communication but wonder what's so bad about the other missteps. At first glance, some of these antilistening responses may seem innocuous, and others may even appear to be beneficial. When you like someone's idea, why not say so? Is it so bad to offer a bit of advice when you have useful knowledge or experience to contribute? Is it wrong to reassure people when they're worried? What's the harm in asking a question now and then? After all, we're doing that right now.

Although advising, questioning, and the like are considered missteps to communication, they don't inevitably damage the flow of conversation.

These behaviors often are appropriate and constructive. *It's not their use but their abuse that causes problems.*

These responses carry a high risk of derailing the conversation when used:

- Too soon.
- Too emphatically.
- Habitually.

- **Too soon.** The difference between a misstep and a constructive response is often a matter of timing. *Each misstep occurs when the "listener" switches from listening to speaking before the speaker has finished expressing herself.* In other words, these substitutes for listening inevitably are *interruptions.* Many conversations are burdened with misstep-laden interruptions. MIT Professor Emeritus Edgar Schein spent much of his professional life observing work conversations. "In general," he reports, "interrupting others is one of the more common and more destructive kinds of communication behavior. Most people have relatively little awareness of how often and how crudely they cut in on others."[6]
- **Too emphatically.** The more forcefully a person criticizes, advises, disagrees, and so on, the more likely the conversation will deteriorate.
- **Habitually.** An occasional misstep may be only mildly disruptive. But most of us rely on certain missteps over and over again. We resort to them not because they're appropriate, but because they've become *habitual.* For example, investigators discovered that on average people interrupt each other approximately twenty-one times in a half hour conversation.[7] That's pretty habitual!

In addition to hindering communication, these missteps tend to put a damper on relationships. As author and rhetorician Paul Swets observed, "One listening mistake after another — slowly, gradually, imperceptibly — can build a wall of resistance between people."[8]

Frequently Used Missteps

This chapter will help you recognize your most frequently used listening missteps. Once you are aware of the responses you often use in place of listening—as well as how they interfere with communication and the damage they can do to relationships—we think you'll be motivated to replace the ineffective substitutes with the real thing.

DISAGREEING/AGREEING

Disagreeing and agreeing are discussed together because in both instances the "listener" prematurely evaluates the speaker's statement—in one case negatively and in the other positively.

Many listeners are quick to evaluate what's being said, and, before the speaker has fully made her point, words of agreement or disagreement fly from the "listener's" lips. If someone complains that "these weekly meetings are a waste of time" right off the bat, many "listeners" will agree or disagree. They might concur saying: "I couldn't agree more!" Or they might take issue with the statement and reply: "How can you say that? Don't you remember how chaotic things were before we had these meetings?" By horning in with their opinion so quickly, this type of "listener" is apt to cut a speaker off before he has finished making his point.

Also, by agreeing or disagreeing prematurely, a "listener" often misses significant specifics of the speaker's message. The sentence "these weekly meetings are a waste of time" could mean a number of things. The speaker might be implying that the meetings are too long. Or that the same people keep dominating the discussions. Or that the team leader should be more (or less) directive. Or that hidden agendas undermine fruitful discussion. By breaking into the conversation prematurely, the "listener" is unlikely to fully understand what the speaker is trying to communicate.

Some people are especially inclined to disagree with what others say. They immediately put the speaker's idea on trial to see if it's wanting. They "respond more frequently with 'but' than 'aha.'"[9] It's a huge turnoff to those who work with you or live with you if your typical response to what they say is to overlook the merits of their ideas and to focus on any perceived weaknesses.

We're not suggesting that you never agree or disagree with other people's ideas. There will be times when you need to express concerns about an option that's being considered or a decision that's being made. Not all ideas are good, and even the most promising ones may benefit from being honed through give-and-take with people of different outlooks. Also, when you like someone's idea, it's usually helpful to let the person know it. The point we're making is that, while disagreeing and agreeing have legitimate roles to play, these behaviors short-circuit communication *when used too soon, too emphatically, and/or habitually.*

People sometimes ask, "What's left for me to do if I don't agree or disagree with someone's statement?" Executive coach Samuel Culbert suggests, "Instead of thinking 'O my God, I've got to set this person straight,' you can scratch your head and wonder, 'What's causing this smart-enough person to see things differently?'"[10] Then listen open-mindedly to find out why that person's point of view makes sense to her.

CRITICIZING

Psychologist Carl Rogers concluded that one of the reasons we don't listen very well is our "tendency to judge, to evaluate, to approve or disapprove the statements of the other person."[11]

People often feel obliged to point the finger of criticism—how else will others improve? Many managers and team leaders give far more corrective than appreciative feedback.

Married partners often assume that the role of intimate critic is part of the package. Psychologist John Gottman's research on behaviors that foster marital longevity and those that erode couple relationships enabled him to predict with 94 percent accuracy which of the couples he interviewed would divorce within three years. Gottman's research provided him with a crucial criterion: Harsh criticism of one's partner is a major predictor of divorce.[12]

Many parents believe it is their mission to point out the fallacy of their children's ways; otherwise, the kids will never grow into responsible adults. One researcher found that when parents talk to their children, the ratio of criticisms to compliments is an overwhelming twelve criticisms to one compliment.[13] Worse still, the ratio of criticisms to compliments in the typical secondary school classroom is an appalling eighteen criticisms to one compliment. The consequences are deplorable. An excess of criticism deflates self-esteem, impedes communication, and stifles rapport. The criticisms may be well-intentioned, but those good intentions are seldom realized.

Candice Carpenter, co-founder of iVillage.com, tells about a number of mothers who were exchanging information about problems with teenagers. They made the radical agreement not to criticize their teens about anything. One would think this would only make things worse. However, at month's end, the teens had all improved! The mother's lack of criticism had broken the cycle of disapproval and noncooperation.[14]

Criticizing works against a prime goal of listening, which is for the speaker to have a nonjudgmental atmosphere in which to express her thoughts and feelings. It's a rare but heartening experience to talk about what is uppermost on your mind without the "listener" trying to straighten you out. *A basic principle of listening is that we "cannot help a speaker experience being understood while we provide the experience of being judged."*[15] So when you listen, offer the speaker a pair of non-judgmental ears.

QUESTIONING

People often equate listening with asking questions and assume that questioning is a good way of showing interest in the speaker. Consequently, many people are taken aback when they find questioning on a list of listening missteps.

Questions tend to steer the conversation in the direction the questioner thinks is best. However, it's usually more effective to let the speaker make her point in her own way. After all, the speaker knows what she wants to say, and the listener doesn't. When looking back at an interview with President John F. Kennedy, journalist Theodore White said, "Had I listened more closely rather than pushing my own questions on him, I might have had a more productive interview."[16]

Most people prefer to talk without being pumped for details—at least until they've expressed their basic idea. So don't let your curiosity hijack the conversation. Refrain from, or at least greatly limit, your questions as the person's message unfolds.

When the speaker is finished, it may be appropriate to ask a few questions to fill in important details or to shed light on whatever is unclear to you. Chapter 11 offers guidelines for questioning effectively. And Chapter 12 teaches the how-to's of creating productive questions, as well as how to organize them into an integrated sequence when that's appropriate.

Although questioning has constructive uses, it inhibits communication when used:

* Too soon.
* Too emphatically.
* Habitually.

ADVISING

Advising is the fix-it misstep where the listener offers a solution prematurely—often as soon as the speaker has given a brief overview of the problem. Some people love to dispense solutions. MIT's Schein asks, "What is more satisfying than giving advice?" And the noted fifteenth-century moralist and memoirist La Rochefoucauld stated, "We give nothing more generously than advice." For some people, dispensing advice is about as automatic as a knee-jerk response.

It's easy to see how people could slip into giving advice. When someone talks about a problem he's facing, most "listeners" want to be helpful. So they're tempted to offer suggestions about what to do—which makes them feel like they're doing the other person a favor. Cartoon character Charlie Brown, when surrounded by members of his baseball team, all of whom are telling him what to do, complained, "The world is filled with people who are anxious to act in an advisory capacity."[17]

As you've undoubtedly experienced from well-given advice you've received, some counsel can be useful to the recipient. But there is appropriate, sensitive, and skillful advice giving, and there's inappropriate, insensitive, and unskillful advice giving. Too often, the advice that's offered is:

- Inappropriate
- Inapplicable

And it may be:

- Taken as an insult
- Be an unintended inducement to dependency

- **Inappropriate.** Giving advice is ill-considered when someone wants to talk about a predicament he's in but isn't looking to you for a solution. As a wife commented about her husband, "When I tell him about a problem I'm having, instead of empathy, he gives me unasked-for advice."
- **Inapplicable.** It's been said that most advice is autobiographical. People often say, "Here's what *I* would do if *I* were you" and explain how they would solve the problem. This rarely helps because the person receiving the advice is different from the advice giver. A course of action that might work for the self-appointed guru may not work for the recipient of the advice who has different talents to work with and different weaknesses to shore up or work around. As Benjamin Franklin noted, "[W]e *can give Advice, but we cannot give Conduct.*"[18]
- **Taken as an insult.** A person may wrestle with a dilemma for weeks or even months before talking it over with a colleague,

spouse, or friend. Despite all that thought, he's still stumped about how to deal with the situation. However, the typical advice giver offers a solution immediately after hearing a brief summary of the problem. The person on the receiving end of such an astounding display of instantaneous problem solving often feels put down and probably thinks, "You don't even fully understand the problem yet!" As the saying goes: "Unsolicited advice is the junk mail of life."

◆ **An unintended inducement to dependency.** Many people who say they want self-reliant kids and self-starting employees undercut their goal by creating dependency through excessive advising.

If you don't offer advice when someone discusses their problem with you, what can you do? Often the best option is to continue listening—be a sounding board rather than a suggestion box. Your listening can help the speaker gain a more objective perspective on his problem, do his best thinking about it, and arrive at a solution that plays to his strengths and fits his lifestyle.

Of course, there are times when offering advice may be appropriate. Just make sure you're not just doling out advice or giving it too soon, too emphatically, or habitually. And when offering advice, you could accompany it with a disclaimer like, "This is what I think" or "In a somewhat similar situation, this worked for me . . ." to indicate that you realize that you are stating an opinion that may or may not fit the other person.

REASSURING

People are often astonished to find reassurance on a list of listening missteps. However, when you are reassuring someone, you are talking when it probably would be more appropriate to be listening. Furthermore, when you look closely at the effects of reassurance, we think you'll find that it has a poor track record. For one thing, words of reassurance rarely lift anyone out of the doldrums. A third-grader whose family was moving to a distant city was distraught at the thought of leaving all her friends. Her mother told her, "You'll make lots of new friends in Chicago." That parental effort at reassurance did nothing to diminish the daughter's anxiety. Think of your own experience. When was the last time you felt less apprehensive because someone said,

"Don't worry. Things will work out."

Reassuring someone generally comes down to minimizing another person's strongly held concerns—trying to talk them out of feeling as they do, which by the way, rarely if ever works. For example, when a person is discouraged over a botched assignment, the "listener" often soft-pedals the screw-up:

Everyone makes mistakes.

You're being too hard on yourself.

Anyone would have done what you did.

It can't be that bad.

I'm sure it will work out.

Supposedly comforting statements like these tend to undercut the person's effort to cope with his difficulties. The very discomfort that reassurance attempts to alleviate can be a powerful stimulus for learning from the situation and for mustering up the willpower to turn it around.

When someone is down in the dumps, it's enormously helpful for a friend or colleague to listen empathically to her predicament. But when a "listener" reassures someone who is discouraged, the latter will likely assume that the "listener" simply doesn't understand the degree of difficulty she is experiencing. Rather than lift another person's spirits, our reassuring words may leave her feeling misunderstood and isolated.

Psychologists point out that *reassurance often is a subconscious, self-protective device that people use to avoid experiencing someone else's pain.* It is a way of *seeming* to comfort a person while actually trying to talk her out of feeling the way she does. We seem to intuit that if we really listen, truly tune in to the depths of a person's discouragement or heartache, we will be dragged down emotionally too.

The assessment that the person doing the reassuring is the one who benefits seems reasonable when we think about the discrepancy between the way most of us handle our own discouragement and the upbeat way we urge others to manage theirs. Humorist Don Marquis observed:

There is always a comforting thought in time of trouble when it is not our trouble.

If reassurance frequently is unproductive or even counterproductive, how can you comfort a person who is disheartened? We find a clue in the derivation of the word *comfort* from two Latin words, *con* and *fortis*. When combined, the words mean "strengthened by being with." Genuine comfort is provided when, instead of offering shallow consolation, you listen empathically to the person's concerns, which will likely reduce the sense of isolation he may be experiencing and may help him grapple his way out of a difficult situation.

DIVERTING

It's highly probable that a diversion is being launched when you hear phrases like:

That reminds *me* of the time when *I* . . .

You think that's bad, last week *I* . . .

Speaking of . . . , *I* . . .

I know what you mean, *my* manager . . .

In a way it's not surprising that diverting would be a frequent temptation for many people. When someone starts talking about a challenge she's facing, it's a good bet that you'll start thinking about one that *you've* been through or are wrestling with. If she describes what she did last weekend, you'll undoubtedly be reminded of *your* weekend activities. That's the way the human mind works. And when your mind makes these associations, you're so eager to talk about them that you often burst into the conversation describing your experience without realizing that the other person hadn't finished talking about what was on her mind. A harried wife came home from work and muttered, "What a day! I don't think one more thing could have gone wrong." Before she could unburden herself, her husband said, "I know exactly how you feel, my day was unbelievable"—and related all the ins and outs of his problems at work. In one sense, you could say they were both talking about the same topic: a bad day at work. But the wife wanted to talk about *her* bad day, and the husband wouldn't wait to talk about *his* bad day—two very different conversations.

One-upmanship is a species of diverting that gets old in a hurry. When you tell about an enjoyable experience, this type of diverter is apt to break in to describe a far better time that he once had. If you tell about a recent mishap, a diverter is apt to interrupt, saying something like "Wait till you hear what happened to me," and delve into an account of a troublesome situation that he experienced, which, of course, was far worse than yours. Whatever may have happened to you, these diverters are quick to let you know that it's *nothing* compared to what *they've* experienced.

If you do much diverting, it won't be long before people assume you are self-centered and have little interest in what they have to say. That's no way to build relationships. And you'll soon find that conversation with you is slowing to a trickle. So discipline yourself to listen intently to the other person until you are sure he has finished what he has to say. Then, if you want to add something, feel free to tell your experience or make your point.

The Missteps in Action

It's one thing to read descriptions of the missteps people make when it would be more appropriate for them to listen and quite another to observe the missteps in action. Let's eavesdrop on a father's misstep-ridden conversation with his thirteen-year-old son, Darren, whose lacrosse team just lost a close game to its biggest rival. You'll see every one of the listening missteps in action.

Darren is walking across the field to meet his dad, who had been watching the game.

> DARREN: (With tears welling up in his eyes.) I was terrible. I'm the reason we lost the game.
>
> FATHER (disagreeing): No you weren't, you were good!
>
> DARREN: I was not! I missed both the goals I tried for. If I had made even one of them we would at least have had a tie game.
>
> FATHER (reassuring): No one expects you to win the game by yourself. However, a little more practice, and you'll do better.
>
> DARREN: You don't understand.
>
> FATHER (disagreeing): I do too understand.
>
> DARREN: Just stop it, will ya Dad! (Darren turns and starts to walk away.)
>
> FATHER (criticizing): You are just too stubborn to listen to reason.

As you'll see in Chapter 9, when one person in a conversation has moderately strong to very strong feelings, the other person needs to take the listening role, at least until the speaker's feeling level returns to normal. In the preceding situation, Darren was so disappointed with his performance that he was incapable of listening to reason at that moment. Therefore, it would have been appropriate for his dad to take the listening role. Instead, as often happens, his father continued talking. Since both Darren and his dad were focused on talking, neither was paying much attention to what the other said or felt. They were having "a dialogue of the deaf."

SKILLED LISTENING IS THE BEST ALTERNATIVE TO MISSTEPS

Let's see how that situation would likely have played out if Darren's father had listened empathically to Darren's great disappointment about his role in his team's loss. As you'll see here and learn more about in later chapters, a good listening response typically restates the essence of the speaker's statement *briefly* and *in the listener's own words*.

DARREN: (With tears welling up in his eyes.) I was terrible. I'm the reason we lost the game.

FATHER (listening response): You're really disappointed.

DARREN: I missed both goals I tried for. If I had made even one of them we would've at least have tied the game.

FATHER (listening response): You feel responsible for the loss.

DARREN: Yeah, that sure would have been better than a loss. If only I had made that last play.

FATHER (listening response): If only . . . (Sigh) (Commenting) Maybe next time.

DARREN: Yeah . . .

FATHER: (Puts an arm around Darren's shoulder, and they walk to the car in silence.)

"YOU JUST TOOK AWAY MY WHOLE LISTENING REPERTOIRE!"

When hearing a presentation about the missteps people often make when listening, many look back with regret. They dwell on communication that went awry and important relationships that were strained because of their use of the missteps. They say things like:

No wonder my kid doesn't talk much to me.

I always thought of myself as a good listener and didn't realize that I often short-circuit communication by the way I listen.

Several responses that you identified as missteps were things that I thought help a conversation and I've been using them pretty consistently.

It's like suddenly knowing the enemy and discovering that it's me.

How did I get to be forty-three years old without discovering that these are missteps?

You just took away my whole 'listening' repertoire. What else is there to do?

The next chapter presents a proven strategy for diminishing your use of the missteps of listening.

7

Reducing Major Missteps

> Habit is habit and is not to be flung out of the window by any man but coaxed downstairs a step at a time.
>
> — MARK TWAIN

NOW THAT YOU'RE acquainted with the six major missteps of listening, it's time to develop a plan for reducing their negative impact on your listening. In this brief chapter, we show how to target and significantly reduce your use of a misstep that's impairing your listening.

Guidelines for Reducing Your Use of a Listening Misstep

Here's how to decrease your reliance on a misstep that's hampering your listening effectiveness:

- Target *one* misstep that impedes your listening.
- Replace the targeted misstep with good listening.
- Overcome the misstep in stages.
- Strive for progress, not perfection.

Target *One* Misstep That Impedes Your Listening

Although just about everyone uses more than one misstep, it's counterproductive to tackle more than one at a time. Once people learn about the missteps and the harm their use can do to communication and ultimately to relationships, many are tempted to try to eliminate several at the same time. *Repeated experience has shown that tackling more than one misstep at a time is a recipe for failure.* Be wise, and conservatively select one misstep to work on. People generally focus on the misstep that most bedevils their listening. However, feel free to choose a different criterion for selecting a misstep to work on.

From the following list *select one misstep to work on*:

- Disagreeing/agreeing
- Criticizing
- Questioning
- Advising
- Reassuring
- Diverting

When you decrease your reliance on that misstep, you'll find that your listening will have improved significantly. Then, if you decide to improve your listening still further, you may decide to target another misstep.

Replace the Targeted Misstep with Good Listening

Research shows that simply trying to break a bad habit is rarely effective. Psychiatrist Maxie Maultsby, Jr. asserts, "People cannot just get rid of a habit; [they] have to replace [the] old habit with a new habit."[1] And renowned family therapist, Salvador Minuchin, found that, "Trying to stop something usually doesn't work. What works is starting something else."[2] At several points in Chapter 6, we mentioned that skillful listening is a good replacement for several of the missteps under discussion. Actually, that's true of all the missteps. Thus, when you catch yourself about to use a misstep, employ skilled listening instead. As you find yourself listening more and better, you'll find that you'll be using the missteps less and less. (You'll learn the skills of listening, as well as important applications of quality listening, in Chapters 7 through 22.)

Overcome the Misstep in Stages

When ridding themselves of a given misstep, people often find themselves proceeding through four stages:

STAGE 1: HINDSIGHT

Early in your attempts to eliminate a misstep, you'll probably realize *after the occurrence* of the misstep that you used it, despite your firm resolve not to. "Darn," you say to yourself, "there I go again!" People frequently become discouraged when they realize that, despite their best intentions and strong effort, they just used the very misstep they've been struggling to manage.

Important tip: Rather than criticizing yourself for using the misstep, *celebrate the fact that you recognized your use of it.* That's the crucial first step to overcoming the power of a dysfunctional habit. Seasoned listening coaches know that it's an encouraging sign when you begin to become *aware* of your use of the misstep—even if you didn't avoid using it. It's important to reinforce even minor progress in your diminishing use of a misstep. So tell yourself, *"Good work for noticing it!"*

STAGE 2: MIDDLESIGHT

With persistence, you will arrive at the second phase of conquering an antilistening habit. At this point, you'll often realize that you are using a misstep just as the words leave your mouth. It may not seem that you are improving because you are still using the misstep. But this is a significant advance: *Now you are often catching yourself in the very act—almost soon enough.*

STAGE 3: FORESIGHT

When you reach this stage of greatly reducing your use of a misstep, *you become aware that you are about to use the antilistening response in time to refrain from uttering it.* You have developed a proficient replacement for the antilistening response that you used habitually for years.

STAGE 4: FREEDOM FROM HABITUAL USE OF THE TARGETED MISSTEP

Free at last! You are no longer in the grip of this detrimental habit, and your listening will have improved appreciably. Now you are in a better position to apply the more constructive responses that you'll learn in future chapters.

Time to celebrate! But don't allow yourself to become overconfident; you still need to remain vigilant, or you're apt to backslide.

Strive for Progress, Not Perfection

The habit you've decided to break has undoubtedly been a part of your life for a very long time, and by now is second nature to you. So it will be close to impossible for you to immediately and completely eliminate that deeply ingrained habit. Benjamin Franklin wrote of his struggle to overcome his habitual pride: "Struggle with it, beat it down, stifle it, mortify it as much as one pleases, and it is still alive and will every now and then peep out and show itself." Be realistic: *Make progress your goal, not perfection*. And be patient with yourself as you gradually reduce your use of the targeted barrier.

Final Tips

Be prepared to experience setbacks as well as successes. For every two steps forward you'll often take one step back. Since improvement will undoubtedly be slower than you wish, *keep reminding yourself that you are making progress*.

Be especially vigilant in important or stressful conversations. When you or the other person is more stressed than usual, or if the conversation is particularly significant, the use of missteps will tend to increase.

When you decrease your reliance on the targeted misstep, you'll find that your listening has improved significantly. Then, celebrate your progress. Of course, if you choose to make the effort, you may select another misstep to work on.

8

Skill-Based Listening

Skill—the ability to do something well.
—OXFORD AMERICAN DICTIONARY

M OST PEOPLE DO *ordinary listening*—the kind that's used every day by people who picked up the way they "listen" from the mainly untrained and unskilled "listeners" who've populated their lives from infancy on. Ordinary "listeners" aren't aware of the trouble spots that bedevil the talking–listening process discussed in Chapter 5. And they're generally unaware of the commonly made listening missteps that were the focus of the last two chapters. Although ordinary "listening" enables people to muddle their way through many conversations, it often leads to serious miscommunication. And all too frequently, it leads to strained relationships.

This chapter describes skill-based listening—a way of listening that enables you to successfully cope with the imperfections that mar the speaking–listening process while providing a positive alternative to using the missteps discussed in the two previous chapters. In contrast to ordinary "listening," this chapter describes what skillful listeners do in conversations that are important to one, both, or all parties.

Good listeners:

- Use a set of skills
- To accurately understand the speaker's thoughts
- And feelings

- From the speaker's point of view
- And restate the essence of the speaker's message
- Until the speaker has fully expressed the point he's making.

Let's take a closer look at each of these phrases that define what good listeners do.

Use a Set of Skills

There's a widely held assumption that listening well is an aptitude that some people are born with and others aren't. However, that assumption has been found to be false. With instruction such as you'll find in this book, combined with diligent practice, anyone of sound mind can become a capable listener. Rather than being an innate gift, *good listening is a cluster of skills that can be learned.* Virtually anyone can master this crucial set of abilities. Having an effective set of listening skills frees you from making random responses to what people say to you and enables you to respond appropriately.

To Accurately Understand the Speaker's Thoughts

When listening, you obviously want to comprehend the thoughts, facts, and ideas the speaker is conveying. To do that, you need to bring an open mind to what's said. Clearly, being charitable to the other person's point of view doesn't necessarily entail agreement with the speaker. However, when you really listen, you must be willing to change your mind when you hear new data that sheds fresh light on the matter. Even when much of what's being said appears to you to be incorrect, listen for a grain of truth in it and benefit from learning that. As actor Alan Alda said, we "need to listen with a willingness to be changed."[1] We're not saying that you'll always learn something new that changes your thinking, but it's smart to be open to that possibility. At the least, you'll learn what's on the mind of the person who is talking to you.

And Feelings

Important as it is to understand the speaker's thoughts, it can be as important and sometimes more important to sense what she's feeling. The speaker's feelings indicate how strongly her thoughts are held. They affect a person's decisions and motivation for action. And they may influence the outcome of the conversation, as well as the quality of the relationship between you and your conversational partner.

Many managers think it's foolhardy to attend to other people's feelings. For instance, in one of our *Listening Skills* workshops, the trainer finished a presentation in which he described how to listen to a person's vehemently held feelings. An agitated participant burst into the presentation, saying, "I don't want to hear one more word about listening to feelings. What a way to run a business! We're here to be productive and get the job done in the shortest and most efficient way. If someone's feelings get hurt along the way, so be it. Maybe he shouldn't be here if he's so thin-skinned."

This kind of resistance to listening to feelings is not unusual. In fact, you may be experiencing some of that yourself. Before you toss out the idea, however, give it a chance. Wait until you've read up to and then through Part IV and experimented with that more detailed explanation of how to respond to a speaker's feelings. Then see what you think.

Of course, in many interactions, people's emotions are low-key, and the listener can focus mainly on the content of the conversation. But when the speaker's feelings are strong, it's wise to respond to them. The chapters in Part IV provide you with the tools for doing that effectively.

From the Speaker's Point of View

When you truly listen, you focus on understanding the speaker's point of view. This is the most challenging part of listening—really grasping the speaker's perspective—especially when his thoughts or feelings are quite different from yours. As mentioned earlier, we're not suggesting that you should necessarily agree with the speaker but that, *when listening, your job is to clearly understand what the speaker is trying to convey until he has fully made his point.* Until then, refrain from assessing whether you agree or disagree with what he's trying to get across. Once you fully and accurately understand the point the other person is making, you'll find yourself in a better position to make your own evaluation of its accuracy and worth when that's important to you or the speaker.

To correctly grasp what the speaker is driving at, you need to put your own thoughts and feelings on the back burner. In his highly regarded book *The Road Less Travelled*, M. Scott Peck, MD, writes:

An essential part of listening is the temporary . . . setting aside of one's own prejudices, frame of reference, and desires so as to experience, as far as possible, the speaker's world from the inside.[2]

And George Miller adds:

In order to understand what another person is saying, you must assume it is true and ask yourself what it may be true of.[3]

It often takes considerable mental effort to extricate yourself from your own frame of reference and immerse yourself in that of another person. Here's a description of one man's struggle to get into his boss's frame of reference: Joseph Swidler, chairman of the Federal Power Commission during the Kennedy administration, described a time when he thought that the president was not giving Swidler's agency enough support. With thoughts of resignation in his mind, he set out for the White House to tell the president how resentful he felt. On the way, he started thinking about the president's problems: "Berlin. Laos. The Congo. Disarmament. The Middle East. The foreign aid bill. Khrushchev. All those burdens. And minute by minute as he approached the office he felt his anger lessen, until by the time the President's door opened, he heard his own voice saying, 'What can I do for you, Mr. President?'"[4]

Of course, one of the president's major challenges is to understand the frame of reference of other world leaders. This requirement was very apparent during the thirteen days of the Cuban missile crisis, which created "the greatest danger of catastrophic war since the advent of the nuclear age."[5] Records from the period show that President Kennedy was constantly imagining himself in Khrushchev's situation in an effort to make decisions that would not cause the Soviet leader to lose face with his own people. Robert Kennedy said when thinking back on that period, "A final lesson from the Cuban missile crisis is the importance of putting ourselves in the other country's shoes."[6]

From writer and educator Peter Elbow, we learned a few questions that help us temporarily set aside our frame of reference in order to discover the value in statements that seem uncongenial to some of our current assumptions and beliefs. Instead of saying, "No way!" or "What a dumb idea" or "You can't be serious!" we try to ask ourselves:

Wait a minute, there must be something sensible here: How can I see the validity in it?

She must be seeing something I can't see. What am I missing? How can I retrieve her insight?

In what sense or under what conditions could her words be true?[7]

When we thoughtfully consider these questions, we usually learn something that we otherwise would have missed. At the same time, we typically gain greater rapport with the speaker—not a bad payoff for putting our frame of reference on hold for a few moments.

And Restate the Essence of the Speaker's Message

A *reflection* is a very brief summary of a portion of a conversation or, in some cases, a summary of the whole interaction. During *casual chats*, reflections can help the flow of conversation but tend not to be essential to the dialogue.

In discussions that are important to you and/or the other person, however, these succinct recaps help keep all parties to the conversation on the same page and make the conversation more accurate, more efficient, less stressful, and more gracious.

As you read further, you'll see that this way of listening is not only highly effective; it's about 180 degrees removed from the relatively inept "listening" that's so common in our culture.

Until the Speaker has Fully Expressed
the Point He's Making

A speaker commonly makes a few comments and, *intending to say more*, pauses to catch his breath or briefly think about how to phrase the next part. Unfortunately, the average "listener" often interrupts the momentary pause to say whatever is on his mind, thus prematurely driving the original speaker into the listener's role. This back-and-forth switching of conversational roles is very inefficient and is the source of much miscommunication.

Skilled listeners keep the conversation focused on the speaker until he has finished making his point. One way to do this is to *treat pauses as commas and listen for what comes next*. When the pause continues a bit longer—about six or seven seconds, consider that a conclusion of that part of the other person's comments and feel free to interject your thoughts.

Because this way of listening may be new to you, you may feel awkward and not like yourself as you try on the "new" way of listening. The feeling of awkwardness, discomfort, and self-consciousness are feelings most of us feel when we try to break old habits and learn new skills of any kind. Take a deep breath and hang in there because these unwanted feelings will soon be replaced by a sense of appropriateness, ease, comfort, and increased rapport.

To Develop the Ability to Listen Well, Follow the Learning to Listen Pathway

Learning to listen in this way is a journey well worth taking, but it's still a journey. There are four sections of the pathway.

At the outset, most learners are *unaware* of the way they listen, how inept it is, and that there is a better way. Many readers might describe themselves as *unaware* at this point.

With exposure to material such as you're reading, you may become *aware* that you are not a really capable listener and that maybe there is a better way.

As you begin using the listening skills taught in this book, you may *feel unnatural*. "How awkward," you think. "This isn't me," you say.

But if you hang in there, you move to the next step of the journey where you become *skillful*. You've developed the skills of listening, and you know when and how to use them. And by then you'll be competent at using them and will be delighted in the improvement in your conversations.

The final step of the journey occurs when your new skills become such an integral part of who you are that *you feel completely natural when you use the skills*. In fact, you'll feel unnatural if you don't use the skills. You will have become a truly capable listener.

9

Whose Turn Is It?

There is a time to be silent and a time to speak.

–ECCLESIASTES 3:7

PERHAPS THE FUNDAMENTAL of interpersonal communication that's most ignored is the issue of which party should have the floor. Although people engage in all kinds of conversations, most folks use one of two *habitual approaches* to participating in them. Some tend to take the floor and do most of the talking. For instance, the late actress, talk show host, and brash comedian Joan Rivers described her style as, "I enter talking." And she often kept the verbal onslaught going for some time. Other people tend to listen their way into and through virtually every conversation. But repetitively taking the same general approach with very different people, in a variety of situations, and when conversing on very dissimilar topics, is a formula for conversational mismanagement.

Good communicators avoid these conversational gaffes by taking a *situational approach to beginning their interactions*. Instead of using one or the other habitual ways of commencing, they align their approach with the circumstances of the specific interaction. To do this quickly and effectively, it helps to have a sound method for assessing whether to initiate primarily with the talking mode or with the listening mode in a given exchange. A suitable choice at the outset can set the stage for a constructive and fruitful conversation.

A Guideline for Knowing
When to Listen and When to Talk

The eighteenth-century Irish author and politician, Sir Richard Steele, devised an easy way to figure out the appropriate approach to take in any significant conversation. In *The Spectator, no.* 49 (April 26, 1711), he wrote:

> It is a secret known but to few, yet of no small use in the conduct of life, that when you fall into a man's conversation, the first thing you should consider is, whether he has a greater inclination to hear you, or that you should hear him.

That's still pretty much the case today.

The Communication Skill Selection Question

That guideline is as valuable today as it was when Steele wrote it more than three hundred years ago. Its usefulness today, however, is blunted by the eighteenth-century language, which in our time comes across as stilted and archaic. So we contemporized the wording and condensed the guideline for easier recall.

At the beginning of each conversation (and at key junctures during the interaction), ask yourself the communication skill selection question: *"Whose need to talk is greater?"*

- When *the other person* has the greater need to talk, *you listen.*

- When *you* have the greater need to talk, *you talk.*

Perhaps you are thinking, "Why waste the reader's time with this guideline? It's just common sense." Although making a conscious decision about whether to listen or to talk in significant conversations may be common sense, it certainly is not common practice. If a majority of people in an organization routinely followed this guideline, their increased productivity would be noteworthy and esprit de corps would certainly be heightened.

Steele's guideline has you ask yourself the communication skill selection question *at the beginning of your conversations*. However, it's also useful to keep that question in mind as the conversation progresses. During the course of a conversation, be alert to the possibility of a shift in people's need to talk. Once the speaker has expressed her point of view, her wish to talk generally diminishes. And if the speaker said something that triggers strong feelings in the listener, the latter will probably want to state his opinion. By being attentive to both the other person's and your own shifting needs to talk, you'll be able to interact appropriately throughout the conversation.

To remind themselves whose turn it is to talk, some people copy the Communication Skill Selection Guide shown in Figure 9-1 and locate it in one or more places where they can refer to it occasionally.

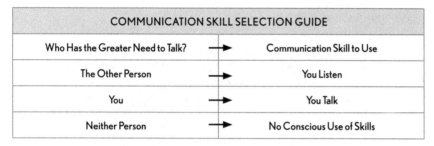

COMMUNICATION SKILL SELECTION GUIDE	
Who Has the Greater Need to Talk? ➡	Communication Skill to Use
The Other Person ➡	You Listen
You ➡	You Talk
Neither Person ➡	No Conscious Use of Skills

FIGURE 9-1. COMMUNICATION SKILL SELECTION GUIDE.

Postpone Serious Conversations
if You Are Unable to Be Fully Present

It's also important to *know when not to listen*. There will be times when the situation calls for you to listen but you aren't able to devote the single-minded attention to the other person, which is essential for effective listening. You may be in a tight time bind. Perhaps you have a splitting headache. Or your own pressing concerns may be so strong that you aren't able to or don't choose to set them aside in order to focus exclusively on the other person's issues. Attempting to listen when you're not up to it compromises your ability to empathize. On those occasions, postpone the conversation because good listening takes focus, energy, and empathy.

When Both People Have a Strong Need to Talk

You can be sure that there will be times when both you and your conversational partner will concurrently have a strong need to talk. When this occurs, there's often an unruly, unpleasant, and unproductive exchange. Rather than let the conversation degenerate into a brouhaha, you can use the communication skill selection process to determine a constructive way to achieve a productive and equitable outcome. In these situations, too, the Communication Skill Selection question is invaluable:

"Whose need to talk is stronger?"

When both people have a strong concurrent need to talk:

- use conflict resolution skills

- and/or cooperative problem-solving skills

Using listening skills to resolve conflict and engage in cooperative problem solving is taught in our book *People Skills: How to Assert Yourself, Listen to Others, and Resolve Conflicts*, Part IV.

When *neither person* has a strong need to talk, it doesn't matter who talks and who listens. Just aim for a fairly even give-and-take so that no one dominates the interaction.

How to Determine When the Other Person Needs to Talk

When looking for the answer to the question "Whose need to talk is greater?" watch for signs of a greater than normal intensity of the other person's body language—higher energy than usual, louder voice, greater rapidity of speech, more intense body language. When you see any of these signals, pay close attention. The person's body language seems to be signaling that something out of the ordinary is going on for her, and she may have a need to talk about it. Those signs generally are indicative of feelings of excitement, anger, shock, amazement, or some other kind of emotional intensity that generally calls for you to listen empathically.

- Less than normal intensity of the other person's body language— the signals of low energy, soft voice, slow speech, and subdued body language—may indicate sadness, hurt, disappointment, worry, annoyance, grouchiness, or just being out of sorts. When you see any of these signals, you need to pay attention. They often indicate that something may be wrong and that the person may need to talk about it. Or at the very least she may not be ready to listen to you. Time for you to stop talking and start listening.

• At times *the content* of what the other person is speaking about may indicate that she has a need to talk. For example:

- A challenging new project

- A hard decision she's facing

- The illness of someone close to him

The simple question "Whose need to talk is stronger?" will facilitate getting off to a good start in any conversation. And it can be useful during the conversation as needs change.

10

Focus Your Attention

Our simple attention, offered to another person, is the most underused of human resources, one of the least costly, one of the most freely available, and—without a doubt—one of the most powerfully beneficial.

—KATHLEEN SINGH

AS AUTHOR AND researcher Sherry Turkle noted, "Conversation . . . is derived from words that mean 'to tend to each other, to lean toward each other.'"[1] Good listeners focus their undivided attention on the speaker—giving him their full postural alignment, mental concentration, and emotional responsiveness. This skill, known as *attending*, is the body language of listening. It's a nonverbal way of showing the speaker, "The floor is yours and I'm all ears."

This chapter describes the important benefits that attending contributes to your listening and describes the specific how-to's of effective attending. It also teaches the companion skill of using *encouragers*—one- to three-word statements or empathic sounds like "Mm-hmm" that enable a listener to participate audibly in the conversation without distracting or interrupting the speaker.

Paying Attention Pays Off

Good attending delivers many benefits. For instance, it:

Demonstrates that you are interested. Psychologists John Gottman and Clifford Notarius write:

> The most common mistake people make is to think that the secret to good conversation is to be interesting. It is not. The secret is not to have interesting things to say, but *to be interested*, genuinely interested, in the person you're talking to and to show it.[2]

Helps the speaker think more clearly and speak more fluently. Behavioral scientists found that when listeners change from doing ordinary "listening" to being physically, mentally, and emotionally attentive to their conversational partner, "speakers tend to . . . 'come alive' in communicating their message."[3] You can easily do your own investigation. When you notice that you have become distracted and inattentive when someone is talking to you, start giving that person your full physical and mental attention. I think you'll be amazed at how the conversation perks up.

Diminishes the wandering mind problem. Distractions happen, and if you're like most listeners, you'll sometimes drift off on a mental vacation when someone is talking to you. Attending is a good antidote to the wandering mind problem. When you stop whatever you are doing, face the speaker, and lean into the conversation, you are shutting out many potential distractions and are reinforcing your inner resolve to maintain your attention on the speaker and his message. Then, too, eye contact fosters improved concentration. Sports psychologist James Loehr finds that, "When you are visually focused, you tend to be more mentally and emotionally focused."[4]

Increases the listener's access to information. Your success at work is highly dependent on the information you receive, and being fully engaged in your conversations increases the amount and quality of information coming to you. Good attending invites the speaker to go deeper into the conversation and to share more valuable data.

Helps the listener better understand the speaker's message. In addition to increasing your concentration on the conversation, attending positions you well for observing the speaker's body language, which is an important supplement to his verbal communication.

Enhances the listener's relationships. It says a great deal to someone when you stop what you are doing, turn to face her, and demonstrate with your attending that she is your highest priority at the moment. The relationship effect of attending is at least as crucial on the home front as in the workplace. "Attention," as the saying has it, "is the food of love." Family therapist Salvador Minuchin says,

> Attention. Genuine attention.
> That's not too much to expect from a marriage.[5]

Yet people often grow careless about attending to the people who are central in their lives. Humorist Helen Rowland wryly noted that when a girl marries, "she exchanges the attentions of many for the inattention of one." Although husbands may tend to be more negligent than wives, it's not uncommon for both partners to become less attentive to one another over time. When that happens, quality conversation and affection erode.

Once begun, attending is self-reinforcing. Your ability to continue attending is aided by the speaker's increased clarity of thinking and fluency of speaking. And, if your mind does stray, it usually returns to the conversation in short order because your posture and visual focus are directed toward the speaker.

Inept Attending and Nonattending
Distance Relationships and Stifle Communication

When a person who is talking to you senses that you are inattentive, she'll likely feel devalued and her motivation to keep talking with you will soon decline. John invited Larry, his business associate, to join him for dinner at a restaurant in hopes of having an important conversation that would have been difficult to have at work. Bad idea. Larry noticed someone he knew, waved vigorously and intermittently, kept an eye on who was with that person. People coming and going caught his attention too. He was so distracted by his surroundings that not only was it impossible for John to have his intended conversation, but he began to feel as though Larry was interested in everyone and everything but him. Although Larry was unaware of it, the relationship took a hit because of his nonattending behavior.

In another situation, an engineering manager often leafed through papers when employees talked with him. One of the employees complained to a friend, "When I talk to him, I feel unimportant. What I have to say is less significant to him than his paperwork."

Multitasking in the Presence of Another Person Is a Blatant Kind of Nonattending

As we've seen, when conversing with another person, unless they're merely chatting about incidental matters, *quality listeners give their undivided attention to the speaker*. Even when it's just chitchat, it's important to keep your focus strictly on the person who's talking to you, or the relationship will begin to sour. However, due in part to the enormous pressure that people today experience to do more in less time, many are increasingly engaging in multitasking as opposed to unitasking. For example, while conversing on the phone, many people do such things as work on email or check their social media feed.

The rapid proliferation of digital devices in recent years has vastly increased the amount of multitasking that people can engage in wherever they are and whomever they're with. And huge numbers of people now engage in multitasking even when it makes them inattentive to the person or persons they are with. *Phubbing*—snubbing someone you're with by using your mobile phone—is a new term for this practice that's rapidly gaining widespread use. A study of more than 450 U.S. adults by Baylor University Professor James A. Roberts found that 46.3 percent of their partners phubbed them, and 22.6 percent said the phubbing caused relationship problems:

> We found that the ones who reported higher phubbing fought more with their partners and were less satisfied with their relationship than those who reported less phubbing.[6]

Few people, it seems, stop to consider that when they are with a person or are having a phone conversation with someone *and are concurrently engaged with a digital device*, they are "thinging" the person they're conversing with—treating him as an object, a nonperson. In the words of philosopher Martin Buber, that's treating the person as an *it* instead of relating to him as a *thou*.[7]

THE DOWNSIDE OF MULTITASKING

Ironically, multitasking isn't all it's cracked up to be. Way back in the first century BCE, the Roman slave Publilius Syrus realized, "To do two things at once is to do nothing." His insight has been confirmed again and again by researchers at leading universities.

Actually, *multitasking is a delusion*. MIT Professor Sherry Turkle spent thirty years researching and writing about people's relationship with technology. She stresses that when we try to multitask, we pursue an illusion. "When we think we are multitasking, our brains are actually moving quickly from one thing to the next, and our performance degrades for each new task we add to the mix. Multitasking gives us a neurochemical high so we think we are doing better and better when we actually are doing worse and worse."[8]

Extensive scientific investigation indicates that, with extremely rare exceptions, when a person is multitasking he'll be wasting much time, he'll be considerably more error prone, and he'll be more stressed out at the end of the day.

The evidence is in: Multitasking is virtually always an inefficient way of operating. And in interpersonal communication, phubbing is "the antithesis of good listening." As psychiatrist M. Scott Peck observed, "You cannot truly listen to anyone and do anything else at the same time." And, as already noted, attending to one's digital device instead of focusing on the person you are with shallows the relationship.

When to Attend

When doing everyday activities with others, it's natural to listen informally and not be very concerned about your body language. But when a significant topic comes up or when feelings become intense, give your conversational partner your full physical, mental, and emotional attention. Why? Because you can't do two things at once if one of them is quality listening. Don't even think about multitasking when someone is talking to you. Turn away from your phone or computer, set your paperwork aside, stop whatever else you are doing, and focus your undivided attention on the speaker. If you are busy at an urgent task and aren't able to set it aside at the moment, explain that you are busy now and negotiate a time when you can give the conversation the attention it deserves.

How to Attend

Position yourself in a way that enhances your attentiveness and communicates your single-minded focus on the speaker and his message. Silence your electronics, as noted, and:

- Stand or sit at an appropriate *distance* from the speaker.
- *Face* the speaker.
- Maintain an *open position*.
- *Lean* slightly into the conversation.
- Maintain a relaxed yet alert *posture*.
- Maintain comfortable *eye contact* and engaged *facial expressiveness*.
- Use small, responsive *gestures*; avoid distracting gestures.

STAND OR SIT AT AN APPROPRIATE DISTANCE FROM THE SPEAKER

In the United States, the typical conversational distance between friends is two to four feet. For most business and social conversations, four to twelve feet is the norm. In other parts of the world, observe the typical distance at which good listeners sit or stand from the speaker in these types of situations and do likewise.

FACE THE SPEAKER

You don't necessarily need to be squared off, directly across from the speaker. People often are more comfortable sitting or standing at a bit of an angle from their conversational partner.

MAINTAIN AN OPEN POSITION

Keep arms and legs relaxed and uncrossed when listening. Speakers are likely to interpret a physically closed position (such as crossed arms and/or legs or ankles) as a sign that the listener is not receptive to what's being said. You'll miss much of what you're told when your body is in a closed position. Researchers found that when people listen with arms crossed, they learn 38 percent less than folks who assume an open position.

LEAN SLIGHTLY INTO THE CONVERSATION

People are sometimes told, "Sit back and listen." Bad advice. Instead, sit up, lean slightly forward, and listen. A somewhat forward lean, with both feet flat on the ground and facing the listener, communicates interest and energizes the conversation. Don't overdo it, though. Sitting or standing in ramrod, military fashion appears rigid and uninviting. What you are aiming for is *a posture of relaxed alertness*.

MAINTAIN COMFORTABLE EYE CONTACT

Most people in our culture associate eye contact with caring, understanding, empathy, and warmth. Researcher and social psychologist Michael Argyle says that good listeners make eye contact about 80 percent of the time. Eye contact that's comfortable for the speaker creates a visual bond with her. However, make sure your gaze is comfortable for the other; you don't want to come across as staring the other person down.

Visual attention to the speaker demonstrates respect. In fact, the term "respect" derives from a word that means "to look at."[9] Remember, though, that prolonged eye contact is uncomfortable for most people. So gently shift your gaze, perhaps to a gesturing hand, and then back to the face, with a glance to the eyes, and so forth.

GET AT EYE LEVEL WITH THE PERSON YOU ARE LISTENING TO

When the speaker is on her feet, stand with her; when seated, pull up a chair for yourself when that's possible. Place yourself as close to eye level as you can.

A good example of someone who takes the importance of attending to heart is our physician. He is a very tall gentleman who, when entering the examining room, greets his patient with a warm smile and a handshake. Then he sits on an adjustable stool and with a barely noticeable move, he adjusts the stool, usually downward, to position himself at eye level with the patient.

USE SMALL, RESPONSIVE GESTURES AND AVOID DISTRACTING ONES

Conversations are enriched when the listener makes small movements of the head and hands that are in sync with the speaker's message and mood.

These small movements indicate that you are tuned in to what's being said. Head nods are a good example. They are an unobtrusive way of communicating that you are paying attention. If you don't nod at all, people are liable to wonder if you are still there. These small responsive gestures are more important than you might think. For instance, researchers found that candidates who nod their heads during an interview get the job more often than those who don't.[10]

AVOID DISTRACTING HABITS

Playing with a paper clip, jangling keys, tapping a pencil, glancing at your watch, and drumming your fingertips on the desk or table are all distracting habits that serve no purpose.

Cultural Variables

What constitutes effective attending differs from culture to culture and even from one subculture to another. For instance, Americans of European extraction tend to look away from the person they are talking to and look toward the person they are listening to.[11] Many African Americans do the opposite.[12] In our diverse society, good listeners adapt their attending to the way the speaker prefers to interact. If you think the speaker is uneasy with something about your body language, try to inconspicuously change the manner of your attending until you find an approach that the speaker finds comfortable.

Wholehearted Concentration

Being preoccupied with the behaviors related to listening, as we've been discussing thus far in this chapter, may make attending seem mechanical—as if merely following a certain set of postural and gestural practices will result in good attending. But obviously if you are mentally or emotionally absent, the impact of your distraction will seriously undermine your attending. Skilled listeners use good attending skills, *and* they are fully focused on the speaker. They are attuned to her and provide a sustained presence throughout the conversation. Fortunately, attending and the other skills taught in this book will help you stay mentally and emotionally involved in the conversation.

Karen Horney, founder of the American Institute of Psychoanalysis, captured the rich meaning of this aspect of listening with the phrase "wholehearted attention." She noted that high-quality attention entails concentrating "all one's faculties in the situation."[13] True attending costs the listener effort and concentration. That's why the phrase "paying attention" is so apt.

Former President Bill Clinton personifies this quality of attending. Someone who observed him at several public forums says whether "you were a head of state or a bell clerk, when you were talking with Bill Clinton he acted as if you were the only person in the room. Every fiber of his being, from his eyes to his body language, communicated that he was locked into what you were saying." [14]

Don't Purposely Nonattend to a Speaker

When someone wants to talk and you're busy, purposely nonattending to the speaker in hopes that he'll see that you're occupied and refrain from interrupting you doesn't work. That common way of handling these predicaments usually backfires. The speaker probably won't notice that you are in a time crunch and may assume from your body language that you are rude or that you don't like him.

Rely on words in these situations: Explain that you're pressed for time at the moment and arrange another time that's convenient for both of you. Use words, not dismissive body language, to handle these situations. It's a polite way of achieving your goal, and what's probably more important is that it's not likely to chip away at the relationship.

There may be one or more people who waste your time with frequent verbal meanderings. When someone repeatedly interrupts what you are doing with irrelevant chitchat, you may have to assert yourself in order to change that annoying habit. Chapters 8–10 of our book *People Skills: How to Assert Yourself, Listen to Others, and Resolve Conflicts* teach assertion skills that can help you put an end to these unproductive interruptions.

Environmental Factors Conducive to Listening

In addition to the body language of attending that we've been focusing on, conversations are often impacted significantly by the environment in which they are held. On some occasions, you may have little choice about where the conversation will take place. But with forethought, you'll probably be able to negotiate an appropriate location for the anticipated conversation.

Savvy conversationalists hold important discussions in settings that are favorable to good communication. Here are some things you can do to converse in a relatively nondistracting environment that supports the upcoming conversation:

Decide whose turf—yours, theirs, or neutral. People usually are more comfortable in their own territory, so if you know in advance that a conversation will be primarily about the other person's agenda, her space may be the best place to meet. Sometimes it makes sense to meet in your area—especially if that enables better control of interruptions and distractions. When a conversation is likely to be difficult, it may be preferable to meet on neutral turf. When you want to minimize power or status differences, consider meeting in a conference room rather than in your workspace.

Assure privacy. For important conversations, seek a location where other people can't overhear what's being said. Cubicles in open office environments generally offer little privacy and no way of shutting out distractions. If you work in that kind of environment, consider going to a conference room or other suitable location for conversations that are important or that could be difficult.

Arrange the seating to facilitate communication. Many workspaces are set up to expedite the tasks the employee does when alone and are not likely to be conducive to face-to-face communication.

If you work at a desk, move out from behind it when someone is talking with you. A desk is not only a large physical barrier, but in the eyes of people lower on the totem pole, it may also be a symbol of authority and a reminder of the distance between your rank and theirs, which may impede the openness of the communication.

Supplement Your Attending with Encouragers

An important part of the listener's job is to stay out of the speaker's way without lapsing into noninvolvement. *Attending helps you do that silently, while the companion practice of using encouragers enables you to demonstrate your attentiveness audibly as well.*

WHAT ENCOURAGERS ARE

Encouragers are one- to three-word statements or empathic sounds like "Mm-hmm" that enable a listener to participate in the conversation without distracting or interrupting the speaker.[15] Encouragers blend into the background of the interaction and don't add to or subtract from the content being discussed. They're spoken in a manner that doesn't imply agreement or disagreement with the speaker's comments. But they're important listening tools: they keep a conversation two-way and therefore more invigorated.

Here's a sampling of encouragers—words, phrases, and sounds—that contribute to the speaker's sense that you are paying attention to and are involved with what she's saying:

I see.	Uh-huh.	Go on.
Got it.	Really!	No kidding.
How about that!	Interesting.	Sure.
Wow!	Yeah.	Oh.
Unbelievable.	Hmm.	No way!
My goodness!	You betcha.	Tell me more.

Good listeners distribute encouragers throughout a conversation. Sometimes they're used more frequently in the early part of a conversation to help it gain momentum. In phone conversations, encouragers can provide a partial substitute for eye contact and facial expressiveness.

HOW TO USE ENCOURAGERS EFFECTIVELY

You undoubtedly use some encouragers already. Here's how to assure that this aspect of your listening is effective:

- **Make sure you are attending well.** Encouragers are most effective when supported by good attending.
- **Use a variety of encouragers.** If you use the same one over and over again, the speaker may experience it as a distracting mannerism. The preceding list can help you add to your repertoire.
- **Enhance your encouragers with vocal and facial empathy.** A bland sounding "Uh-huh" won't do much for the conversation. If

emotions are an important part of what's being said, respond to the speaker's feelings with a tone of voice and body language that lets the speaker know that you are attuned to what she's feeling.

When appropriate, intersperse encouragers with reflections. (Part III of this book teaches when and how to reflect what you're told.)

Don't Be Misled by the Simplicity of These "Big-Little" Skills

Encouragers and attending are *"big-little"* skills. *Big*—in that they can make a significant impact on a listener's effectiveness. *Little*—because they are very brief and require the least effort and skill to implement. Improvements in your attending and use of encouragers can enhance your listening significantly.

11

Be a Great Asker

> The four greatest words in one's vocabulary are, "What do you think?"
>
> —ANONYMOUS

> Some readers may wonder about the inclusion of chapters on the use of *questioning* in a book about *listening*. Although questioning is not the same as listening—nor is it a subskill of listening—we include two chapters on questioning because we think of listening and questioning as *companion skills* that are often used in tandem when a person is seeking information. Skilled communicators often alternate between adept questioning and respectful listening.

"THE IMPORTANT THING," said Einstein, "is not to stop questioning. Curiosity has its own reason for existence." Leadership experts Warren Bennis and Burt Nanus write, "Successful leaders, we have found, are great askers, and they do pay attention."[1] Management consultant Caroline Webb adds, "Merely by saying, 'Tell me more about that,' you'll be in the top ten percentile of listeners that anyone will meet today."[2]

Questions are incredibly useful work tools. They can help you learn a new procedure, discover which of your products or services is needed by a prospect, understand the reasons for a customer's dissatisfaction, determine whether or not the person you are interviewing is the best candidate for the job, or uncover the reason for last month's slump in productivity.

And asking an insightful question or two can lead to a strategic break-through. For instance, at a critical juncture of semiconductor maker Intel's history, CEO Andy Grove turned to cofounder Gordon Moore and asked this question: "If we got kicked out and the board brought in a new CEO, what do you think he would do?" Grove's question shifted Moore's point of view from that of a co-founder of the corporation to that of an objective outsider. With this alteration of mindset, Moore unhesitatingly gave the revolutionary response, "He would get us out of memories." (Computer memories were their major business at the time!) Grove then asked this follow-up question: "Why shouldn't you and I walk out the door, then come back and do it ourselves?" Metaphorically, that's just what they did, which positioned the corporation for its remarkable success in the years following.

Asking well targeted questions can be important in one's personal life too. Effective questioning will help you acquire the knowledge needed for important decisions like dealing with a child's problems at school, evaluating medical treatment options, making major purchases, researching sound investments, and so forth.

Although all of us ask questions on a daily basis, effective questioners are few and far between. Someone asked theologian Martin Luther, "What was God doing before He created the world?" Annoyed by the banality of the question, the reformer replied, "He sat under a birch tree cutting rods for those who ask nosey questions."[3] In our own day, effective questioning is still the exception rather than the rule. Although journalists supposedly have mastered the skill of questioning, many of their interviews are marred by inane questions. During Lyndon Johnson's administration, the White House correspondent of The *New York Times* interviewed the president and asked about an internal White House procedure. Johnson laughed and said, "Here you have a chance to interview the President of the United States and the leader of the free world. And you ask a chickenshit question like that."[4]

The purpose of this chapter is to help you develop effective questions and ask them in a way that obtains needed information and/or stimulates the other person's thought without straining the relationship. Here are five keys to being a great asker:

- Hear the speaker out.
- Limit the number of questions you ask.
- Create productive questions.
- Use an effective questioning process.
- Act when you receive an actionable response.

Hear the Speaker Out

It's usually best to listen completely to what the speaker has to say before asking questions. Inept "listeners" often derail conversations by prematurely butting in with questions. These interruptions often cause the questioner to miss useful information that she would have obtained had she continued listening. So, when someone is talking to you, listen until he has finished speaking. Then if you need further information, you've earned the right to ask further questions.

Limit the Number of Questions You Ask

"Less is more" is a useful guideline when it comes to asking questions. No one likes to be hammered by a barrage of questions. And excessive questioning is an inept approach to acquiring information. As noted in Chapter 5, when too many questions are asked, they're likely to become barriers to communication. Additionally, investigators found that asking numerous questions often diverts the discussion away from the primary issues.[5] Furthermore, researchers learned that the amount of information obtained soon decreases when the number of questions asked increases.[6] Police investigators discovered that it's normally less effective to guide a person through an interview with questions than it is to allow people freedom to explain things in their own way. When an investigator plies the witness with one question after another, the witness generally becomes more passive and is less likely to volunteer potentially important information that the questioner doesn't think to inquire about.[7] So strenuously discipline yourself to limit the number of questions you ask.

Create Productive Questions

Obviously, the caliber of the questions you ask will impact the usefulness of the responses you get. Because this matter is so important, the next chapter is devoted entirely to developing and sequencing fruitful questions.

Use an Effective Questioning Process

Productive questioning often involves more than merely popping a question; it frequently entails using a six-step process:

1. Develop the question.
2. Ask the question.
3. Provide thinking time.
4. Listen carefully to the reply.
5. When appropriate, reflect the reply.
6. Take action when you receive an actionable response.

DEVELOP THE QUESTION

People can be overly casual about the phrasing of their questions and often have to state two or three of them before they muddle their way to approximately what they wish to ask. Study the next chapter because, when you apply its content, you'll obtain much improved information from the queries you make.

The more threatening a question seems to the person being asked it, the more defensive he's likely to become, and the information he provides is apt to be scantier and less reliable than it otherwise would be. So, when wording your question, consider how it will be taken by the person receiving it. Hard issues sometimes need to be faced, and difficult questions may need to be asked. With contentious issues, it's especially important to phrase your inquiry as tactfully as you can to avoid provoking self-protective reactions. Think yourself into the other person's situation. Then phrase and ask your question in a way that will be as palatable as possible.

ASK THE QUESTION

Once you've developed your question (and a preface to it when that's appropriate), you're ready to ask it. S. I. Hayakawa, a language scholar and former United States senator, emphasized that good questioners "avoid all implications (whether in tone of voice or wording) of skepticism or challenge or hostility. They must clearly be motivated by curiosity about the speaker's view."[8]

PROVIDE THINKING TIME

Once you've asked a question, be silent. Don't say another word until the other person has responded. The recipient of a question may take a few moments to think about how he'll answer. Silence makes many people feel anxious. To relieve their own stress, questioners sometimes repeat the question, perhaps in slightly different words, or ask another question. Don't make that mistake!

Realize that:

Silence is the questioner's ally!

William Ury, cofounder of Harvard Law School's Program on Negotiation, found that:

> Only half the power of a . . . question lies in the question itself. The other half can be found in the pregnant silence that follows as the [other person] struggles with the question and mulls over his answer. A common mistake is to deprive him of this creative time.[9]

LISTEN CAREFULLY TO THE REPLY

Having put considerable thought into framing your question, make sure you concentrate on the response. Although it's important to craft good questions, two-time Pulitzer Prize winner David McCullough—an outstanding questioner—says, "It's much more important to listen when you are interviewing than to worry about what questions to ask."[10]

Redbook's former senior editor Andre Fontaine's message to journalists applies to anyone who uses questions to obtain information:

> Reporters can't afford to listen like normal people; they must work at it. You recognize that most people aren't very articulate, that their words are a screen that often shadows or distorts information which is very clear in their own minds. You have to penetrate this screen and see the idea as clearly as your source does. It takes work.[11]

WHEN APPROPRIATE, REFLECT THE REPLY

When someone replies to your query, it's often useful to reflect his response. A reflection at this point often encourages the other to elaborate what he was driving at, so it's frequently a good substitute for asking another question. Reflections also add variety to the conversational process and reduce the likelihood that the person being questioned will feel like he is being interrogated. They transform what might have seemed like an inquisition into a dialogue. The skills of reflective listening are taught in Chapters 13–18.

Act When You Receive an Actionable Response

When you ask someone a question, respect her response. If she makes a helpful suggestion, thank her, put it to work, and a bit later follow up and let her know that you're implementing it.

Even when a suggestion doesn't seem usable, the respondent was undoubtedly trying to help. So you could respond to the remarks with an acknowledging comment like, "Hmm. Interesting idea. I hadn't thought about it that way."

> This chapter presented six keys to being a great asker. Chapter 12 will help you further develop your information-gathering expertise in that it describes how to develop productive questions and presents well established ways of sequencing them effectively.

12

Creating and Sequencing Productive Questions

> I would like to find the guy who first said, "There is no such thing as a stupid question," and force him to sit through the monthly meeting cycle of any major corporation.
>
> —MARK MCCORMACK

THE PREVIOUS CHAPTER presented keys for developing and asking questions and highlighted the importance of taking action when you receive an actionable response. This chapter helps you put that information to optimal use by providing:

- Guidelines for creating productive questions.
- Methods for sequencing multiple questions effectively.

Guidelines for Creating Productive Questions

How you phrase a question can make a significant impact on the usefulness of the response you get. As the saying goes, "You can't get a clear answer from an ambiguous question."

We've found four guidelines to be especially helpful in developing productive questions:

1. Consider creating an alternative question to the one you first think of.
2. Preface the question.
3. Decide whether to ask an open-ended question or a closed-ended question.
4. Arrange multiple questions in a productive sequence.

CONSIDER CREATING AN ALTERNATIVE QUESTION TO THE ONE YOU FIRST THINK OF

When asking a question, many people just fire off the first question that pops into their mind. Instead, it's usually preferable to first determine specifically what you want to ask about. Then think about how to phrase it. Steve Cole, VP of research and development at HopeLab, a nonprofit that fights to improve children's health using technology, gives this example: "Any time in life you're tempted to think, 'Should I do this OR that?'" he suggests asking this alternative question: "Is there a way I can do this AND that?"

Psychiatrist Alfred Adler's biographer and close friend, Phyllis Bottome, wrote that when a patient came to see the famous psychoanalyst, he did not ask himself:

> as most doctors would, "How ill is he?" but always [the alternative question], "How much in him is still healthy?"

For he believed that the basis of the cure would be the power of the man's resistance rather than the power of the illness itself.[1]

PREFACE THE QUESTION

A preface can serve one or both of two purposes.

* A preface typically frames the question in a way that enables the respondent to understand more clearly what information you are seeking.

   PREFACE: I need to make any adjustments to the new system by December 31.

   QUESTION: How is the new system working?

- When a question is being asked that the respondent might have hoped to avoid, a preface may soften the impact somewhat and perhaps make a tough question more palatable.

   PREFACE: We need to coordinate with Pete's schedule.

   QUESTION: What are your plans for sending the prework to him?

Unfortunately, researchers find that although prefacing many of one's questions would enhance numerous queries, few people preface their questions.[2]

Here's an easy way to figure out how to preface a question. Mentally complete the following sentence starter:

The reason I ask is . . .

When you complete that sentence, you'll have the preface to your question. For example, an executive planned to ask his managers how the division could reduce the amount of inventory on hand. Not wanting to risk their becoming defensive by dropping that question on them out of the blue, he decided to begin with an explanatory preface. When preparing for the meeting, he said to himself, "The reason I ask is . . ." and completed the sentence with the words, "because I've just received a directive to reduce our inventory by at least 10 percent." That gave him his preface:

   PREFACE: I've just received a directive from the division VP to reduce our inventory by at least 10 percent.

   QUESTION: What can we do to decrease inventory by that amount without reducing the quality of our service?

Obviously, a preface is seldom needed when the context and purpose are already perfectly clear to the other person.

DECIDE WHETHER TO ASK AN OPEN-ENDED QUESTION OR A CLOSED-ENDED QUESTION

You probably understand the distinction between these two important types of questions. Here we briefly recap that difference; then we'll describe how to create and use both types of questions. For simplicity's sake from here on we'll refer to open-ended questions as open questions and closed-ended questions as closed questions.

Open questions invite fairly expansive answers. They're typically used to:

- Gain an *overview* of a situation.
- Obtain *the respondent's opinion.*
- Or learn about his feelings.

They typically generate longer and more thoughtful responses.

Closed questions solicit very brief and specific answers, such as "Yes," "No," "Maybe," or "I don't know." This type of question helps you discover *specifics facts,* by calling for *succinct one- to three-word responses.*

Before framing your question, determine whether an open question or a closed question will generate the information you want. Often a combination of the two types of questions will provide you with the best information.

GET THE BIG PICTURE WITH OPEN QUESTIONS

Open questions are good tools for initiating a discussion or for obtaining an overall description of a situation and for eliciting the other person's opinion or feelings. They typically begin with one of these question starters:

What?   What if?   Why?   How?

However, be cautious about using questions starting with "Why" as in, "Why did you make that decision?" Questions starting with the word "Why?" often come across as being judgmental, and the recipient may become defensive and less cooperative.

Fortunately, "Why" questions can be reworded to "What" questions, which enables you to receive the needed information without the likelihood of putting the respondent on the defensive. Here are a few examples.

Why didn't you do it?
What factors led to your decision not do it?

Why haven't you finished this project?
What difficulties have you encountered that delayed the completion of this project?

Why didn't you finish the project today?
What factors led you to change your mind about finishing the project?

Also avoid questions that are excessively open-ended such as, "What's new?" People generally respond to excessively open-ended questions with blandly uninformative answers like, "Not much." The commonly used but overly open-ended, "How're things going?" predictably calls forth uselessly vague responses like, "Fine" or "Good" regardless of how the person actually feels.

A touch of creativity can produce a different and often a more useful answer than a more prosaic question. When the Gallup organization wanted to identify high-performing managers, its interviewers could have asked:

OPEN QUESTION: Who are your best managers?

Instead they phrased their query this way:

OPEN QUESTION: Which of your managers would you dearly love to clone?[3]

The latter, more creative wording would likely generate more out-of-the-box information.

The number of situations in which open questions are useful is practically endless. Here are a few examples.

When a person's body language suggests that she wants to talk. If you infer from someone's nonverbals that she might want to speak but for some reason isn't saying anything, encourage her with an open question. For your preface in this sort of situation, you could briefly and nonjudgmentally describe her body language. Then ask a question that invites her to elaborate:

PREFACE: You look a bit discouraged today.

OPEN QUESTION: What's going on to get you down?

When keeping the air time balanced. It can be off-putting when someone dominates the conversation. So if you suddenly realize that you've been doing more than your share of talking, use an open question to invite the other person to tell about her thoughts or experiences.

PREFACE: Well, that catches you up on my news.

OPEN QUESTION: How did your daughter's big game turn out?

We've seen that a preface is often used to set the context for an open question. However, when the respondent understands the context, there's no need for a preface. In the following examples, assume that the context is understood by the respondent and that no preface is needed.

When transitioning from small talk to the point of the conversation, you can, after a few minutes of pleasantries, use a question to shift to the substance of the conversation:

OPEN QUESTION: What's on your mind today?

When soliciting suggestions for improvement. When a division manager at a multioffice supply company visits a store, he gathers employees in small groups and asks:

OPEN QUESTION: What have you noticed that needs attention or change in the company that I might not have noticed?

When inviting different viewpoints:

OPEN QUESTION: I'd like to hear some additional perspectives on this matter.

When negotiating an objective:

OPEN QUESTION: For this objective, what would be a home run for you?

More examples of open questions:

What are you working on these days?

What are your thoughts about this?

What led up to the crisis point?

What is your worst-case scenario?

What have you thought of or done so far?

Would you lay out the pros and cons of that approach?

How does this square with your experience?

What other options do you see?

How does that translate into action?

What's your reaction to this recommendation

What do you like best about this plan?

What are some of the things that could go wrong?

Anything else we should talk about before deciding?

OPEN STATEMENTS

You can inject a bit of variety into your information gathering by occasionally interspersing an open statement into a sequence of questions. As the name suggests, open statements are information-gathering statements rather than questions. And they can generate the same information as a similar question would while adding a welcome bit of variety to your inquiry. They begin with sentence starters like:

Tell me about . . .

I'd like to hear your reaction to . . .

Describe . . .

> OPEN STATEMENT: *Tell me about* your experience at the exposition.

> OPEN STATEMENT: *I'd like to hear your reaction to* the president's speech.

> OPEN STATEMENT: *Describe* the problems you think we may have overlooked.

Many open questions can be converted to open statements to give a bit of variety to your questioning. For example:

> OPEN QUESTION: What have you thought of or done so far?

> OPEN STATEMENT: Tell me what you've thought of or done so far.

OPEN QUESTION: Would you lay out the pros and cons of that approach?

OPEN STATEMENT: Describe the pros and cons of that approach.

You'll undoubtedly find that when you become more skillful at asking open questions and using open statements:

- You will receive better information.
- Your asking will encourage the respondent to speak more forthrightly.
- Your conversations will be characterized by more give-and-take.

Despite the incredible usefulness of open questions, Dorothy Leeds, the author of several books on questioning, found that "only one of twenty questions managers ask is phrased in an open style."[3] So there's a good likelihood that you'll be able to significantly improve your information gathering by using more and better open questions.

LEARN IMPORTANT DETAILS WITH CLOSED QUESTIONS

Closed questions help you delve into the specifics. They promote concreteness and clarity. And they invite very succinct one- to three-word responses. They lead off with one of these question starters:

When?	Where?	Who?	Which?	Would?
Could?	How much?	How many?	How often?	Do you?
Will you?	Can you?	Are you?	Does . . .?	

CLOSED QUESTION: Which would you like—the blue one or the red one?

CLOSED QUESTION: When did that start?

CLOSED QUESTION: Who was present?

CLOSED QUESTION: When you say seven days, do you mean seven calendar days or seven business days?

CLOSED QUESTION: What time is the meeting?

CLOSED QUESTION: Can this responsibility be delegated?

CLOSED QUESTION: How much time will that take?

CLOSED QUESTION: Will your other responsibilities suffer?

CLOSED QUESTION: Do you like that approach?

As noted, once you ask a closed question, the other person will usually answer "Yes," "No," "Maybe," "I don't know," or something nearly as brief. Since the answer to a closed question consists of only a word or two or three, the conversational ball is back in the asker's court in a split second. It all happens so quickly that the questioner is often at a loss about what to say next. What's most likely to come to mind is another closed question. Researchers found that one closed question tends to beget another, which begets yet another. That's rarely, if ever, a good way to obtain information. And the person being bombarded with a string of closed questions will probably feel that he's being grilled and is likely to become less communicative and somewhat miffed by the interrogation. Also, a series of closed questions tends to switch the agenda of the conversation from the speaker to the listener. Therefore, good listeners carefully ration their use of closed questions and are very purposeful about using them.

Although the misuse of closed questions occurs frequently, when it's time to focus on concrete details, closed questions are the way to go. During a briefing with the head of Mexico's largest bottling company, former Coca-Cola CEO Doug Ivester was told that the company's products were distributed by tens of thousands of mom-and-pop retailers. Ivester then asked a savvy closed question:

So which are they—moms or pops?

The resulting investigation revealed that a large percentage of the retailers were moms. So the answer to that closed question resulted in an incentive program devised to reward the most productive moms—an initiative that helped lift sales by 13 percent.[4]

Methods for Sequencing Multiple Questions Effectively

Often you'll need to ask several questions in order to get sufficient information about the issue or situation you are inquiring about. The most common approach used to ask several questions about a topic or incident is to spontaneously ask questions as they pop into the asker's mind. This random approach to asking multiple questions typically results in chaotic information gathering and greatly reduced recall. It's far more productive when asking several questions about a given issue or situation to sequentially organize the questions prior to the interview. Knowledgeable questioners often use one or the other of two question-sequencing models: *the Funnel Sequence* and *the Inverted Funnel Sequence*. Each of these formats aids you in arranging a number of questions in a productive sequence. In important interactions, that type of preparation can be enormously helpful even though some of the planned questions may need to be altered or scrapped in the give-and-take of conversation. Since the Funnel Sequence seems to be used more frequently, we will look at three examples of this way of sequencing questions.

THE FUNNEL SEQUENCE

The Funnel approach to information gathering proceeds from the general to the specific. It begins with one or more open questions that invite the interviewee to think about and state his general ideas, opinions, and/or feelings about the topic or situation being discussed.

Closed questions are asked further down the funnel to unearth specific information. They're employed to surface the nitty-gritty of what you need to know.

For instance, in a teacher training practicum, the coach sat in the back of the classroom while the trainee taught his or her first class. In the tutoring session at the close of the workshop day, the coach used the funnel format. Here's a condensed version of the sequence of open questions she used. (Because the coach's students knew the context for the questions, prefaces to the questions were not necessary.)

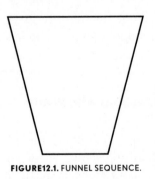

OPEN QUESTION: How useful was the session for you?

OPEN QUESTION: What do you like about what you did?

OPEN QUESTION: What would you do differently if you could repeat the session?

FIGURE12.1. FUNNEL SEQUENCE.

CLOSED QUESTION: Do you need any help from me?

Of course, in productive conversations there's usually lots of interaction between the questions.

A Funnel Sequence can contain quite a few questions. Here's a set of debriefing questions that's great for harvesting learnings and fostering improvements at work. It's equally useful on the home front when talking with your significant other or having a conversation with a child. And it generates a more interesting and informative conversation than the customary "Where did you go?" "Out" What did you do?" "Nothing."

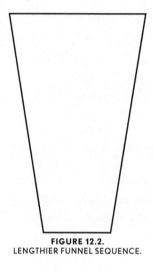

FIGURE 12.2.
LENGTHIER FUNNEL SEQUENCE.

OPEN QUESTION: How did it go for you?

OPEN QUESTION: What went well?

OPEN QUESTION: What was most difficult?

OPEN QUESTION: What worked?

OPEN QUESTION: What didn't?

OPEN QUESTION: When you do this again, what will you do differently?

CLOSED QUESTION: Which of these learnings will you apply in your next [sales call, basketball game, etc.]?

On the other hand, the Funnel Sequence can be as brief as two questions:

FIGURE 12.3.
VERY BRIEF FUNNEL SEQUENCE.

OPEN QUESTION: What did you learn from that?

CLOSED QUESTION: When will you start using that information?

THE INVERTED FUNNEL SEQUENCE

As the name implies, this framework of questioning begins with a narrow scope and broadens as the conversation proceeds. Inverted Funnel questioning moves from the particular to the general—from a tree to the forest, so to speak. It typically begins with one or more closed questions and moves to one or more open questions.

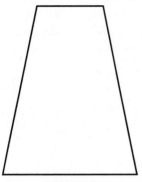

FIGURE 12.4.
INVERTED FUNNEL SEQUENCE.

CLOSED QUESTION: How many months in the past year did Aaron miss his sales goal?

CLOSED QUESTION: By how much did he miss his target each time he fell short?

OPEN QUESTION: What do you see as his strengths and weaknesses in selling?

OPEN QUESTION: How can you as his manager help him overcome his weaknesses and develop his strengths further?

There's much spontaneity in productive conversations, and, as a questioner, you need to be responsive to the other person's remarks. But even as you bounce off the speaker's reply with your next query, the preparation of having thought your way through your sequence of questions will help you extemporaneously come up with further questions that will help you collect more and/or better information.

This chapter and the previous chapter showed how to create and use productive questions in a way that enables you to gain information effectively and to avoid seeming like you are bringing back the Inquisition.

You have now completed Part II and are ready to move on to Part III, where you'll learn the purpose and nature of this crucial communication ability, as well as discover how to master two of the basic skills of this crucial ability.

PART III

REFLECTING CONTENT

Reflections are
"the most useful
yet least used response
in interpersonal communication."

—GERARD EGAN

13

Reflective Listening: Antidote to Miscommunication

Letting people know that I understand what they are saying to me is a kind of oil that lubricates the entire communication process.

—GERARD EGAN

WHAT MOST DISTINGUISHES effective listening from average listening is a cluster of skills known as reflective listening. This family of skills is sometimes termed *active listening* because, unlike the passivity of typical listening, these skills provide a proactive way of grasping the speaker's message and demonstrating to him that he has been understood.

What Reflections Are

Reflections are:

*Concise restatements
of the crux of the speaker's message
using the listener's own words*

Reflections provide a sounding board for the speaker. They let the speaker know how his message landed on his conversational partner so that he can clarify any misunderstandings—or know that part has been received reasonably correctly. And, if he has more to say, reflections encourage the speaker to continue expressing what he's thinking and feeling.

Reflective listening has an unusual history. It's been traced back to the University of Paris in the Middle Ages where the format for theological debates was for each speaker to summarize what the previous speaker said to the latter's satisfaction prior to stating his own point of view. However, in the tumult of that or later periods, the practice of reflective listening seems to have disappeared.

As mentioned in the preface, Dr. Carl Rogers rediscovered and refined the skill of reflective listening. Several other psychologists contributed useful nuances. This book in general and Part III in particular are greatly indebted to Rogers's seminal contributions to the knowledge of how to listen effectively.

Over a period of forty-two years, the authors of this book have spent much of our professional lives designing, revising, and intermittently tweaking reflective listening training programs for use in workplace conversations. We also developed and led workshops in listening for college teachers, public school educators, State Department of Mental Hygiene professionals, couples, parents, and a host of other populations. So what's contained in this and the following nine chapters has a rich history of development and a breadth of application that we believe will help you perform better at whatever your job may be and create greater rapport with others in all manner of relationships.

Skeptical? Learn the skills well, read Chapter 22, put the skills to the test—then decide.

When to Reflect

Reflective listening is useful in interactions that are of considerable importance to one or both parties to a conversation. A conversation is considered to be important when *either person* or *both people* feel a need to talk. For example, reflective listening is called for:

- When the *other person* has a somewhat strong to very strong need to talk.
- When *both you* and *the other person* feel a strong need to talk.
- To *recap a significant conversation or a major part of it.*
- When you are *seeking information.*

- *Before taking an action that has been agreed upon.*
- *As an integral part of several other communication skills, such as influence skills, feedback skills, conflict resolution, and cooperative problem solving—to mention some of the many applications.*

Four Types of Reflections

There are four subskills of reflecting. Each subskill feeds back a different aspect of the speaker's message:

1. Paraphrases reflect the *thoughts, ideas, and opinions* that were expressed in the speaker's comments.
2. Reflections of feeling reflect the *emotional overtones* of the speaker's statements and demeanor.
3. Reflections of meaning reflect the *content + the emotional overtones* that were expressed in the speaker's verbal and nonverbal messages.
4. Summary reflections briefly recap *a whole conversation* or *a significant part of the conversation.*

We explain how to use each of these four subskills of reflective listening in the following six chapters of the book.

The Pre-Step to Reflective Listening: Decide to Reflect

A problem many people encounter when first learning to reflect is *deciding to reflect* when the conversation calls for it. Instead of reflecting, people new to using this set of skills *often reply* to the speaker *rather than reflect* what was said. After all, they've been doing that all their lives, and deeply entrenched habits are notoriously hard to break.

So, for most people, a critical pre-step to the process of reflective listening is to *break the habit of replying* when you find yourself interacting with someone who has a fairly strong need to talk. You do that by making *a decision to reflect*. When you sense that someone's feelings are a bit more intense than normal, remind yourself, "This is a time to reflect." After a while, you'll probably find yourself instinctively deciding to reflect when that's appropriate.

The Four-Step Reflective Listening Process

Years ago, Ed Lisbe, one of our master trainers, determined that if we were going to teach people how to reflect, we needed to explain how one goes about it: *What is the inner process by which one turns another person's long paragraphs into a single succinct sentence using one's own words.* The problem was we didn't know *how* we came up with a reflection—*the inner process* we went through to develop one. So our approach to teaching reflecting just followed a monkey-see/monkey-do process. We'd typically explain how to do reflections, show a modelling tape demonstration and then do a live demonstration, and finally have the group members pair up and practice the skill that was just taught.

Ed, however, continued puzzling about the inner process of reflecting and finally figured out the inner steps we were unconsciously taking to make our reflections:

Step 1: Take it in.

Step 2: Sort it out. } The inner process of reflecting

Step 3: Sum it up.

Step 4: Say it back succinctly and in your own words.

Each of the four types of reflecting uses the same four-step reflective listening process, which is a boon for people learning how to listen reflectively. So, take your time now and memorize the steps. You'll get reinforcement in several subsequent chapters as you learn to reflect content (factual information), reflect feelings, reflect meanings (facts + feelings), and make summative reflections, which recap a whole conversation or a major part of one. Here is a fuller explanation of the four steps involved in making all four types of reflections.

1. TAKE IT IN

Reflective listening begins with accurate reception of what the speaker said. If you don't receive the message accurately, your reflection is bound to be off the mark. To correctly understand what you are told, set your own thoughts and agenda aside so that you can give your undivided attention to comprehending the speaker's point of view.

Focus on the speaker's frame of reference. A major task for the listener is to understand what was said from within *the speaker's frame of reference.* In Japanese writing, the symbol for listening puts the character for *ear* within the character for *gate*. It's a graphic way of showing that, above all else, *listening entails seeing things from the speaker's point of view.*

The challenge we face in understanding others is that each of us has spent a lifetime developing our own frame of reference. We live within that mental set most of the time every day. Our minds are jam-packed with our own experiences, opinions, biases, issues, feelings, values, agendas, and so forth. When someone presents his or her idea, our own notions about that subject are likely to be activated. Instead of focusing our mental energy on understanding the other person's position, our thoughts are apt to be dominated by our own mindset—thus coloring our reception of what we take in. Furthermore, our frame of reference has become such a part of us that much of the time we are unaware of its influence. So taking in the speaker's message can be more of a challenge than is commonly realized.

It's especially difficult to put ourselves in the other person's shoes when we disagree with what's being said or when we think we're being criticized. When I (Bob) used to visit my elderly widowed mother during the last decade of her life, she often greeted me with, "Why don't you visit more often?" I thought I was doing pretty well at making time to see her, so what I took as criticism stung. I unwisely responded by launching into a defensive explanation that I visit every week, that my work has me travelling a lot, and so on and on. As you can imagine, my yeah-but's didn't enhance these interactions. Her complaints, combined with my protracted recital of excuses, made those conversations much less engaging than they might have been.

What happens in a given conversation often influences future interactions between the same people. Often a *pattern* develops so that when the same twosome converse, they're likely to keep repeating the same dysfunctional dynamic. *Though the content of their communication may vary, they have essentially the same conversation over and over again.* My mother and I had fallen into that trap. For some time, nearly all our conversations followed the same wearisome routine. Husbands and wives often get stuck in this type of relationship-depleting pattern. Parents frequently get into these go-nowhere ruts with their kids. These repetitious interactions are commonplace at work too.

One day when driving to my mother's apartment for a visit, I decided to set aside my frame of reference and do my best to understand hers. It became obvious that what she said revealed her loneliness and the fact that she loved and missed me—her only child. This time, rather than go into another lengthy explanation, I simply reflected, "You miss me and wish I would come by more often." Though she continued talking a little longer about wanting me to visit more, my mother now talked in a more disclosing than accusing manner. Finally we were free to enjoy conversations that weren't marred by petulance on her part and defensiveness on mine.

The ability to sense the other person's angle on things is also a powerful asset in the workplace. In his book, *Mind-Set Management: The Heart of Leadership*, Samuel A. Culbert asserts:

> before you can lead, manage, or team up effectively you must comprehend the mind-sets of the people with whom you deal.[1]

2. SORT IT OUT

Figuring out the main thrust of what's being said can be challenging. Much of the time the speaker is likely to be winging it. Sometimes he'll beat around the bush, making it difficult for the listener to identify the real issue. And at times the speaker will drift off on a tangent, and it may be challenging to know whether this information is merely a digression or relevant to the main thrust of his message.

Even when the speaker remains on track, the listener can easily get waylaid. A speaker may give an example when making a point. But illustrative stories can be so intriguing that they hook the listener's interest to the point where he gets stranded in the details and misses the point. When you get overly engrossed in the specifics of an example, ask yourself, "What's the *real point* of what she's saying?"

3. SUM IT UP

A good reflection is *a highly condensed summary* of what was said: the shorter, the better. Long, flabby reflections tend to be less focused and therefore less helpful than lean reflections. What artist Georgia O'Keeffe said about her field is equally applicable to reflective listening:

> It is only by selection, by elimination, by emphasis that we get at the real meaning of things.

Additionally, very succinct reflections energize the conversation. And they quickly return the conversational ball to the speaker, where it belongs.

So condense your reflections. Boil them down. Compress them so you can make your recaps as brief as possible while retaining the crux of the message.

4. SAY IT BACK SUCCINCTLY AND IN YOUR OWN WORDS

When you think you've grasped the crux of a brief segment of the conversation, say it back very concisely, *using your own words.* This step is the speaking part of reflective listening. Rather than saying "I know what you mean" or words to that effect, *demonstrate your understanding by succinctly feeding back your sense of what was communicated.* When you reflect what you heard, the speaker will know whether or not you got the message she was trying to get across. Thus, on-target reflections often save time by eliminating needless repetitions by the speaker. And, even more important, the speaker will feel *heard,* which can be a pleasant rarity in today's world.

Some people find it helpful to photocopy the following outline of the reflecting process and glance at it from time to time to remind themselves of the four steps of reflecting.

Step 1: Take it in.

Step 2: Sort it out. } The inner process of reflecting

Step 3: Sum it up.

Step 4: Say it back succinctly and in your own words.

Resistance to Reflecting What You've Been Told

When attending a training course to learn a better way of employing a skill that they've been using for many years, people are often reluctant to learn the new and improved methods. That's certainly the case for many who are sent to listening skills training programs. On the one hand, most participants can see that communication missteps actually do derail conversations and decrease rapport. They buy into the fact that interactions are enhanced when an attentive listener focuses his mental concentration and body language on her conversational partner. But *people's skepticism often kicks in when they begin to learn reflective listening.* Most objections to reflective listening fall into one or more of the following categories:

1. It doesn't feel natural.
2. It's too mechanical!
3. People will react negatively if I repeat what they just said.
4. If I restate what was said, the speaker will think I agree with him.

IT DOESN'T FEEL NATURAL

For many people, reflecting seems like a very strange way to listen to someone. It's counterintuitive, often requiring one to do the opposite of what comes naturally to most people. Of course, that's true of many other skills such as golf, tennis, swimming, skiing, and so on.

"You'll never catch me listening that way," objected one of the listening skills workshop participants. "It doesn't feel natural." Using reflective listening feels unnatural to many people when they're first learning and using the skill. We've heard that objection so often, we sometimes reveal this pre-prepared visual when that objection is raised:

Naturally It Feels Unnatural.

Then we comment somewhat as follows.

Habit is often referred to as second nature. Because we're so accustomed to our habits, they're comfortable to use—they *feel* "natural." If you've ever tried to improve your golf swing, tennis serve, or backstroke, you'll undoubtedly recall how awkward—how unnatural—the new behavior felt at first. So it's to be expected that it will feel awkward—or as people often say, "unnatural"—when trying a new way of doing something like listening that you've done in a different way time and again since your preschool days.

M. Scott Peck reminds his readers that it is "natural . . . to never brush our teeth. Yet we teach ourselves to do the unnatural."[2] Talk show host Barry Farber says, "God may have given us the game of golf just to teach us that often what 'feels' natural and harmonious is wrong, even disastrous."[3] Similarly, a ski instructor tells beginning students: "If it feels right, it's probably wrong. And if it feels wrong, it's probably right."

Learning a new and improved way of doing something generally means leaving an area of your comfort zone. It means enduring the stress associated with breaking long established habits and building new skills and abilities to replace them. So expect that the new listening skills you'll be learning will feel unnatural for a while. And realize that, with practice, using these new and improved ways of listening will begin to feel as comfortable as the old less effective ways once did. Additionally, they'll certainly deliver more satisfactory results.

IT'S TOO MECHANICAL!

People sometimes complain that if they follow specific steps and guidelines when listening, they'll lose their individuality and spontaneity in conversations. One mother in a parenting class protested, "If I'm reduced to using formats for the way that I speak when I respond to my daughter, I might as well be a robot."

She put her finger on a real concern. Some listeners follow reflecting guidelines in such a simplistic, unimaginative, and formulaic way that they do sound like robots. However, the guidelines for reflective listening are just that—*guidelines*—not laws. Once you become skilled at reflecting, your listening can be imbued with your personality as well as informed by the guidelines. Later in this part of the book, you'll see how conversational ways of phrasing and voicing your reflections can rid you of any tendency to sound like a robot. Then, too, it's good to remember famed dancer Martha Graham's dictum: "The aim of technique is to free the spirit."

Of course, there'll be times when it will be appropriate to set the guidelines aside and respond in whatever way your judgment suggests. The development of reflecting skills should expand your options, not limit them.

Also, as our friend and former colleague Rick Brandon, PhD, likes to point out, it's important to distinguish between a person's listening *skill* and his listening *style*. A *skill* like reflecting is a developed ability that's based on certain *guidelines*, which help you obtain superior results in that activity. By contrast, a person's listening *style* is the expression of the individual's unique personality and creativity that permeates his listening. Effective listeners follow the guidelines for reflecting, but their style of reflecting—their timing, word choice, intonation, facial expression, and the like—is distinctly their own. So when a person reflects what her conversational partner is saying, her reflections should be imbued with the stamp of her own personality.

It's like that with any skill—people who excel at a skill blend their personal style with the best practices of the discipline. As golfing great Arnold Palmer was reported to have said:

> There is no such thing as one correct swing that every golfer should try to imitate. In fact the "perfect swing" myth keeps many golfers from playing great golf. Instead, every swing should be as individual as the golfer himself . . . . Although certain swings share certain basics, in many ways they can vary tremendously.

Even more than golf, listening is a distinctly personal activity, and while every person's listening will benefit from mastery of the basics, it should also bear the earmarks of her own individuality.

PEOPLE WILL REACT NEGATIVELY IF I REPEAT WHAT THEY JUST SAID

Many people are incredulous when we suggest that in important conversations they reflect what was said as soon as they have a good feel for what the speaker is driving at and that they continue to reflect what they're being told every so often throughout the conversation. At this point we often hear statements like:

> You're telling me that I should keep saying back to a person what he just told me? No way! I'd look like a fool. The other person would complain, "I just said that."

That never happened to either of us in more than forty years of reflecting. So that seems to be a low-probability concern. That kind of a response probably indicates not that the reflection is in the listener's own words but that the listener is merely parroting back what the speaker just said.

In the unlikely event that someone makes that kind of a comment, you can reflect his concern, then make the truthful response, "It's my way of trying to be sure I understand what you mean. Did I get that right?" *If* you've developed good rapport with that person *and* have followed the guidelines in the next chapter for getting off to a good start in using these new-to-you listening skills, it's unlikely that you will run into much, if any, resistance.

IF I RESTATE WHAT WAS SAID, THE SPEAKER WILL THINK I AGREE WITH HIM.

Of course, it's possible that once in a great while someone may assume that your reflection means that you agree with what she's saying. Should that occur and you want to be clear that you have a different opinion, keep reflecting until she has finished speaking. Then state your opinion or understanding of the facts. For instance:

> I'd like to tell you my point of view on that.

> My ideas are a bit different than yours.

What Reflections Do For Conversations

Reflections are the best conversational tools for showing that you understand what was said and for preventing misunderstandings. Here are some of the many ways they contribute to productive and satisfying conversations.

Reflective listening helps the listener:

- Concentrate on the message.
- Remember what was heard—since saying something aloud strengthens recall.
- Collect more and better information.
- Understand a situation before reacting.
- Obtain a more open-minded hearing for the listener's input.
- Gain a few brief but still useful moments to think before making a reply.
- Maintain emotional control—during tense interactions reflective listening tends to have a somewhat calming effect on both parties.
- Confirm agreements.
- Demonstrate a people orientation.

Reflective listening helps the speaker:

- See that the listener is paying attention and is intent on understanding what she is saying.
- Realize that the listener understands what she's said so far.
- Make her point without interruption.
- Crystallize her thinking through hearing her thoughts stated more concisely and in different words.
- Gain deeper insights into the matter under discussion.
- Discover her own solution to the challenge or problem she is discussing.
- Feel valued as a result of being listened to.

Reflective listening helps both the listener and the speaker. Whatever facilitates a more effective interaction usually enhances the conversational experience for both listener and speaker, so actually *all of the items on the preceding two lists tend to be advantageous to both parties.*

Two additional benefits that derive from reflective listening are especially useful to both the speaker and the listener. Competent reflections:

1. Focus the conversation on the central issues.
2. Correct misunderstandings on the spot, further saving time and needless effort due to problems caused by miscommunication.

That's a huge bundle of benefits that can result from reflecting significant aspects of the speaker's message.

Although reflections can be used in casual interactions, they're invaluable when dealing with subject matter that's important to one or both people, as well as when the conversationalists are wrestling with emotion-laden issues. The bottom line is that *whenever you have a significant conversation at work, at home, or anywhere else, reflective listening is a must-have set of skills for making the most of the situation.* Think of reflective listening as *a communication quality control device.*

Unfortunately, as UCLA's Dr. Gerald Goodman noted, reflective listening is "the missing link in communication because so few people reflect what they hear."[4]

Here are examples of two conversations:

1. One when ordinary "listening" was used
2. One when reflective listening was used

1. EXAMPLE OF A CONVERSATION IN WHICH ORDINARY "LISTENING" WAS USED

Let's eavesdrop on a conversation in which it would have been appropriate for the listener to have used reflective listening but in which the listener used her "old ears."

JOE: Remember the Fullerton project my team and I started last January?

LISTENER: Vaguely.

JOE: Well, anyway, what an unbelievable mess that turned out to be. If anything could go wrong, it did.

LISTENER: How come you let things get so out of hand?

JOE: It wasn't my fault. First my key player left the company without giving any indication he was leaving.

LISTENER: Oh come on. There must have been signs that he was unhappy.

JOE: Who said he was unhappy? He just got a better opportunity with more money elsewhere.

LISTENER: Whatever.

JOE: That's exactly what happened.

LISTENER: Okay. I'm not saying it didn't.

JOE: You sure sounded like you didn't believe me.

LISTENER: You don't have to be so thin-skinned about everything.

JOE: I'm not thin-skinned. . . . Well, I gotta go now. Got another meeting.

2. EXAMPLE OF THE ABOVE CONTENT WHEN REFLECTIVE LISTENING IS USED

JOE: Remember the Fullerton project my team and I started last January?

LISTENER: Yeah, wasn't your deadline end of March?

JOE: It was actually March 15. Anyway, what an unbelievable mess that turned out to be. If anything could go wrong, it did.

LISTENER: Everything went south?

JOE: That's putting it mildly. First my key player left the company in the middle of the project. The technical parts we ordered to move forward never arrived, and we had to reorder, which made it impossible to keep our March 15 commitment.

LISTENER: It was one thing after another.

JOE: You got that right. I felt like I blew the whole job and when I tried to explain the situation to my boss, he wasn't happy.

LISTENER: Hard for him to accept.

JOE: Yeah. Feels like I'm between a rock and a hard place. I lost a lot of credibility with my boss, and the irony is none of it was my fault.

LISTENER: Things were out of your control, and now your boss is down on you.

JOE: Yeah. Now I have to figure out how to salvage things.

LISTENER: You want to start correcting a bad situation.

[Pause and transition from exploring the problem to resolving it.]

What have you thought of or done so far about the problems?

Teaching point: *Reflecting can help people move from complaining to action.*

This chapter provided an *overview* of the reflective listening skills that are essential abilities for competent listening. Next you'll learn the *four skills* of reflecting:

1. Paraphrasing (reflecting content)
2. Reflecting feelings
3. Reflecting meanings (content plus feelings)
4. Summary reflections (wrapping up a segment of a conversation or recapping the entire conversation)

14

Paraphrase What's Important

> [W]ords have a different connotation for you than they do for me. Consequently, I can never tell you what you said, but only what I heard. I will have to rephrase what you have said, and check it out with you to make sure that what left your mind and heart arrived in my mind and heart intact and without distortion.
>
> —JOHN POWELL

THIS IS A key chapter. The other subskills of listening taught in the next three chapters build on what's taught here. So take your time and take it in.

The chapter has two parts:

1. What paraphrasing is.
2. How to paraphrase.

What Paraphrasing Is

Paraphrasing, as the term is used in this book, is a skill that involves:

- *Summarizing* the *factual part* of the speaker's message—the data, ideas, thoughts, opinions, and the like.

- *Saying a summary back* to the speaker in the listener's *own words.*

Focusing exclusively on the factual aspect of communication is what distinguishes paraphrasing from the other skills of reflective listening. Paraphrasing is useful in conversations that have a low to moderate level of intensity, require accuracy, and are important to one or both parties.

Regarding the worth of this skill, psychologist Marshall Rosenberg notes:

> If we have accurately received the other party's message, our paraphrasing will confirm this for them. If, on the other hand, our paraphrase is incorrect, we give the speaker an opportunity to correct us. Another advantage of choosing to reflect a message back to the other party is that it offers them an opportunity to . . . consider what they've said.[1]

In response to an on-target paraphrase, the speaker typically confirms its accuracy by saying, "Right," "Exactly," or something in that vein. Or she might nod "Yes" or in some other manner indicate that the listener correctly captured what she said. Here's an example:

SPEAKER: After yesterday's interviews, I was pretty confident that I'd select Blaine for the vacancy. But the more I think about it, the less sure I am. At that time I was focusing on the importance of technical skills, and Blaine seemed to be the clear-cut choice. But as I consider the need for teamwork with coworkers and collaboration with other departments, I'm less sure.

PARAPHRASE: You're questioning Blaine's people skills.

SPEAKER: Right. We could run into big problems if . . .

The speaker continues talking, and the listener paraphrases the next segment of the message. And so on.

When the speaker discusses a problem and your reflections are concise and on target, the speaker often solves the problem himself. At other times, when he has finished speaking and hasn't solved the problem, it's appropriate for you to add your input.

DISTINGUISH BETWEEN PARAPHRASING AND PARROTING

Some people think they are paraphrasing when they are merely parroting what was said. However, the two ways of responding are worlds apart. A paraphrase is a brief restatement of the speaker's message, *using the listener's wording*. By contrast, a parroted response is essentially a vocal carbon copy of what the speaker said; it could have been given by a tape recorder. Parroted responses soon will begin annoying the speaker.

Note the difference between a parroted response and a paraphrased response:

> SPEAKER: Lately, I've had second thoughts about the job offer. I'm not sure I'm the right person for this particular responsibility. It seems to call for skills I don't have.

> PARROTED RESPONSE: You're having second thoughts about the job offer because you're not sure you are the right person for this particular responsibility. It seems to call for skills you don't have.

> PARAPHRASE: You wonder if you're right for the job.

Parroting—regurgitating the speaker's message—is a gross caricature of paraphrasing. And it's a real conversation stopper. It only takes a few parroted responses to make the speaker want to end the conversation in a hurry.

How to Paraphrase

As with each of the other reflecting skills, paraphrasing is a four-step process that's preceded by the listener's decision to feed back what she heard.

Pre-step: Decide to paraphrase.

Step 1: Take it in.

Step 2: Sort it out.

Step 3: Sum it up.

Step 4: Say it back.

You'll note that these are the same four steps that were presented in the previous chapter. Here you'll learn how to apply these steps when listening to the factual part of the speaker's message.

PRE-STEP: *DECIDE* TO PARAPHRASE

Most people need to make a conscious decision to paraphrase; otherwise, they're unlikely to do it. This is especially the case when they're new to paraphrasing. When someone makes a statement, the untrained "listener" instinctively tends to respond with his opinion instead of reflecting what was said. For instance, if you start telling the average listener your opinion of the current administration in Washington, his reactive mind is likely to immediately shift its focus to his opinion of the administration, and he'll probably state that rather than paraphrase what you just said. Of course, as soon as he makes a statement, he will have prematurely and inappropriately switched from the listening role to the speaking role.

In workshops, we sometimes do an activity that demonstrates the tendency of many people to *reply* to what was said instead of *reflecting* the speaker's comment. The trainer tells the group that she will call out one word, and each participant's role is to instantly answer with whatever word comes to mind. She adds that the procedure will be repeated several times using a different word each time. The trainer begins by saying, "Up." Without exception, participants say, "Down." The trainer says, "Wet." With one voice the group says, "Dry." The trainer says, "Black." The unison reply is, "White." And so forth. Participants are astounded at how uniformly reactive everybody is.

That same tendency is often at work in our everyday conversations. During a weekly team meeting, one member might say, "These weekly meetings are a waste of time." Most listeners would immediately assume they know what the speaker means and instead of paraphrasing, they typically would *reply* to what was said. Some might concur, saying something like, "I couldn't agree more!" Others might disagree: "How can you say that? Don't you remember how chaotic things were before we started having these meetings?" In other words, there's a good probability that the "listener" will reply—state her own point of view. By contrast, a skilled listener would likely pause briefly to give the speaker room to speak further. Then, when the speaker finished making her point, the listener would paraphrase that aspect of the message. And so on.

In short, unless newcomers to reflective listening make a conscious decision to practice this skill, it's unlikely that they'll paraphrase what's been said. People's reactive minds seem to ricochet—almost automatically—off the speaker's statement and into their reply. Consequently, *the biggest challenge most people face when beginning to paraphrase is deciding to do it.* Therefore, at the outset of important conversations, decide to paraphrase. Refrain from replying until you are sure the other person has fully expressed the point she was making.

1. TAKE IT IN

Once you are listening from within the speaker's frame of reference, search for the crux, the kernel, the essence of her message. Sometimes that can be difficult to ferret out. The main point sometimes is obscured by a clutter of anecdotes or irrelevant side issues. The listener's job at this point is to penetrate through any distracting details to get at the essence of the message. You may find it helpful to ask yourself: "What's the essence/point of this part of what's being said?"

2. SORT IT OUT

When tracking down the central issue, you may be faced with two or more ideas and will need to figure out which is more important or how they relate to one another. If you put too much emphasis on the less significant part of the message, you'll miss what the speaker is driving at.

There's a story, perhaps apocryphal, about Orville and Wilbur Wright who, after many tries, finally achieved what no one had ever accomplished before. On December 17, 1903, near Kitty Hawk, North Carolina, they achieved manned flight. Elated by their success, they wired the momentous news to their sister Katharine, "We have actually flown 120 feet. Will be home for Christmas." Katharine ran down the street and breathlessly handed the telegram to the newspaper editor. He read it and, smiling, said, "How nice. The boys will be home for the holidays."

Assuming the account is accurate, that editor missed one of the great scoops of the century because he zeroed in on the least important part of the message and overlooked the big story.

3. SUM IT UP

A good paraphrase is very concise. Reflecting is a boiling-down endeavor, a process of creative deletion. Pare away everything but the essence of the message. Here's the transcript of a recording of Dr. Carl Rogers' succinct paraphrase of a young mother's cluttered description of how she solved a parenting problem:

CLAIR: I would come home from work, and walk in the door . . . [and] the first things I'd see would be coats and books and baseball mitts and dirty glasses and cookie crumbs. The kids were glad to see me but I'd begin with "Good heavens, what's going on? Pick this up and put that away," and I'd be punishing and ugly and the kids didn't like me and I didn't like me and they felt guilty and ashamed. I began to think about it and I realized that they really didn't notice the things, because if I pointed to them they would pick them up and if I didn't point to the thing three feet away they didn't see it. It was strange. But they really didn't see it. And so I called a meeting . . . and for the first time really owned this as my own problem. *I* have a problem. I can't bear to have the house cluttered the way it is.

(ROGERS HAS TAKEN IN THE *MESSAGE, SORTED IT OUT, AND IS NOW READY TO SAY IT BACK.*)

ROGERS: It wasn't a problem to them but it was very much a problem for you.

CLAIR: Exactly. They . . .[2]

As usually happens with a good paraphrase, Clair confirmed the accuracy of the reflection ("Exactly") and continued her account.

4. SAY IT BACK

This is the speaking part of listening. Instead of saying, "I know what you mean," demonstrate your understanding by feeding back your sense of the crux of the message, as Dr. Rogers did in the example. That way, the speaker will know whether or not you understood the point she was trying to get across and will be able to correct any misunderstanding that may have occurred. Here are three keys to wording your paraphrase effectively.

Keep it brief. You want your reflections to fit into the flow of the speaker's talk. So aim for the most concise recap you can make. Paraphrasing is a boiling-down procedure, an exercise of creative deletion. Your task in paraphrasing is "to make a long story short." Leave out as much as you can. Don't use long prefaces like, "What I think I hear you saying is . . . ." Toss out some of the clutter. *Summarize your understanding in one succinct sentence.*

Use your own words. Although you are trying to focus on the speaker's perspective, the paraphrase needs to be in your words.

Start with a you focus. "You focus" is a shorthand way of saying that, since you are trying to sum up the speaker's message, you need to word your paraphrase in a way that keeps the spotlight on the speaker's thoughts, issues, problems, experience, or concerns. Many people have a habit of doing the opposite: They chime in with their own thoughts as soon as the speaker pauses. We've found that using you-focused sentence starters helps beginners at paraphrasing keep the focus on the speaker's point of view:

From your standpoint . . .	Sounds like you . . .
Your sense is that. . .	In other words, you . . .
You think . . .	You're concerned that . . .
As you see it . . .	So, for you . . .

Avoid using the word "I" in your paraphrases since that will likely lead you into responding with your point of view rather than paraphrasing the other person's concern. *Note that the preceding examples use the words "you," "your," or "you're"—not "I."*

If you think you need to use *sentence starters* for a while, limit them to two, three, or at most four words. When a person uses bloated and overused starters like, "What I think I hear you saying is . . ." or "If I understand what you are getting at . . ." the speaker may think you are playing amateur psychologist.

Don't rely on the same sentence starter all the time. We've known people who begin every reflection with the same words such as, "You're saying . . ." What a turnoff!

USE AN APPROPRIATE TONE OF VOICE AND BODY LANGUAGE

When paraphrasing effectively, your body language and tone of voice should show interest in and acceptance of the speaker and should pretty closely match the speaker's energy level and feeling tone. Voice and body language should be compatible with the speaker's delivery and the content of the conversation.

END YOUR PARAPHRASE WITH A DOWNTURNED VOICE

It is important to word and deliver your paraphrase as a statement rather than as a question. Doing so involves using a downturned voice at the end of the paraphrase.

Many people have been taught to turn their voice up at the end of a paraphrase. That weakens the effectiveness of the paraphrase (or any other reflection). The listener's upturned voice at the end of a paraphrase transforms it from a paraphrase into a question. As a result, the listener is no longer following the speaker's lead but is now (often unintentionally) directing the conversation with questions; she has switched from listening to talking—typically before the speaker has finished what he wished to say.

At first, this four-step method of paraphrasing may seem a bit like a paint-by-the-numbers approach to learning how to listen. However, we and our colleagues found this to be the best way to master reflective listening. Before long, you'll find yourself internalizing the process, and your paraphrasing will flow naturally and in your own style.

SOMETIMES YOU NEED TO BREAK IN TO PARAPHRASE

When talking, people generally pause from time to time to catch their breath, think about what they'll say next, or perhaps to give you a chance to respond. These pauses give you openings to paraphrase what was said.

However, you'll undoubtedly encounter some monologers who seldom pause, making it difficult to get a paraphrase in edgewise. To have an interactive conversation with one of these folks, you'll likely have to break in.

You can use your body language to alert the speaker of your intention:

- Sit up a little straighter.
- Lean forward and open your mouth, indicating that you're about to speak.

If these signals are not responded to by the speaker you can say something like:

> You're giving me a lot of information. I want to be sure I understand what you're telling me.

Then paraphrase what he just said.

How Paraphrasing Enhances Conversations

In the last chapter, we saw the many benefits that reflective listening contributes to one's conversations. Now we'll focus on the specific ways that paraphrasing increases conversational effectiveness.

PARAPHRASING GREATLY REDUCES MISCOMMUNICATION

When you say back a brief recap of what you heard, the speaker knows whether or not you accurately received the message she was trying to communicate. If miscommunication occurred, she can immediately correct it. Although there's no such thing as zero defects communication, paraphrasing what the speaker says will help you get as close as possible to that elusive goal. That's reason enough to paraphrase what you're told. However, paraphrasing can improve your communication in several additional ways.

PARAPHRASING DIMINISHES THE WANDERING MIND PROBLEM

In Chapter 10, we saw that, when using ordinary ways of "listening," people tend to drift off now and then on mental vacations and miss some or much of what was said. It's not surprising that this would be a problem for many listeners. Modern scientific studies of the brain concluded that evolution equipped humans with a highly distractible brain. (Many school teachers probably think that insight was a no-brainer!) The highly distractible brain often served our prehistoric ancestors well; when they were feasting on an animal they had just killed, they dared not concentrate too exclusively on their feast lest a predator attack and and make a feast of them.

Unfortunately, when it comes to listening, the problem of distractibility is a major liability. The human brain processes information about four times faster than the average person speaks. And the typical person uses that time poorly. With all that surplus time on its hands, the mind is apt to soon wander off on extraneous thoughts.

When you paraphrase, however, you put that extra time to good use as you try to accurately understand what's being said, identify the central thought being communicated, and figure out how to send a condensed and reworded version of that thought back to the speaker. With your mind preoccupied by the demands of paraphrasing, the wandering mind problem becomes virtually nonexistent.

PARAPHRASING OFTEN SAVES TIME

Psychologist Marshall Rosenberg founded and served as director of Educational Services for the Center for Nonviolent Communication—an international peacemaking organization. He developed Nonviolent Communication Skill Training and taught it in sixty countries around the world. In the early 2000s, for example, he taught Nonviolent Communication workshops and led peacemaking negotiations in about thirty-five countries a year. Paraphrasing was a key tool in those workshops and negotiations. He found (as we and others who teach paraphrasing have found) that:

> Some people resist paraphrasing as a waste of time. One city administrator explained during a practice session, "I'm paid to give facts and solutions, not to sit around doing psychotherapy with everyone who comes into my office." This same administrator, however, was being confronted by angry citizens who would come to him with their passionate concerns and leave dissatisfied for not having been heard. . . .
>
> Paraphrasing tends to save, rather than waste, time. Studies in labor–management negotiations demonstrate that the time required to reach resolution is cut in half when each negotiator agrees, before responding, to accurately repeat what the previous speaker had said.[3]

Paraphrasing makes conversations more focused and therefore more efficient by reducing the speaker's repetitions and digressions. That in itself can save a bundle of time. Paraphrasing also saves time by enhancing accuracy. It's a key skill for enabling you to do things right the first time so that you don't have to spend time redoing them.

Furthermore, when people experience the higher-quality communication that your listening generates, they're likely to start letting you know about problems early on—before they grow into bigger problems.

So rather than think of paraphrasing as a drain on your time, look at it as an investment in quality communication and relationship building which, over the long haul, will save time and be a significant contributor to your effectiveness.

PARAPHRASING INCREASES THE LISTENER'S RETENTION OF WHAT WAS SAID

We know that thoughtful repetition aids memory. As with each of the other reflecting skills, paraphrasing helps you anchor what you heard in your memory.

PARAPHRASING STRENGTHENS YOUR RAPPORT WITH THE SPEAKER

Another benefit of paraphrasing is that it increases your rapport with the speaker. When people talk to you, they want to feel that you are focusing on what they're saying. Your paraphrasing assures the speaker that you are making a disciplined effort to understand what she means. When she hears your on-target paraphrase, she knows she's been understood—a feeling most of us wish for but experience infrequently.

GET OFF TO A STRONG START

If you've not been doing much paraphrasing prior to reading this chapter, consider skipping ahead and reading Chapter 22 before applying this skill. You'll find useful start-up pointers there. You might then read Chapter 15. After working with those skills for a while, begin reading the remaining chapters of the book.

15

Listen Through the Pauses

I waited while you spoke,
I listened to your reasoning;
while you were searching for words,
I gave you my full attention.

–JOB 32:11

JOURNALIST NATHAN MILLER once said that "conversation in the United States is a competitive exercise in which the first person to draw a breath is declared the listener." Although Miller was obviously exaggerating, we thought he was on to something and decided to investigate what happens when a speaker pauses momentarily, whether to catch a breath or for other reasons. From our consulting and training work, we had video and audio tapes of a large number of conversations that clients said we could use for research purposes. We studied them to see how frequently people pause when they're talking, how long the pauses usually last, and what generally happens when a pause occurs. We also reviewed communication scholars' findings about conversational pauses. Then we experimented with various ways of handling pauses effectively. We found that when you understand the basic facts about pauses and know how to manage them effectively, your listening will become much more productive.

Six Little-Known Facts About Conversational Pauses

Although we experience hundreds of pauses in the typical day, few people know how to make the most of them. That's a shame because these concise silences can contribute significantly to our conversations. Here are some facts that have helped us realize the importance of these significant silences.

1. PAUSES ARE PLENTIFUL IN MOST CONVERSATIONS

Pauses abound in most conversations. The speaker talks a bit, pauses to catch his breath, then says a little more, hesitates a moment or two to determine how to phrase the next part, then continues. These pauses reoccur throughout his talking. Then, when he's had his say, he pauses a bit longer than usual and perhaps glances at the listener to indicate that he has concluded his remarks or at least that part of them.

2. MANY PEOPLE ARE UNCOMFORTABLE WITH PAUSES

Lots of folks are ill at ease with conversational pauses and feel an urgency to fill these brief silences with comments—even when they have nothing in particular to say. Ending the uncomfortable silence often is their only goal. Prematurely terminating a potentially productive pause, however, is an interruption—a listening misstep. Good listeners discipline themselves to listen through most silences.

3. THE TYPICAL PAUSE IS VERY BRIEF

Many people experience the typical conversational pause as being uncomfortably long. However, UCLA clinical psychology Professor Emeritus Gerald Goodman found that:

> The typical amount of time between when one person in a conversation stops talking and the other person starts is about nine-tenths of a second. About the amount of time it takes to say, "Silence."

Despite the brevity of the typical pause, many listeners become uncomfortable with these briefer-than-one-second silences, and they barge into the talking role to terminate the uncomfortable quiet. By contrast, good listeners discipline themselves to listen through these brief moments.

4. PAUSES GENERALLY ARE MORE SIGNIFICANT MOMENTS THAN IS COMMONLY REALIZED

Mark Twain, who was an artist at using words, said:

> The right word may be effective, but no word was as effective as a rightly timed pause.[1]

And the composer Claude Debussy said, "Music is the space between the notes."

5. PAUSES OFTEN OCCUR AT KEY MOMENTS IN A CONVERSATION

The silences in our conversations are often significant moments, and it's important to manage brief moments well. Goodman points out the significant impact these brief moments of silence contribute to our lives:

> Silences regulate the flow of listening and talking—and the rhythm of our listening and talking regulates the flow of our thinking and feeling. Our conversations are full of these almost automatic regulators, these talk traffic signals. We rarely recognize them as they regulate the give-and-take of attention. To understand that silences govern our attention is to know that they shape the quality of our conversation, and, ultimately, our relationships. . . . Silences are to conversations what zeros are to mathematics—nothings, yes, but crucial nothings without which communication can't work.
>
> I want you to see that these little slivers of quiet in a conversation—where someone pauses, where people switch turns talking, or when thoughts stop while thoughts are collected—are not trivial. When they're not there in the appropriate places, conversation loses its easy flow.[2]

6. THE AVERAGE LISTENER MISHANDLES MANY PAUSES

The way these brief, scarcely noticed moments of silence are handled can have a major impact on conversation. In fact, we found that:

Pauses are especially important moments in conversation because they are the places where the listener is most likely to *interrupt* the speaker.

Many listeners experience a pause in a conversation as an unpleasant vacuum that needs to be filled instantly. They're uncomfortable with even a very brief silence during a conversation. So when the speaker pauses, the average listener's discomfort builds quickly, and in a split-second she's liable to say the first thing that comes to mind which, as mentioned, usually turns out to be an interruption.

With run-of-the-mill listening, the speaker and listener switch roles just about every time the person who is speaking hesitates for a moment before continuing. For example:

- You say what you think.
- When you pause, I break in to say what I think.
- When I pause, you chime in with your comments.
- After you've said a bit more, I jump back in with my opinion.
- Back and forth it goes.

Figure 15.1 is diagram of a typical conversation, which shows that within a few moments you can't tell which person is the speaker and which one is the listener!

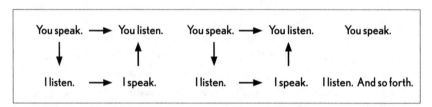

FIGURE 15.1. A TYPICAL CONVERSATION.

Conversational ping-pong like that may be OK for casual chats in which neither person has anything substantial to say. But in conversations that are significant for either person, it's inappropriate to repeatedly shift back and forth between listening and speaking. Switch-track conversations are disjointed and inefficient. Yet the average listener typically falls into the back-and-forth conversational pattern even when the speaker has a great deal of energy about what he's saying.

Good Conversationalists Listen Through Pauses

When the speaker pauses, especially in substantive conversations, a good conversationalist continues listening. His attention remains focused on the speaker, leaving space for her thoughts to "marinate" in case she wants to say more.

In any conversation that's more important than chitchat, listen until the speaker has said all she wants to say on the subject—or at least that part of the topic. When she has fully made her point, it's your turn to speak. Author Nancy Kline, who has greatly increased our awareness of the importance of pauses, writes:

> If you are lucky, when you are listening to someone, they will suddenly go quiet . . . . This is a privileged moment for you: don't ruin it. You may well feel awkward when the quiet first sets in. You may have been taught that at times like these you must speak, that you must "rescue" the person from the apparent mounting embarrassment of having nothing to say. Yet when a person is thinking out loud and is suddenly quiet but is not stuck, the quiet is alive. Neither the person nor the quiet needs rescuing. They need attention only—and more quiet.[3]

Figure 15.2 is a diagram of a conversation in which the listener stays focused on the speaker.

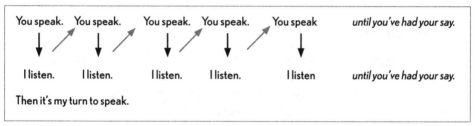

FIGURE 15.2. A YOU-FOCUS CONVERSATION.

Bestselling author and inspirational speaker Zig Ziglar sums it up this way:

> Listen—Pause—and Listen![4]

Tips for Listening Through Pauses

You'll be better able to listen effectively through these fleeting moments of silence when you:

- Avoid three common misunderstandings about pauses.
- Make good use of pauses.

AVOID THREE COMMON MISUNDERSTANDINGS ABOUT PAUSES

Here are some key facts about pauses that run counter to most people's understanding:

Your Sense of the Length of a Pause Is Probably Greatly Exaggerated

Researchers discovered that *listeners tend to experience pauses as vastly longer than they actually are:*

> Studies show that when interviewers estimate the length of a period of silence they typically magnify it by a factor of 10 to 100.[5]

When you estimate the length of a pause realistically, you'll be much less likely to rush to fill what you misperceive as an awkward silence. The pause may feel uncomfortable to you, but it rarely seems awkward to the speaker.

The Speaker Owns the Pause

The average listener takes it upon himself to end many pauses. But that's usually inappropriate. The *speaker* owns the pause. After all, it was the speaker—not the listener—who temporarily stopped talking and thus created the pause. He surely can add to what he's just said, invite your comments, change the subject, or break the silence in some other way. *It's inappropriate for the listener to assume responsibility for managing the speaker's pauses.*

Normally, a Pause Is a Productive Time for the Speaker

The speaker may need to catch her breath, and once that's done, she'll continue speaking. Perhaps she's taking a moment to think as she struggles to explain a complex problem or difficult concept. Occasionally, a speaker will fall silent because she's trying to figure out what to say next or how phrase it. At other times, she may be deciding what to disclose and what to withhold. Or she may be pausing to deal with strong emotions. Perhaps the process of talking about her situation generated new insights, and she is taking a few moments to integrate them into her thinking. So it's typically best to continue listening through the pause. In fact, conversational research reveals that a speaker's most significant comments often come immediately after an uninterrupted pause.

MAKE GOOD USE OF PAUSES

Pauses are not periods to be merely waited out but are opportunities to be fully mined. As Plutarch advised in the first century BCE:

> In all cases, then, silence is a safe adornment . . . and especially so, when in listening to another he . . . waits for the speaker to pause, and, when the pause comes, . . . allows an interval to elapse, in case the speaker may desire to add something to what he has said, or to alter or unsay anything.[6]

In *Listening with the Third Ear*, psychiatrist Theodor Reik, concludes: "The active power of silence . . . works upon the [speaker] encouragingly, *and works even more strongly than words could.*"[7]

How to Take Advantage of Conversational Pauses

- **Attend to the speaker.** Attending shows the speaker that you are listening intently while she is thinking.
- **Observe the speaker's body language.** When you are not distracted by someone's words, you can concentrate even more on what his nonverbals are communicating.
- **Mull over what's been said.** Pauses provide an opportunity to catch meanings that would otherwise be missed. William Isaacs of MIT's Sloan School of Management notes that when listeners make good use of silences, the meaning of the speaker's message generally becomes clearer.[8] Pauses provide time to mentally review what you've been told, assess whether you've gotten to the heart of the matter, and understand more deeply why what you've been told is important to the speaker.

When a listener uses pauses in these ways, he'll be too busy to feel uncomfortable with the silence. So there'll be less temptation to interrupt the speaker.

> This chapter concludes Part III. The next five chapters equip you to "read" and respond to the whole gamut of feelings that you'll encounter in future interactions.

PART IV

READING AND REFLECTING OTHER PEOPLE'S FEELINGS

It's irrational to expect everyone to be "rational."

–JAMES CREIGHTON

16

Why Listen to People's Feelings?

Granted, it is not easy to deal with feelings. But it is certainly difficult to get anything accomplished without dealing with them.

—THOMAS QUICK

E MOTIONS ARE AMAZING things. They are the "unquenchable origin of every act more complicated than a reflex. . . . In all cases, emotions are humanity's motivator and its omnipresent guide."[1] Feelings lift us up, adding color and pizzazz to our lives—but our emotions also drag us down in the dumps. They provide the drive that makes achievement possible—yet they sometimes undermine our effort by sapping our energy or eroding our morale. Feelings are at the heart of love, friendship, and compassion for others—but they sometimes lead to defensive, vengeful, or other destructive behaviors that tear relationships apart. When used well, our emotions are a tremendous asset for vital living. As psychologist Robert W. Levenson put it:

> Emotions are short-lived physiological phenomena that represent efficient modes of adaptation to changing environmental demands.
>
> Psychologically, emotions alter attention, shift certain behaviors upward in response hierarchies, and activate associative networks in memory. Physiologically, emotions rapidly organize the response of different biological systems including facial expression, muscular

tonus, voice, autonomic nervous system activity, and endocrine activity to produce a bodily milieu that is optimal for effective response.[2]

People in our culture tend to underestimate the importance of feelings. We tend to downplay the emotional and herald the rational. But, as this chapter demonstrates, our emotions are a hugely important part of our lives. Unfortunately, few of us are as adept as we'd like to be in understanding and handling our own feelings or the emotional aspects of our interactions with others.

> Although psychologists often distinguish between feelings and emotions, the distinctions are unimportant for the purposes of this book. So, as is the custom in everyday life, we use the terms "feelings"[3] and "emotions" interchangeably.[4]

Emotions Permeate Our Lives— for Better or Worse

To keep this chapter to a manageable length, we'll confine ourselves to commenting briefly on the influence feelings have on our performance and satisfaction in the following realms:

Learning

Thinking

Communication

Relating to others

Decision making

Taking action

Performing successfully at work

We'll also note the impact of emotions on one's health and longevity.

Feelings Affect Our Learning— for Better or Worse

Psychologist C. R. Snyder of the University of Kansas found that the level of a student's hope as a freshman was a better predictor of a student's academic grades than his or her score on the SAT test. Given about the same range of mental abilities, emotional intelligence accounted for the difference between the higher-scoring students and the lower-scoring ones.

Feelings Affect Our Thinking—for Better or Worse

Like fire and water, feelings are good servants but bad masters. That's certainly true of the relationship between our thinking and our feelings. It's common knowledge that one cannot think clearly in moments of great anxiety, anger, or ecstasy. That fact undoubtedly led to the often held beliefs that one's thinking should be divorced from one's feelings and that employees should park their feelings at the gate when they come to work. But thinking and feeling are inseparably interconnected. Saint Augustine spoke of their relationship as: "The mysterious alliance of intellect and feeling." And recently, famed neuroscientist Antonio Damasio emphasized, "Emotion is in the loop of reason all the time."

Our experience is always emotionally loaded. Edward de Bono, the noted physician, psychologist, creativity expert, and inventor adds:

> If emotions and feelings are not permitted inputs in the thinking process, they will lurk in the background and affect all thinking in a hidden way.[5]

Feelings Affect Our Communication—for Better or Worse

Emotions have a major impact on the nature and consequences of our conversations. When people move beyond small talk, they typically talk about things that are personally meaningful to them and thus have an emotional coloration. Feelings often affect what is said—as well as what is withheld. A person who is trusting of the listener and feels strongly about an issue is likely to speak candidly. But when anxiety or distrust prevail, people are more likely to hold back their thoughts, go along with the majority, or operate with hidden agendas.

Our feelings also affect the way we deliver a message. An idea expressed by someone whose conviction is evident is more persuasive than the same point made by someone whose delivery is halfhearted. Important messages should usually be delivered with the appropriate emotional tone as well as with words that accurately convey the sentiment. And, of course, when negative emotions surge out of control, what's said is likely to be contaminated by exaggeration, loaded words, sarcasm, or other obstacles to clear and accurate communication.

On the receiving end of communication, effective listeners are emotionally attuned to the speaker. The speaker's feelings communicate important data; they tell you what's behind the words that were spoken, and they underscore how intensely or mildly he feels about what he's saying. On the other hand, when a listener is flooded by strong negative emotions, she tends to be incapable of receiving information accurately let alone of responding constructively. Communication expert William Howell concluded:

> More than any other factor, the feelings that are generated between people determine the consequences of their conversation.[6]

Feelings Affect Our Relationships—for Better or Worse

Emotions are at the heart of our most important relationships, both at work and in our personal lives. Feelings of trust, respect, and empathy enhance our ties to others. In contrast, feelings like anxiety, distrust, hurt, fear, and dislike undermine rapport. Psychologist Donald Sanzotta concluded:

> If I were asked to offer the single most important guide to interpersonal relations, it would be this; don't underestimate the role of emotions.

Feelings Affect Our Decisions—for Better or Worse

Decision making and mismanaged feelings are a dangerous mix. Everyone, it seems, can think of bad decisions made when they were carried away by anger, anxiety, enthusiasm, or even infatuation. But to try to banish feelings from decision making would be to "throw out the baby with the bathwater." Decision making is an inherently emotional activity. When trying to determine which of several options to select, feelings come into play, helping us determine which alternative is better and which ones are less desirable. In the final analysis, the most important decisions we make—what career to follow, what job to take, whom to marry, which house to buy—are based on or at least strongly influenced by our feelings.

When making complex decisions, complete and unambiguous information is seldom available—and the obtainable facts may be open to alternative interpretations. Paul Otellini, former CEO of Intel told the *Atlantic Monthly,* "[W]hile we like to speak with data around here, so many times in my career I've ended making decisions with my gut, and I should have been following my gut." Similarly, when an interviewer asked Steve Jobs, "What is the role of intuition in your job?" Jobs replied:

> It's critical. It's extremely critical. The most important things in life, whether they're personal or professional, are decided on intuition. I think you can have a lot of information and data feeding that intuition. You can also do a lot of analysis. You can do a lot of things that are quantitative in nature. But in the end of it, the things that are most important are always gut calls.

Feelings Affect Our Actions—for Better or Worse

The words *"emotion"* and *"motive"* both derive from the Latin root, *motere,* "to move." Emotions are our motivators; they provide the impetus for our action, and they are the horsepower for our behavior. Throughout the ages, noted intellectuals and practitioners of innumerable disciplines have asserted that feelings like enthusiasm, confidence, and determination drive our achievements. Historian and philosopher Georg Wilhelm Friedrich Hegel concluded:

> We may affirm absolutely that nothing great in the World has been accomplished without passion.

Ferdinand Foch, the French Marshall who halted the German march through France in World War I, said, "The most powerful weapon on earth is the human soul on fire." And David Hume, considered by many the greatest of Enlightenment scholars, claimed that although reason guides ideas, math, logic, and fact, reason is incapable of moving us to act; only emotion stirs us to action.

Wise leaders realize that emotion is essential to implementing decisions and bringing plans to fruition. After being tapped to rescue a floundering IBM, CEO Louis Gerstner said that to make the changes needed to turn the company around, he'd have to "appeal to people's emotions. They've got to buy in with their hearts and bellies, not just their minds." Gerstner's strategy of heightening the emotional emphasis of his turnaround strategy was exactly what was needed, and the huge corporation's rebound was dramatic.

Ordinary people can achieve extraordinary results when fired up by emotion. Take the examples of Cindi Lamb and Candy Lightner. Cindi was driving with her daughter Laura when they were struck head-on by a car speeding at 120 miles per hour. As a result of the accident, her five-and-a-half-month-old daughter became a quadriplegic. The driver of the out-of-control vehicle was a drunken driver. Several months later, a drunken driver with two prior convictions and a still valid driver's license ran over and killed thirteen-year-old Cari Lightner. The driver had been convicted of drunken driving and similar offences three times in four years. Each time the courts were very lenient—the driver who killed Cari still had a valid driver's license. Two days prior to killing Cari, that driver had been arrested for another hit–and-run while drunk. The driver simply paid bail and went free. A cynical cop told Cari's mother, Candy, "Lady, you'll be lucky if this guy gets any jail time—much less prison."

Candy had been totally apolitical until her daughter's tragic death—"I wasn't even registered to vote," she said. She was divorced and supporting her other two children. But her intense feelings transformed her. Fired by grief and a passionate commitment to do what she could to prevent further tragedies, she and Cindi Lamb created Mothers Against Drunk Driving (MADD) in 1981. As early as the fall of 1982, there were seventy chapters of MADD! On its twentieth anniversary, there were more than 600 chapters; every state was represented, and there were affiliates around the world. The emotions of those two grieving mothers stirred them into incredibly effective action.

Of course, feelings can inhibit action too. People are sometimes "paralyzed" by fear and "blocked" from their best efforts by anxiety. At times, people simply lack the energy to give a project their best effort, and the energy drain could well be caused by the person's feelings. Psychiatrist Stewart Battle says nearly 80 percent of all chronic tiredness stems from emotional fatigue. Fortunately, sound management of our feelings enables us to live up to our full energy potential.

Feelings Affect Our Work Performance —
for Better or Worse

Many people have been conditioned to believe that business interactions should be strictly rational, dispassionate, and objective with no room for emotion. In reality, however, when at work we are bombarded by feelings—our own and those of the people we interact with. Abundant studies have made it clear that feelings have a major impact on one's effectiveness at work. The research of Daniel Goleman and others documented the fact that emotional intelligence is associated with effectiveness in virtually every type of employment. However, the impact of the emotions on one's performance has been evident for centuries. The famed monastic, Saint Augustine (354–430 AD), wrote:

> Experience shows that success is due less to ability than to zeal.

The other side of the coin, as you've doubtless witnessed, is the vocational and business cost of emotional ineptitude, which is enormous.

Although emotional competence improves one's effectiveness in all types of employment, for brevity's sake we'll confine ourselves to noting its impact in two very different types of vocational populations.

SALESPEOPLE

Research on sales effectiveness revealed the surprising fact that neither intelligence nor product knowledge distinguishes high performers from average ones. In large part, success in selling is determined by how salespersons manage their emotions and how well they relate with their customers. MetLife, one of the largest global providers of insurance, annuities, and employee benefit plans, had for years used a selection test designed to identify high-potential sales candidates. However, one hiring season, instead of hiring candidates who did well on the selection test, it hired candidates *who failed the normal selection screening tests but who scored high on a test for optimism.*

The result? *The optimists outsold those who scored high on the selection test by 29 percent in the first year and by a whopping 50 percent in the second year.*

CORPORATE EXECUTIVES

Researchers found that incompetent executives are rarely ineffectual for intellectual or technical reasons; their ineptness is almost invariably due to bungling the emotional aspects of the job. Highly effective executives, by contrast, are adept at mastering the emotional elements of their work.

Intel's former CEO Andy Grove led the corporation through two spectacularly difficult periods. After experiencing those corporate near-death experiences, he stated that a company's ability to survive extreme crises depends essentially on how top management reacts emotionally. In *Secrets of a Corporate Headhunter*, John Wareham concluded:

> The key to understanding the incompetent executive is to recognize that he is rarely incompetent for technical or intellectual reasons, but that his condition is almost invariably *emotional*.[7]

The message from contemporary psychological theory and research, as well as from corporate experience, is clear: Feelings have a major impact on one's interpersonal effectiveness and on one's competence at work. Reading and responding sensitively to people's emotions, rather than attempting to ignore them or underestimate their importance, is crucial to success in one's personal and vocational life.

Feelings Affect Our Health and Longevity— for Better or Worse

The Old Testament Book of Proverbs reminds us that:

> A merry heart is good medicine,
> but a downcast spirit dries up the bones.[8]

Modern medical science has corroborated the belief that positive feeling states enhance one's health. Realistic positive thoughts and an upbeat spirit boost the strength of the immune system and the robustness of the cardiovascular system. Promoting beneficial emotions has an important function in the prevention and treatment of disease across medical disciplines.

The impact of emotional intelligence on our health and longevity is impressively significant. Health authorities estimate that one-third of all visits to primary care physicians are triggered by emotional stress.

Researchers at the Mayo Clinic followed 839 patients who had been classified as optimists or pessimists. At the thirty-year mark of the longitudinal research, significantly more of the optimists than pessimists were still alive.

In another study, 225 medical students took a personality test that measured overt hostility. A quarter of a century later, the angriest of them had five times more heart disease than the least angry ones.

Research in Finland found that hostility may be a better predictor of coronary disease risk than the standard risk factors—cigarette smoking, high blood pressure, and high cholesterol. And a team at Duke University found that getting a high score on a hostility test correlated positively with the severity of coronary artery disease.[9]

The Nuns Study of Aging and Alzheimer's disease is a longitudinal study begun in 1986 and still continuing thirty-one years later. When the 678 Roman Catholic nuns entered the convent of the School Sisters of Notre Dame at an average age of twenty-two, each one wrote an autobiographical essay. Analysis of those essays decades later found that positive emotional content in those early autobiographies predicted which sisters would lead the longest lives. The young nuns who expressed more positive emotions in their autobiographies lived an average of ten years longer than those expressing fewer positive emotions. Furthermore, those expressing positive emotions in their early autobiographies were much more active and alert in their later years.

Researchers who conducted the follow-up studies of the nuns were amazed that writing samples from people in their early twenties would be a reasonably reliable predictor of who would be alive more than three decades after the autobiographical essays were written.

Recent scientific investigation of positive emotions has created impressive evidence of the powerful impact that emotions like happiness, intimacy, love, contentment, honesty, courage, confidence, and optimism have on people's health and longevity, as well as on their overall well-being and life satisfaction. Even stronger research findings conclude that negative states like excessive anger, anxiety, or depression not only greatly diminish one's happiness but also tend to generate illness, worsen symptoms, constrain recovery, and lead to early death.

To sum up, emotions are an inevitable and important part of our lives. They affect virtually everything we do—for better or for worse.

The Grant Study of 268 Harvard College sophomores in the years 1939–1944 was a unique research project due to the long time span of the research. Dr. George E. Vaillant, who has directed the research for decades, wrote that one of the most interesting findings was:

[T]he more at ease the men were with their feelings, the more successful they were at the rest of their lives.[10]

The rest of Part IV provides you with the tools to get on the emotional wavelength of your conversational partner in ways that help him feel understood and that build deeper and richer rapport. The upcoming three chapters provide the how-to's of listening to feelings. You'll learn how to "read" the feelings of others, how to reflect those feelings, and how to reflect both the speaker's thoughts and feelings in one succinct sentence, a skill that's referred to as reflecting meanings.

17

"Read" People's Feelings

> The body is a house of many windows: there we all sit showing ourselves.
>
> —ROBERT LOUIS STEVENSON

THE SUBJECT SAT expressionless at the end of the table, carefully crafting his answers to the FBI agent's questions. Although the person wasn't a prime suspect in the homicide case, the agent asked him a series of questions about the murder weapon.

If you had committed this crime, would you have used a gun?

If you had committed this crime, would you have used a knife?

If you had committed this crime, would you have used an ice pick?

If you had committed this crime, would you have used a hammer?

An ice pick had been used in the crime, but that fact was not public knowledge, so only the killer would know which object was the real weapon.

When the ice pick was mentioned, the man's eyelids came down hard and stayed down until the next weapon was named. The agent instantly understood the significance of the eye-lid behavior he had witnessed, and from that moment forward the minor suspect became the primary person of interest in the investigation. He later confessed to the crime.

The interrogator was Joe Navarro, who, in addition to exposing the ice pick killer, caught master spies and numerous other criminals in his notable career with the FBI. When asked, "What is the secret of your success?" he typically answered, "I owe it to being able to read people."[1]

Nonverbal behaviors are sometimes referred to as *"tells"* because they tell what is going on in the speaker's mind and heart—often more accurately than what is conveyed by the speaker's words. Because body language conveys a lot that words don't reveal, reading it is an essential aspect of effective listening. The ability to "read" body language is ultra important because nonverbals can . . .

Complement   Emphasize   Repeat
Contradict or Replace

. . . the words that are being spoken.

Reading people's feelings is a key listening skill and a strong contributor to a good life. A study of more than 7,000 people in nineteen countries found that those who are adept at identifying people's feelings are better adjusted and more popular than those who are less attuned to the feelings of others. They're also more successful at work and in romantic and family relationships.[2]

Everyone of sound mind and body has some ability to read people's feelings, but in most people this is a skill that's seriously underdeveloped. For instance, at the beginning of our listening skills workshops, the typical participant misses most of the emotional overtones of the conversations they're engaged in. They tend to fix their attention on the factual content that's communicated and miss much or all of the speaker's body language, which conveys much of the emotional meaning of their conversational partner's message. As a result, these people are tone deaf to much of the emotional dynamics of their conversations. And that's an important aspect of many conversations; indeed, it's typically the key part of many of our most important interactions.

Understanding the feelings of others is complicated by the fact that *emotions are qualities that cannot be perceived directly*. In workshops, when a trainer says, "No one has ever seen or heard anger, fear, joy, or any other emotion," it's fairly common for participants to disagree. For instance, one participant said, "I'll prove that feelings like anger can be seen and heard." The participant then screwed his face into a scowl and stomped across the room. He shook his fist in the trainer's face. "There," he said. "You've just seen and heard anger."

But even if the participant actually felt as angry as he acted, no one in the room would have seen or heard one iota of the emotion of anger. *Emotions are inner qualities* that are impossible to perceive directly. What the folks in that room observed was *body language* that's often associated with anger. As psychologists Don Dinkmeyer and Lewis Losoncy explained:

> Behavior is the external event which shows us what is going on inside the person.[3]

So when you want to "read" what a person is feeling, the most reliable information is typically obtained by focusing on her nonverbals. Indeed, when someone's body language is at odds with her verbal message, it's wise to check out whether her body language is providing a more accurate representation of her thoughts and feelings.

Our culture greatly overemphasizes the impact of the verbal and hugely underestimates the relevance of body language. By contrast, when various social scientists sought to determine the comparative importance of each, *body language always out-communicated the verbal messages.*

Three Steps for Formulating Reflections of Feelings

In Chapter 13, we outlined the steps to take when reflecting what's said to you. Then in Chapter 14, you learned how to apply that set of steps when paraphrasing—reflecting the factual aspect of what's said. We'll be following the same set of steps in this chapter as we discuss the three inner steps you engage in when developing a reflection of feelings:

Step 1: Take in the feelings. ⎤
Step 2: Sort out the feelings. ⎬ The inner steps of formulating a
Step 3: Sum up the feelings. ⎦ reflection of feelings

When you've completed these three steps of the inner process of reflecting feelings, you're ready to take the outer step:

Step 4: Say back the feelings succinctly and in your own words.

Here's how to do each of the inner steps of reflective listening.

STEP 1: TAKE IN THE FEELINGS

Of the three steps involved in formulating a reflection of feelings, taking in what the other person is saying generally is the most involved step, and accomplishing it typically requires the greatest amount of time.

Here are three keys to assessing what the speaker is feeling:

1. Be alert to *variations from the person's normal behavior.*
2. Focus on *key indicators of the emotion(s).*
3. Note the *emotional intensity* of the message.

Be Alert to Variations from the Person's Normal Behavior

We humans are creatures of habit. That makes it possible for you to become aware of your conversational partner's characteristic manner of emotional expression. Consider the person's typical, everyday range of verbal and nonverbal behavior to be her *verbal and body language baseline.*

> *When a person's verbal expression and/or body language varies from her baseline, the difference often indicates what the person is feeling.*

Focus on Key Indicators of Emotion to Determine What the Speaker Is Feeling

Three types of indicators of emotion are especially helpful when "reading" what someone else is feeling:

1. Verbal descriptions of emotions and their intensity
2. Body language and other nonverbal indicators of emotion
3. The "language of action"

Verbal Descriptions of Emotions and Their Intensity

Feelings can be expressed in many different ways:

Feeling words: "contented," "relieved," "optimistic," "angry," "worried," "sad," etc.

Phrases (often slang) that suggest what the speaker is feeling: "I've had it." "I was really burned when she said that." "What a downer." "I sure was fired up." "It was beyond belief." "What a gift that was."

Figures of speech that convey feelings. "On top of the world." "That was the frosting on the cake." "Made my day." "Felt like the rug was pulled out from under me." "It's the pits." "Between a rock and a hard place." "Like being stabbed in the back." People often transition into a figure of speech with the word, "Like" or the phrase "It felt like."

An action the person would like to do (but undoubtedly won't): "I'd like to tell her off." "I feel like walking away from the whole project." "I could give him a big hug." "I'd like to wring his neck."

Descriptions of body language that portray their feelings: "The hair stood up on the back of my neck." "My palms were sweaty." "My heart was pounding." "I breathed a sigh of relief."

Swearing: Often a sign that the person's feelings are negative and running high. (But not always—some people just cuss a lot.)

Body Language and Other Nonverbal Indicators of Emotion

In every human encounter, emotions are continuously signaled and received nonverbally. Psychologist Alan Loy McGinnis wryly noted that "even when your mouth is closed you are saying a lot."[4] In fact, many of the most useful emotional clues can be detected in the 90 percent of interpersonal communication that is nonverbal.

Facial Indicators. Saint Jerome (347—420 AD) wrote, "The face is the mirror of the mind, and eyes without speaking confess the secrets of the heart."[5] And in *Macbeth*, William Shakespeare penned:

> There's no art
> To find the mind's construction in the face.

An abundance of modern scientific research has confirmed Charles Darwin's hypothesis that the face is the primary region for the display of emotions. Scientists discovered that the face is lavishly equipped with nerves and a complex network of muscles that enable it to reveal a large range of emotions. In fact, the eighty muscles of the face are able to make more than 7,000 facial expressions.

Although the face is the most emotionally expressive part of the body, it can be an unreliable source of information about someone's feelings since many of the muscles that control facial expression can be consciously manipulated. The lyrics of an old song remind us that someone may be "laughing on the outside" but "crying on the inside." That's possible because some of the muscles that create facial expressions are voluntary—under the person's conscious control.[6]

The eyes are an especially expressive part of the face. In his essay *The Conduct of Life*, Ralph Waldo Emerson commented on the expressive versatility of the eye:

> An eye can threaten like a loaded and leveled gun,
> or can insult like hissing or kicking;
> or in its altered mood, by beams of kindness.
> it can make the heart dance with joy.

Vocal Indicators. The voice, the "sounding board of emotion," is another valuable source of information about the speaker's feelings. A person's voice can *underline* her words. A computer service technician jokingly says he listens to the level of hysteria in his customer's voices prior to scheduling his calls for the day.

Of course, there's an abundance of other body language clues about what another person may be feeling, which you can review in one of the books solely devoted to teaching readers how to read body language.

Additional Clues to What a Person May Be Feeling. While it makes sense to be particularly observant of aspects of body language that can be especially emotionally expressive, don't ignore other indicators. A person's posture, pace, gestures, breathing, and so forth can contribute to your understanding of what she is feeling. Also, when one indicator suggests that a person is experiencing a certain feeling or a particular mixture of feelings, due diligence would have you explore additional indicators for confirmation or disconfirmation.

The "Language of Action"

The actions we take are often triggered by our emotions. So be alert to the possible emotional underpinnings of the actions a person does or doesn't take. Several years ago, anthropologist Edward Hall was given the assignment of assessing the likelihood that various city departments would adopt nondiscriminatory labor practices. He set up hour-long interviews with each department head, and in those interviews the department heads assured Dr. Hall of their willingness to adopt the nondiscriminatory practices.

Despite the unanimous verbal assurances of cooperation, Hall realized that only one department was likely to make the desired changes. The other department heads "forgot" appointments, kept him waiting for an inordinate amount of time, typically cut the length of the interviews to one-fourth or less of the agreed-upon length, and so forth.[7] Based on the administrators' consistently resistant behavior, Hall reported that, despite their verbal assurances, all but one were strongly resistant to adopting the nondiscriminatory practices. His prediction was spot on.

Determine the Intensity of the Emotion

Once you determine the type of feeling the person is experiencing, it's important to take in and accurately label the *intensity* of the emotion. To do that effectively, you'll need to rely on a feeling word vocabulary that enables you to distinguish between various levels of intensity in several families of feelings.

In Figure 17.1, you'll find examples of words that refer to different levels of intensity for six "families" of feelings. You can increase your emotional fluency by studying the chart a few times a week for two or three weeks.

	MILD	MEDIUM	STRONG
ANGER	irritated	frustrated	furious
	annoyed	fed up	enraged
	perturbed	aggravated	seething
FEAR	nervous	scared	terrified
	worried	frightened	desperate
	on edge	apprehensive	panicky
CONFUSION	undecided	confused	bewildered
	unsure	muddled	baffled
	unclear	mixed up	disjointed
SORROW	low	distressed	despondent
	dissatisfied	bummed	hopeless
	displeased	glum	anguished
EXCITEMENT	interested	eager	thrilled
	involved	fired up	pumped
	attentive	enthusiastic	exhilarated
JOY	satisfied	happy	elated
	glad	delighted	ecstatic
	contented	cheerful	jubilant

FIGURE 17.1. INTENSITY OF FEELING WORDS.

STEP 2: SORT THE FEELINGS OUT

In Step 1, you carefully noted what is observable about the speaker's feelings—his body language, vocal indicators, additional clues to what the person may be feeling, and, when available, the language of action. That combination of information will probably provide you with enough information to make a pretty good guesstimate of the person's feelings.

Now, in Step 2, the task is to sort out the information you took in in Step 1 with the goal of making an informed inference about the speaker's current feelings. Two guidelines enhance your ability to do that accurately:

1. Rely on clusters of clues.
2. Realize that the person may be experiencing a mixture of feelings.

Rely on Clusters of Clues

There's a widespread impression that certain nonverbals have a very specific meaning—that folded arms and/or crossed legs, for instance, mean that the person is feeling defensive. But sometimes the person may simply be more comfortable in those positions.

> Rather than leaping to a conclusion based on a single clue, note what the combination of nonverbal indicators suggests about the person's feelings.

Realize That the Speaker May Be Experiencing a Mixture of Feelings

In the realm of emotion, two (or more) different—or even opposing—emotions can exist in the same person at the same time. As psychologist Haim Ginott noted:

> There's a possibility that, where there is love, there is also some hate; where there is admiration, there is also some envy; where there is devotion, there is also some hostility; where there is success, there is also apprehension.[8]

For example, parents may experience some degree of sorrow as well as much joy at the wedding of their only daughter.

People typically assume that a friend or loved one who just received a promotion would be unambiguously happy about the career advancement. However, *Businessweek* reported that ambivalence and anxiety related to a promotion are not unusual.

> A promotion is usually a cause for celebration and pride. But for some, it's a source of deep anxiety, so scary that it eclipses life-altering occurrences like the death of a loved one or a divorce. That's what almost 1 out of 5 business leaders said in a recent survey when asked to choose their "most challenging" life event. Promotion was ranked as "most challenging" by 19% of respondents, followed by bereavement (15%), divorce (11%), moving (10%), and managing teen age children (19%).[9]

STEP 3: SUM UP THE FEELINGS

In Step 1, you took in the speaker's verbal message and nonverbal behaviors. Step 1 typically takes the bulk of the time in working your way through this three-step process. In Step 2, based on the clusters of clues unearthed in Step 1, you determined what the person is really driving at. With the data acquired in Step 1, Step 2 can usually be accomplished rather quickly. Step 3 requires even less time and can be explained in a single sentence:

> Boil down and compress what you sorted out in Step 2, and say it back in one short sentence.

Don't let the brevity of Step 3 deceive you. Condensing what may have been a long, meandering, confusing statement into a concise reflection is a skill that can take considerable discipline to acquire.

The three steps of *reading someone's feelings* are all done silently in your mind. *Reflecting someone's feelings* involves an additional very important step. Once you've mentally created a concise summary of the most recent part of the speaker's message, you succinctly check out the accuracy of what you think the speaker is communicating. The best way of checking whether you are tracking the speaker's feelings accurately is to reflect the emotional aspect of what he said. Reflective listening to a speaker's feelings is vital to being an empathic listener. The next two chapters describe powerful reflective listening skills for use in emotionally laden conversations.

18

Reflect Feelings and Meanings

-----what you try to convey is reality-----

The fact plus the feeling, a total complex experience

of a real world.

— JOYCE CARY

A MESSAGE OF MODERATE or of considerable importance to the speaker typically contains both *facts* and *feelings*. So proficient listeners need to be able to recap the facts accurately. (You learned that in Chapter 14.) And they need to acknowledge the emotional aspects of the speaker's message. That's done by *reflecting feelings*—a key listening skill taught in this chapter. And in this chapter you'll also learn how the feelings and the facts can be put together to make a more complete reflection—*a reflection of meanings*.

Skepticism About Reflecting Feelings

Some participants in our workshops have been dubious about reflecting feelings in conversations with friends and family. An even greater number were convinced that this kind of listening wouldn't pass muster where they work. June, one of the skeptics, put it this way to the trainer who was leading the workshop:

JUNE: Picture me talking with Tony, a peer at work. He's incensed that I didn't get some critical information to him by the agreed-upon time. As a result he missed an important deadline for a consolidated report to his team leader. He's railing at me that he's in the doghouse with his boss. And my schedule has been so tight that I still haven't been able to dig up the information he needs.

   You think I'm going to say to him, "You're feeling angry with me."

[Class chuckles.]

JUNE: No way!

TRAINER: You sense that would have only made matters worse.

JUNE: [Nodding emphatic agreement.]

TRAINER: I would not have responded that way either — it sounded so phony. You'll soon learn that there are many ways of phrasing reflections of feelings. As we work our way through this module, let's see if we can find a satisfactory way of letting Tony know that his feelings about the missed deadline have gotten through to you. Maybe this could help the two of you get to the other side of the problem.

JUNE: Maybe. I'll see . . .

The rest of this chapter contains the type of information the trainer then presented.

Benefits of Reflecting Feelings

When the speaker's feelings, whether positive or negative, become stronger than normal, it's usually appropriate for the listener to reflect them. Doing so benefits both the speaker and the listener.

HOW THE SPEAKER BENEFITS FROM A LISTENER'S REFLECTION OF FEELINGS

Here are several ways a speaker may benefit from your reflections of feelings:

1. Reflections of feelings demonstrate that you're open to listening to the emotional component of the speaker's message. Many listeners become uncomfortable when their conversational partner starts talking about what he's feeling. When you reflect the speaker's emotions, it lets him know that it's OK with you for him to talk about his feelings.

2. Accurate and empathic reflections of feelings let the speaker know that you understand what he's feeling—that you "get" the emotional aspect of what he's saying. Experiencing that attunement is a major benefit of reflecting the speaker's feelings.

3. Reflections of feelings often help the speaker become more fully and more specifically aware of his feelings about the situation he is discussing. This increases his emotional awareness and fosters an enhanced ability to cope with his challenges.

4. When the speaker's unwanted emotions are empathically reflected, they typically decrease to—or nearly to—the person's emotional normal. When feelings soar, thinking tends to stop. Since empathic listening helps the speaker express his feelings, after a few reflections the speaker's heightened feelings begin to subside, and he is more able to understand his situation more accurately and can think and talk about it more productively. Occasionally, the speaker's intensity may temporarily surge a bit higher after a reflection of feelings, but with further reflections, his emotions soon tend to diminish and move toward his normal range.

5. Reflecting the speaker's positive feelings tends to reinforce them. You'll note that this is the opposite effect of reflecting unwanted feelings. For example, when a person is speaking of his happiness and the listener reflects those feelings, the speaker is likely to become even more joyful.

HOW THE LISTENER BENEFITS FROM REFLECTING THE SPEAKER'S FEELINGS

As a listener, you'll receive these benefits from reflecting the speaker's feelings:

1. You'll obtain *feedback* on the accuracy of your reflection. When a reflection of feelings is on target, the speaker typically confirms its accuracy with a nod of the head, "an um-hmm," or some other brief affirmation of the aptness of the reflection. If the

reflection is wide of the mark, the speaker usually corrects it and continues on with the next part of his message.

2. As mentioned, when the speaker is experiencing moderately strong to very strong unwanted feelings, reflecting them generally decreases their intensity. So, in stressful conversations, good reflections of feelings generally reduce tensions significantly, which makes the conversation better for both parties.

3. Succinct, on-target reflections of feelings often pull more concise statements from the speaker. When a speaker is feeling emotionally intense, he's apt to become more long-winded than usual. Fortunately, a listener's brief and accurate reflections of feelings show the speaker that he's been clearly understood so he can move on to what else he wants to say or perhaps transition to listening. So, although reflecting feelings take time, in addition to providing relief to the speaker's heightened feelings, it tends to promote clarity of communication. Thus, in the long run listening to a person's strong feelings ultimately tends to saves time. And it certainly improves relationships.

How to Reflect Feelings

Reflections of feelings share these characteristics with paraphrases:

- Brevity
- In one's own words
- Downturned voice at the end
- Vocal attunement

The difference between a paraphrase and a reflection of feelings is that the former is focused strictly on the factual aspect of the speaker's message, whereas reflections of feelings concentrate on the emotional aspect of what the speaker is saying.

A reflection of feelings often starts with the word "You're" and is followed by a word or phrase describing the feeling that the listener observed. Here's a bare-bones example:

You're _____.
        Feeling word

You're _____relieved_____.
        Feeling word

Does that seem pretty abrupt? We think so too. This is a simplistic example that is used to portray the *structure* of a reflection of feelings. In a moment, we'll move on to how to "conversationalize" your reflections.

INTENSITY OF FEELING WORDS LIST

To aid you in choosing the most appropriate feeling word, we're reprinting the *intensity of feelings words list* (Figure 17.1) that appeared in the previous chapter.

	MILD	MEDIUM	STRONG
ANGER	irritated	frustrated	furious
	annoyed	fed up	enraged
	perturbed	aggravated	seething
FEAR	nervous	scared	terrified
	worried	frightened	desperate
	on edge	apprehensive	panicky
CONFUSION	undecided	confused	bewildered
	unsure	muddled	baffled
	unclear	mixed up	disjointed
SORROW	low	distressed	despondent
	dissatisfied	bummed	hopeless
	displeased	glum	anguished
EXCITEMENT	interested	eager	thrilled
	involved	fired up	pumped
	attentive	enthusiastic	exhilarated
JOY	satisfied	happy	elated
	glad	delighted	ecstatic
	contented	cheerful	jubilant

FIGURE 18.1. INTENSITY OF FEELINGS WORD LIST.

How to Reflect Meanings

When a listener reflects the speaker's meaning (the factual content and the emotional coloration) in one sentence, it's sometimes referred to as "listening in stereo." We think that's an apt expression. As stereophonic sound is much fuller and richer than monophonic sound, reflections of meaning are fuller and richer than paraphrases and reflections of feelings. This is not to say that reflections of meaning are necessarily better than the other ways of reflecting. Each has important uses, and skilled listeners employ each of them appropriately.

Here's a format for reflecting meanings:

You're _____ about (or that) _____.
        Feeling word   *Incident, action, or statement that*
                                           prompted the feeling

When using this format, insert the appropriate *feeling word* in the first blank. Then fill in the second blank with a concise description of the incident, action, or statement that prompted the person's feeling. For example:

You're <u>worried</u> about <u>the effects downsizing may have on employee morale.</u>
  Feeling word   *Incident, action, or statement that prompted the feeling*

You're <u>upset</u> that <u>you weren't consulted on the plan you have to implement.</u>
  Feeling word   *Incident, action, or statement that prompted the feeling*

You're <u>relieved</u> that <u>you got an A– on the final.</u>
    Feeling word   *Incident, action, or statement that prompted the feeling*

For variety's sake, you may want to change the wording of the formula now and then. You can make minor changes by merely changing a word or two:

You seem <u>bummed</u> that <u>your team lost the big game.</u>
      Feeling word   *Incident, action, or statement that prompted the feeling*

You look <u>perplexed</u> about <u>so few people signing up for the trip.</u>
      Feeling word   *Incident, action, or statement that prompted the feeling*

Sounds like you're <u>delighted</u> that <u>your presentation was so well received.</u>
        Feeling word   *Incident, action, or statement that*
                               prompted the feeling

Or you might change the order of the two parts of the reflection:

<u>When your proposal received unanimous approval</u> you were <u>elated.</u>
      Incident, action, or statement   *Feeling word*
        that prompted the feeling

Conversational Reflections of Feelings and of Meanings

When you've mastered using the formatted reflections of feelings and reflections of meanings, it's time to graduate to a more conversational style of reflecting. Unlike formatted reflections, conversational reflections have a colloquial ring to them. They sound pretty much like ordinary speech.

HOW TO "CONVERSATIONALIZE" REFLECTIONS OF FEELINGS AND REFLECTIONS OF MEANINGS

Here are two methods for making reflections of feelings sound more down-to-earth and fit more naturally into your conversations:

- Use a variety of ways of describing the feelings the speaker seems to be expressing.
- Modulate your voice appropriately.

USE A VARIETY OF WAYS OF DESCRIBING THE SPEAKER'S FEELINGS

As in many endeavors, variety is the spice of reflective listening. Here are four ways of spicing up your reflections of feelings. (For your convenience, we are repeating here some content from the previous chapter.)

Use phrases (often slang) that suggest what the speaker is feeling, "You've had it." "It's like your hands are tied." "You were burned when she said that." "What a downer." "Your back's up against a wall." "You were really fired up." "You're on a roll." "It was beyond belief." "Talk about surprised!"

Use figures of speech that convey feelings. "On top of the world." "On cloud nine." "That was the frosting on the cake." "Made your day." "You weren't on the same page." "Felt like the rug was pulled out from under you." "It was the pits!" "Between a rock and a hard place." "Like being stabbed in the back." "Your stomach is doing flip-flops." "You felt like a fish out of water." "You let bygones be bygones." People often transition into a figure of speech with the word "Like" or the phrase "It felt like."

Describe an action the person would like to do to convey the feelings (but undoubtedly won't). "You'd like to tell her off." "You feel like walking away from the whole project." "You could give him a big hug." "You feel like wringing his neck." "You'd like to wash your hands of the whole thing."

Use descriptions of body language that portray the speaker's feelings. "You breathed a sigh of relief." "You were jumping for joy." "It was like the hair was standing up on the back of your neck." "Your heart must have been pounding." "Sounds like you got up on the wrong side of the bed this morning." "You kept a stiff upper lip." "It's like you were bumping your head against a brick wall." "You felt like jumping up and down."

Here's an example of using each of four ways of reflecting the feeling of joy:

Feeling word: You're glad that . . .

Phrase: You're delighted over . . .

Action the person would like to take (but probably won't): You feel like giving him a big hug.

Description of body language that portrays the speaker's feelings: You must have been grinning from ear to ear!

USE CONGRUENT BODY LANGUAGE AND VOCAL INTONATION

Whether responding with a formula reflection or a conversational reflection, when a person's statement has emotional coloration, your body language and tone of voice need to be in tune with the tenor of the speaker's manner and message. Imagine a speaker all fired up and full of energy when telling about a success at work, and the listener says in a bland, monotone voice:

That was exciting.

Now imagine the listener responding with a physical and vocal energy that was similar to the speaker's:

That was exciting!

ANTICIPATE POSSIBLE RESISTANCE TO A CHANGE IN THE WAY YOU LISTEN

Whenever one person makes a significant change in his behavior, people who relate frequently to him are apt to be uncomfortable even when it is an improvement in his way of relating. They may not have thought the old ways were great, but they were predictable and the person's friends, relatives, and acquaintances had learned to live with them.

It's worth repeating that when one person in a relationship changes, especially in one of the basic modes of communication like listening, it tends to put pressure on the other person to do some things differently.

IDENTIFY THE PERSONS AND/OR TYPES OF SITUATIONS BEST SUITED FOR YOU TO GAIN EXPERIENCE WITH REFLECTING FEELINGS AND MEANINGS

When people begin reflecting feelings and meanings, it's advisable to gain a bit of experience using this skill in casual and impersonal relationships before using them in their more important relationships. When developing these skills, consider how to use them in three types of relationships.

- **Outer circle people:** Least important relationships—people with whom you generally have brief and fairly casual interactions, where little or no resistance is expected:
    - Postal clerk
    - Checkout cashier
    - Store manager
    - Car maintenance worker
    - Waiters and waitresses
    - Department store personnel
    - Delivery person
- **Middle circle people:** Moderately important relationships— people you see more frequently and with whom you interact more frequently, where a moderate level of resistance is expected:

▶ Your child's teacher

▶ Home maintenance person

▶ Neighbor

▶ Consultants for insurance, investments, real estate, etc.

▶ Doctor

▶ Dentist

- **Inner circle people:** Longest, most frequent interactions with people you see most frequently, where the highest likelihood of resistance is expected:

  ▶ Family members

  ▶ Closest friends

  ▶ Manager/team leader

  ▶ Coworkers

It may seem strange, but the people who are closest to you could be the most likely to resist your reflection of their feelings. Conversely, the people who are more peripheral to your life are apt to be more accepting of your new way of listening and perhaps may even welcome it right from the start.

But consider this perspective on the likelihood mentioned in the list. Those who are closest to you have the most at stake in their relationship with you and are thus apt to be more wary of changes in your behavior. And conversation is a bit like a dance: When one partner makes changes, the other partner needs to make some coordinated changes.

Skepticism About Reflecting Feelings Revisited

Toward the conclusion of the module on reflecting feelings previously mentioned, Dot returned to discuss June's skepticism about reflecting feelings. The situation June raised was that Tony, her peer, was incensed that she didn't get critical information to him by the agreed-upon time, causing him to miss a key deadline with his boss. June said, "You think I'm going to say to Tony, "You're feeling angry with me"?

Of course, that would have sounded awkward and phony. When June realized that she had optional ways of reflecting feelings, she said she would consider using some of these conversational reflections of feelings in the next conversation with her boss:

Seems like I put you between a rock and a hard place.

Talk about being let down.

You didn't expect that of me.

Reflections of feelings and of meanings are essential skills in crucial conversations. They enable you to function competently in the most stressful interactions. And they enable you to help others obtain greater joy from their positive moments and weather the emotional storms that come to us all at times.

PART V

THINGS TO KEEP IN MIND

[T]o make an end is to make a beginning.

The end is where we start from.

—T. S. ELIOT (*FOUR QUARTETS*)

19

Wrap It Up with a Summary Reflection

Do not disengage and leave a situation still unclear.

—JOE ALEXANDER

YOU KNOW THE problem: When people in meetings are wrestling with an issue, they often raise numerous options, discuss them at length, and seemingly agree on a solution. Afterward, nothing happens. Why? Because it was not clear what was going to be done, who was going to do it, by what time, and what the follow-up would be. When the snafu is investigated, you're apt to hear statements like:

But I thought we agreed to do it this way.

I understood that Alison was going to organize the second stage of the campaign.

I didn't realize you expected the survey to be completed by the tenth.

You thought *I* was going to do it?

Misunderstandings like these waste time, effort, and money. And they can be very hard on relationships. Typically, each person thinks his version of what was discussed is right, and people are apt to react against one another with blame, recrimination, and defensiveness.

This chapter presents the use of summary reflections to avoid this kind of mix-up. Here's what you'll learn:

- What summary reflections are.
- How to make summary reflections.
- Make a summary reflection before acting on a request.
- Ask others to summarize what they're going to do before they take action.
- Make internal summaries.

What Summary Reflections Are

You may be wondering what the difference is between summary reflections and the other types of reflections you've been reading about since they all summarize what's been said.

- The reflections we've covered so far are ways to summarize bite-size pieces of what's been said.
- By contrast, a *summary reflection* recaps long stretches of what's been covered in a meeting or a long conversation. In fact, they are often used to recapitulate the whole interaction.

The best way to assure that everyone is on the same page at the end of a meeting or a long conversation is to wrap up the interaction with a summary reflection. This type of reflection focuses on the central points by rigorously pruning out extraneous material. These reflections provide a highly specific recap of the essence of a meeting or significant conversation—or a major part of those interactions. Summary reflections precisely define what agreements have been reached regarding what is to be done, by whom, in what time frame, and what differences, if any, need to be worked through and what the follow-up will be. Here's an example:

> Here's my take on what we've decided. Starting next Monday, Jake and Andrew will ask the department heads for ideas about streamlining the budgeting process. They'll integrate the ideas they've collected and bring them to me for review by the first of next month. The three of us will then prepare and bring a revision to the next meeting for the team's approval.
> Have I missed something, or does that cover it?

Note how condensed, the summary reflection of an hour-long meeting is boiled down to six sentences.

Although that example is of a summation of a long meeting, it's often useful to tie up loose ends with a summary reflection at the conclusion of significant shorter interactions. Of course, when you're merely passing the time of day, there's no need for summary reflections.

How to Make Summary Reflections

Though making a summary reflection is a fairly straightforward process, the following tips will help your conversations produce the results you want.

MAKE A THREE-PART STATEMENT

It's often useful to use a three-part format for your summaries:

1. Lead-in
2. Summary reflection
3. Check for accuracy

Using the example given earlier, here's what each part of a summary reflection looks like:

1. **Lead-in:**
   Here's my understanding of what we've decided.

2. **Summary reflection:**
   Starting next Monday Jake and Andrew will ask the department heads for ideas about streamlining the budgeting process. They'll integrate the ideas they've collected and bring them to me for review by the first of next month. The three of us will prepare and bring a revision to the next meeting for the team's approval. I'll present the approved version at the next finance department meeting and email the results to each of you.

3. **Check for accuracy:**
   Have I missed something or does that cover it?

When the subject matter is uncomplicated and the speaker's comments are well organized, it's easy to summarize a whole conversation.

The preceding example was a useful accuracy check that certainly didn't require a great deal of mental effort. Other summaries are more of a challenge due to the complexity of the subject matter, the variety of options discussed, or the disjointed nature of the speaker's presentation.

HOW TO CREATE EACH PART OF A SUMMARY REFLECTION

1. LEAD-IN

In relatively few words, let people know that you are going to sum up the discussion or at least the actionable part of it. Phrases like these signal your intent to summarize the conversation:

> This is my understanding of what we're planning to do.

> Here's my recollection of the main points we discussed.

> I'll try to summarize the ground we've covered to make sure we're all on the same wavelength.

> Let me see if I can restate what we decided.

> Note the open, nondogmatic tone of the transitions: "Let me see if I can restate . . ." or "This is my understanding."

2. STATE YOUR SUMMARY REFLECTION

Very succinctly restate the *essence* of what's been said. Brevity is crucial in a summary reflection. In his first meeting with Sigmund Freud, Carl Jung excitedly poured out a jumble of thoughts for three straight hours. Then, to Jung's great astonishment and appreciation, Freud reorganized the contents of the spontaneous outpouring into "several precise headings that enabled them to spend the further hours in a more profitable give-and-take."[1]

Determine how you'll organize the summary. Sometimes you'll recap the conversation in the order in which things were discussed. At other times, it's useful to show how the various parts of the conversation fit together in your mind rather than feed them back in the order the speaker used. Psychologist Gerard Egan makes this important point:

> A summary is not a mechanical pulling together of a number of facts; it is a systematic presentation of relevant data.[2]

During long, complex discussions, it may be helpful to use a memory aid to keep track of key points. When appropriate, take notes. Or keep outlining the conversation in your mind: Each time a new topic is raised, give your memory an assist by inwardly reminding yourself of the major concerns that have been resolved thus far.

At the conclusion of a decision-making meeting, the following outline for summarizing is often used:

Who?

Does what?

By when?

At what cost?

How and when will we follow up?

It's often advisable to document what was agreed to and copy everyone who has a role to play or a stake in the outcome.

3. CHECK FOR ACCURACY

Ask the other person or persons whether they think there were inaccuracies or omissions in your summary:

Is there anything that I've misunderstood or left out?

Have I covered everything?

Is there something you'd like to add?

Does this match your understanding?

By inviting the other person's perspective, you make this a mutual review of the conversation. The other person's participation increases the likelihood of accuracy because he may note points you missed or misunderstood. Getting the other person's perspective also provides an opportunity for him to express reservations that he may not have disclosed earlier.

> The clear allocation of responsibility for action not only assures that action will be taken but provides a test of the decision in that the responsible implementer may raise questions about the decision that had not been raised before."[3]

Better to deal with disagreements now than be blindsided later.

Whether your summary is accepted as is or is corrected, it's advantageous to have both parties arrive at a common agreement of what the interaction accomplished.

Make a Summary Reflection Before Acting on a Request

Recapping what's wanted *before acting on someone's request or instructions* is one of the most useful applications of summary reflections. This simple practice of clarifying agreements will help you do things right the first time so that you don't have to do them over.

Ask Others to Summarize What They're Going to Do Before They Take Action

When you give instructions or make a request of someone, ask the person to sum up what specifically she is going to do. That will prevent many a costly misunderstanding. The late motivational speaker, Earl Nightingale, said that whenever his partner, Lloyd Conant, gave instructions on an important task, Conant would ask the person he was coaching to recap the instructions. It can be done with a simple prefaced question:

> So that we're sure we leave with a common understanding, would you summarize what you are going to do as a result of this meeting?

"The difference," according to Nightingale, "was often astonishing."[4]

Don't make the mistake of asking, "Do you understand?" You'll almost always get a "Yes" because even when the person grossly misunderstands what you meant, she probably thinks she knows exactly what you meant.

There's a beneficial side effect of habitually asking others to restate your requests and instructions. When people realize they'll be asked to recap what you've said, they'll listen much more carefully.

Make Internal Summaries

So far we've concentrated on *concluding summaries*, which wrap up a whole conversation. *Internal summaries* recap a large segment of conversation, such as a major agenda item. When the speaker or group finishes talking about a particular topic, an internal summary helps assure that all parties in the conversation have a common understanding before moving on to the next item.

Another use of internal summaries is to post *accurate and greatly condensed summarized opinions side by side for a more fruitful discussion* of their comparative merits—a very useful tool in negotiations, team meetings, and other forums. Side-by-side summaries of opinions or alternatives are especially helpful when written on newsprint or some other medium so that all can see them. That's an application of the saying, "One dull pencil is worth more than six sharp minds."

TWO USES OF INTERNAL SUMMARIES

1. In lengthy conversations, internal summaries review the progress that's been made, thus providing *a sense of movement* that energizes the conversation.
2. An internal summary helps *relaunch a conversation that's resumed after a break.* The recap heads off much unnecessary repetition, helps build on the accomplishments of the previous session, and generates momentum for the remaining discussion.

Internal summaries typically follow the same format as concluding summaries:

1. Lead-in
2. State your summary reflection
3. Check for accuracy

1. LEAD-IN

Here are some phrases that can help you lead into an internal summary:

So far we've talked about these options.

Let's back up for a minute and review how we got here.

As you see it, are these the key elements of the problem?

One theme you keep coming back to is . . .

What's really important to you is . . .

Your main suggestions are . . .

As I understand it, your position is . . .

Let's see if I can restate your concerns.

2. STATE YOUR SUMMARY REFLECTION

Remember to keep your summary reflection succinct.

3. CHECK FOR ACCURACY

Close with an accuracy check to make sure the other person's take on things matches your understanding.

Some discussions don't need to be recapped. In many others, a concluding summary is all that's required. At times, though, you may find yourself recapping each point that's made, as well as drawing together the whole conversation with a concluding summary.

Begin Now

Here are two ways of easing into making summary reflections:

1. Summarize during telephone conversations. They're especially easy to recap because you can take notes. Also, in the age of the cell phone, many of the people you are talking with are focusing only a fraction of their attention on the conversation. So summaries during phone calls are needed more than ever these days.
2. In small, uncomplicated meetings, practice making an occasional summary reflection.

20

Results-Focused Listening

The optimum solution to an individual's problems rarely comes from the outside; the best answers are usually the ones individuals discover for themselves.

—ANONYMOUS

S O FAR YOU'VE learned the key components of skillful listening. Those skills make it possible for you to understand what a person is trying to get across to you. Having learned the skills of reflective listening, you're able to check out whether you've heard the speaker's message accurately. When you've understood the other person's situation and he seems to have concluded making his point, the question is, "Now what?"

There are two possibilities.

1. No action is needed.
2. Results-focused listening is called for.

1. No Action Is Needed

The speaker is truly done. He is satisfied that he has said all he has or wants to say about this topic. He has run out of steam. He appreciates your investment of time and effort on his behalf, and he's ready to move on. No action is needed.

What have you accomplished? The way you've handled this conversation has contributed to building a positive relationship with that individual. At work, positive relationships are the foundation of productivity and a positive learning culture, while in personal life they're essential for one's happiness—pretty important outcomes.

Of course, if an individual makes a habit of stopping by with a strong need to talk about his concerns and if your work is piling up, be candid and tell him that you don't have the time to talk right now. If his concerns are work-related and part of your responsibilities, make an appointment for a later meeting. Even when the topic is not a work issue, there are undoubtedly times when it will be appropriate to find a time for the conversation. When the topic appears to be just a time waster, be frank and tell him that you can't give the time now to this discussion since you have deadlines to meet.

2. Results-Focused Listening Is Called For

The second option is more complicated because the speaker discloses a real problem that needs to be resolved. You're so used to solving problems that you're likely to get hooked. Like many people, you probably think of yourself as a pretty good problem solver. You want to mentally roll up your sleeves and solve this problem for the person and get on with your day. You may even believe that your problem-solving ability is an essential part of what you're paid for.

Here are just a few reasons why you might want to reconsider any temptation to jump right in and respond to the speaker's problem with your solution:

- The speaker may not have given you all the pieces of the puzzle.
- The speaker may have already tried what you suggest.
- The speaker could have been struggling with this problem for some time and may become defensive when you presume you can solve it in a few minutes.
- The speaker may fall into a "Yes, but" routine.
- When you solve the problems people bring to you, you're likely to be creating dependent relationships.
- You're not developing the person, which is part of your responsibility whether you're an organizational leader or a parent.

The benefits of using results-focused listening are that you avoid all these negatives, and you also strengthen the relationship with the other person because you've formed more of a partnership rather than merely a boss–subordinate relationship. Partnerships are more appropriate in today's team approach to work rather than the old boss–subordinate approach. Another plus to this approach is that you will have helped the speaker increase his self-confidence and sense of resourcefulness.

Overview of the Results-Focused Listening Process

Results-focused listening is the preferred way to respond when people bring their problems to you. There are three sequential steps in this process:

1. Explore
2. Transition
3. Resolve

There are several substeps for each step. Here's an overview of the steps and substeps of the results-focused listening process.

1. EXPLORE

- Reflect until both parties achieve a clear understanding of the problem.
- State the problem.
- State the goal.

2. TRANSITION

- Ask what's been thought of or done so far.
- Reflect what you hear.
- Ask if your input is wanted.

3. RESOLVE (ASSUMING YOUR INPUT IS WANTED)

- Make your input.
- Summarize the agreement.
- Schedule a follow-up (if needed).
- Express optimism (when appropriate).

How to Do Results-Focused Listening

Here are the how-tos for each step of the results-focused listening process.

STEP 1: EXPLORE

Reflect until both parties understand the problem.

An employee begins communicating about a subject of importance to him. You sense his strong need to talk, which is your signal that reflective listening is called for. You reflect what you hear and drastically ration your questions. Keep reflecting until you have a highly specific understanding of his problem or concern.

State the problem.

You very succinctly state your understanding of the speaker's problem in your own words. The speaker usually concurs. If not, explore with further reflections until you and the speaker agree on the statement of the problem.

State the goal.

The problem and the goal are linked; on the flip side of most problems there lurks a goal. The situation wouldn't be a problem unless the person wished things were different. That means a goal isn't being met. Here are two examples of how to transform a problem into a goal.

EXAMPLE 1:

Your *problem* is that Pete's work is mixed—sometimes good, sometimes not.

And your *goal* is to achieve consistent performance.

EXAMPLE 2:

Your *problem* is that you're falling behind in your technical reading.

And your *goal* is to keep up-to-date with developments in your field.

Once you and the speaker understand the problem, a goal statement is easy to create.

Once you've changed the problem statement into a goal statement, you've moved from the likelihood of getting stuck mucking around in a negative situation to the possibility of having a positive and energizing goal to work toward.

When you're able to state the problem and turn it into a goal with relative ease, you can *move into a much more conversational way of expressing the problem and the goal.* For instance, returning to the first example, you could say:

So Pete's work is mixed—sometimes good and sometimes not. That's a
Problem statement
concern, and, as his manager, you want to help him achieve consistency.
Goal

The second example might sound something like this:

You're bothered that you're falling behind in your technical reading, and
Problem statement
you want to keep up-to-date with developments in your field.
Goal

In each of the these examples, there's not a great difference between the formal and the more informal wording, but anything that makes your phrasing more conversational is a plus.

AVOID THIS TRAP

When the problem definition and the goal statement are agreed upon, it's like a siren's call. Here's where many people automatically want to jump in with their solution. Be patient and proceed with the two final steps of the results-focused listening process.

STEP 2: TRANSITION

Ask "What's been thought of or done so far?"

Give the speaker some credit. It's her problem. It's likely that she has been thinking about it for a while, and it's possible that she has tried to solve it. She just hasn't been successful yet. Asking her what she has thought of or done so far gives her a chance to show how she has struggled to work this thing out before coming to you. And it often provides useful information as you move through the conversation.

You can ask, "What has been thought of or done so far?" in a number of ways. Here are a couple of examples:

> You've been working on this for a while. Have you thought or done anything to date that brings you closer to where you want to be?

> Sounds like a challenging situation. You've probably had some thoughts on how to approach it. Maybe you've already done some things to address it.

Reflect what you hear.
Say back the crux of the message. Keep your reflections succinct.

Ask if your input is wanted.
You may recall the old phrase, "Keep the monkey off your back." The picture of a manager going through his day, hearing his people's problems and taking them on as his own was made vivid by picturing the problems as monkey's leaping from the reporting person's back onto the manager's back. At the end of the day, the manager was loaded down with problems that belonged to other people.

Throughout the steps of the results-focused listening process, we've worked at keeping the ownership of the problem with the speaker.
The problem is hers. The monkey is her monkey. It's her responsibility to resolve it. Although it is her problem, the temptation is there for you to take it on. If you can discipline yourself to keep from jumping in with your excellent solutions, you'll be known as a manager who develops his people and one who does not work below his level of responsibility.

However, there will be times when your input is appropriate. With the lessons learned from your years of experience, you may in fact know the best way to resolve the problem. When you think it's appropriate to make some suggestions, first get permission; ask if your input is wanted. This is simple courtesy.

Here are a few examples of how to ask if your input is wanted:

What you're trying to resolve isn't easy.

Would you be open to discussing possibilities I can think of?

Would you like to hear some of my thoughts?

I have some ideas on this matter. Would you care to hear them?

STEP 3: RESOLVE

Make your input.

You've listened through the explore step until you've understood the problem, and you've stated the problem and the goal. You've made the transition of finding out what the person has thought of or done so far. And you've shown courtesy by asking permission to present your ideas. The speaker virtually always says, "Yes." Now you have the green light.

> This is an important crossroads for you. Your input could easily turn into a lecture that will undo all the work you've done to make it a developmental experience for the other person. Or the interaction can continue on the road that will culminate in a positive developmental moment for the other person, as well as getting the problem solved so that it will stay solved.

We find that the speak-check-reflect method often provides the best way of making one's input interactively so that the conversation is a dialogue rather than the one-way lecture that's so prevalent when people share their thoughts with others.

The Speak-Check-Reflect Method

The Speak-Check-Reflect method is a highly effective way of giving your input (see Figure 20.1). It's especially useful when your message is complex or the point you are making may not be viewed positively by the receiver. And it's a very useful tool for making your input when doing results-focused listening.

Here's the method:

1. First, you briefly make a point.
2. Then you ask a "checking question" to get your conversational partner's reaction to the statement you just made.
3. Finally, you concisely reflect the person's response.

Then, your conversational partner may make her input. Or, you may move on to your next point using the Speak-Check-Reflect method.

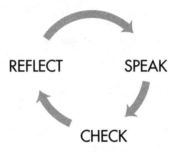

REFLECT   SPEAK

CHECK

FIGURE 20.1. HOW THE SPEAK-CHECK-REFLECT METHOD LOOKS.

LISTENER SPEAKS: Joe Hauck is particularly strong in the areas where you say Pete is inconsistent. You could set up a coaching opportunity for Pete by having him partner with Joe on the upcoming XYZ project.

LISTENER CHECKS: How does that sound to you?

SPEAKER: That's a possibility. My concern is how to position that kind of thing. How do you bring Hauck into it, and what do I say to Pete?

LISTENER REFLECTS: You're wondering how to position it with each of them.

SPEAKER: Yeah.

LISTENER SPEAKS: If you see merit in going that route, these are the details you need to work out. [Gives the details.]

LISTENER CHECKS: Are you comfortable doing that?

SPEAKER: Yeah, that's doable.

LISTENER REFLECTS: Sounds like a plan.

LISTENER SPEAKS: It would be useful for you to have a conversation with Pete telling him about the inconsistency problem that you have observed and how you propose to help him correct that. And remember to reflect to his reaction. We want him to realize this as a positive move on your part to help him develop.

LISTENER CHECKS: What's your reaction to doing that?

SPEAKER: These conversations are never easy. I'll have to do some planning on how I want to handle it.

Using the Speak-Check-Reflect method when you give your input keeps you from saying too much too soon. It reminds you to keep focused on listening to the speaker. And it leads you to reflect his reaction before adding more information.

Summarize the agreement.

To make sure you haven't wasted your time, it's wise to nail things down with a clearly expressed understanding of who does what, how, and by when so that everyone leaves the room with the same understanding.

Then use the last two procedures of the resolve step:

1. Schedule a follow-up on the issue under discussion if needed and
2. Express encouragement when appropriate.

Results-Focused Listening Process

Results-focused listening is an alternative way for you to operate when people bring their problems to you. Here's a review of the step-by-step process.

1. EXPLORE

- Reflect until you both understand the problem.
- State the problem.
- State the goal.

2. TRANSITION

- Ask what's been thought of or done so far.
- Reflect what you hear.
- Ask if your input is wanted.

3. RESOLVE (ASSUMING YOUR INPUT IS WANTED)

- Make your input (by using the Speak-Check-Reflect method).
- Summarize agreement.

- Schedule a follow-up (if needed).
- Express optimism (when appropriate).

Here's another example of a conversation in which the listener uses results-focused listening:

THE SITUATION

A nineteen-year-old freshman pre-med college student, home on spring break, approaches his mother saying he wants to give her an update on what's up at school.

1. EXPLORE

Reflect until both parties achieve a clear understanding.

LUKE: This is pretty big, Mom. Maybe you want to sit down.

MOM: [Sits down.] OK. I'm ready.

LUKE: I'm 99 percent sure that I won't be attending medical school.

MOM: You're right, Luke, this is pretty big. Tell me more.

LUKE: Well, I suffered through Organic Chemistry I and Physics, and I hated every second of them. Now I'm suffering through Organic Chemistry II, and that's no better.

MOM: Really painful for you.

LUKE: Awful. I get good grades, but I just hate it!

MOM: Good grades don't make it easier to stomach.

LUKE: Right. I literally wake up every day and hate what I'm studying. I find myself thinking all the time about ways to get out of what I thought I wanted.

MOM: It's that bad.

LUKE: Real bad. I've tried the "grind through the petty stuff" so that my ultimate goal of becoming a doctor can happen, but I'm not sure that I'm up for studying years of things I don't like. And I'm stressed about realizing that I may not be cut out for being a doctor after all.

MOM: It's unsettling finding medicine might not be for you.

LUKE: Yeah. I'm trying to keep an open mind right now. Maybe medical school after all — maybe not, maybe change my major — maybe not. I don't know.

State the problem.

MOM: You're in a tough spot because after being so sure you wanted to be a doctor, you're having major doubts about it.

State the goal.

MOM: And what you want is to find a direction that you can feel excited about and dedicated to whether it's in medicine or not.

LUKE: Exactly. It's not easy.

2. TRANSITION

What have you thought of or done so far?

MOM: Well, Luke, you probably have some thoughts of your own about this. I wonder if you've done anything to date to move things along.

LUKE: Not a lot. I know that I'll complete the courses I'm in this semester. I don't want to lose those credits.

MOM: Losing credits doesn't make sense to you.

LUKE: No way. And I know this may sound fuzzy right now, but what I think I might want to do is be an advocate for people who can't advocate for themselves. Maybe in a not-for-profit organization.

MOM: You may want to help unempowered people.

LUKE: Right. I know I want to make a difference to people, and I'm confident that there are many ways I could do that.

MOM: You're excited about exploring other options.

LUKE: Yeah.

Ask if your input is wanted.

MOM: Would you like to hear some of my thoughts?

LUKE: Sure.

MOM SPEAKS: My first thought is that it's good you found this out now rather than having second thoughts in medical school.

MOM CHECKS: [Pauses.]

LUKE: Exactly.

MOM SPEAKS: We're on the same page about that.

MOM SPEAKS: You're coping with a lot right now. The good news is time is on your side. Using it to explore possibilities makes all kinds of sense. You'll need time to look into different options, time to think through each one. Maybe get a few internships in some of the fields that focus on advocating for others.

MOM CHECKS: How does that sound to you?

LUKE: Yeah, I've got at least two years to keep my options open. Some of the upperclassman I know learned a ton in internships. I've actually thought about exploring a couple of internships.

MOM REFLECTS: The internships might give you some insight.

LUKE: Yeah.

MOM SPEAKS: It would probably make sense to explore your options. And you seem to have a lot of respect for your advisor. You might want to give her a heads-up on this.

MOM CHECKS: What do you think about that?

LUKE: I'm on board about continuing to explore what being a doctor is really like and seeking internships in different fields, but I'll skip bringing my advisor into this. I have no need to discuss this with her.

MOM REFLECTS: So no advisor, but you want to look into internships.

LUKE: Yeah.

Get agreement on next steps.

MOM SPEAKS: OK. Here's what I heard. You decided to slow down, take your time, and start exploring other career options while you continue to learn more about medicine as a career. You're particularly interested in fields where you would be advocating for others who can't advocate for themselves. Getting some internship will be part of your approach.

MOM CHECKS: Did I miss something?

LUKE: No, I don't think so. I don't know where any of this will take me ... politics, policy, administration. I just don't know, but I'm not worried. I might even see my advisor. She's alright.

Schedule a follow-up.

MOM: You're okay with living with ambiguity for a while. I'm glad you felt you could talk this over with me. How about we discuss the situation again just before you go back to school, maybe next Sunday afternoon.

LUKE: Sounds good, but after the game, okay?

MOM: Sure, right after the game.

Express encouragement:

MOM: I have to tell you, this is a bit of a surprise for me, but you've made clear what's going on with you. I know this is a challenge to work out, and I want you to know that I have confidence in your ability to land right where you want to be.

Keeping It All Straight

The process we've suggested may have you thinking, "Give me a break. You start talking about three steps and then turn it into ten steps. How am I to keep all that straight?"

Try looking at it this way.

1. EXPLORE

What we refer to as the explore step is what you would ordinarily do in trying to understand the speaker's problem. Even if you never heard the word "explore," you would try to understand the problem so that you could work with it. The only new part for you is that we suggest that you reflect what you hear to assure that you correctly understand the problem.

State the problem.

You would probably quite naturally state your understanding of the problem and get feedback on it before you tried to solve it.

State the goal.

What we've added is turning the problem statement—what they are trying to avoid—into a goal statement—what they are trying to accomplish. That contributes forward motion to the discussion.

2. TRANSITION

Ask what's been thought of or done so far.

Doesn't it make sense to find out what the person has thought about or done so far before you add your thoughts on the issue? You don't want to hear, "Well, I tried that and it didn't work."

Reflect what you hear.

Again, this is to assure accuracy.

Ask if your input is wanted.

When the time comes for you to add your recommendations, asking permission is a nicety—a common courtesy.

3. RESOLVE

Make your input.

Regarding putting forward your ideas, the new part is do it in bite-size pieces and check the person's reaction to what you've said. If you don't invite the speaker's reaction to your suggestion, you're flying blind. It could be that the person is having a negative reaction to what you've been saying, and it's wise to learn what that is before winding up the conversation.

Summarize the agreement.

This is always a good idea when concluding an important conversation.

Express optimism (when appropriate).

Most people can use the feedback that others believe in them and their ability.

This chapter concludes the skill development part of the book. However, when it comes to empathic listening, important as good skills are, more is needed—the listening spirit—which is the subject of the next chapter.

21

The Listening Spirit

> If it is simply a reflection, that's no good. That's just a technique. It must be a desire to understand empathetically to stand in the other person's shoes and to see the world from his vantage point.
>
> —CARL ROGERS

SO FAR, WE'VE talked primarily about the *skills* of listening. But one of the dangers people are likely to run into when improving their listening is becoming so focused on the skills that their listening becomes rather mechanical. Important as these skills are, their effectiveness depends on something deeper.

Carl Rogers, whom we've referred to several times in this book, emphasized that *respect, empathy,* and *genuineness* are three "core conditions" that undergird quality listening. We think of this combination of facilitative qualities as the "listening spirit." This is the foundation on which effective listening rests.

Today, sixty-some years after Rogers published his findings, it is firmly established that this triumvirate of characteristics greatly enhances listening. *Respect* is the foundation. *Empathy* demonstrates caring and informs connections with the speaker. *Genuineness* is being your true self, interacting without pretense. Listeners who show respect for others and who are empathic and authentic in their dealings with them are much more effective in their listening than those who are deficient in these qualities. Of course, what you want to strive for is using proven listening skills while relating respectfully, empathically, and genuinely. This chapter describes each of these core qualities that undergird effective listening—and virtually all other forms of constructive interaction.

Respect

WHAT RESPECT IS

Many people think respect is a feeling of deep admiration for someone for their commendable abilities, qualities, and/or achievements. That's not what we mean by it. As we use the term, *respect does not need to be earned by good conduct: It's the way human beings ought to be treated.* Respect does not mean you should necessarily like or agree with the other person. It means taking the other person's point of view seriously, realizing that each person has her own wisdom. Listener respect involves interacting considerately with the speaker regardless of your personal feelings about the individual or the content of his message. It offers the speaker the courtesy of listening without interrupting. It is being open to his idea, which requires holding your own ideas lightly. It sometimes is wondering about what lies behind that "smart enough person's" thinking. Even in highly emotional conversations, the respectful listener hears the other person out. Negation and conflict management experts Roger Fisher and Daniel Shapiro state:

> Listening for merit in another's point of view can transform the way you listen.[1]

WHAT RESPECT CONTRIBUTES TO INTERACTIONS

Respect is an amazingly powerful quality. International mediator William Ury says: "Respect . . . . is the key that opens the door to the other's mind and heart." He adds:

> An obvious reason to give respect to the other is *because it works.* In my own work as a mediator in ethnic wars, I have had to deal with leaders who have blood on their hands. I do not approve of their behavior, I may not like them personally, but if I want them to accept a No to violence—bring about a ceasefire, save the lives of children—the only way I have found that works is to approach them through basic human respect.[2]

Abraham Lincoln, one of our greatest presidents, was noted for treating others respectfully even when they acted rudely and disrespectfully toward him. For example, Edward Stanton, a leading politician of the era, put the president down in the most abusive terms. He described President Lincoln to others in such terms as a "low cunning clown . . . the original gorilla." Despite Stanton's many put-downs, Lincoln treated Stanton respectfully and picked him to be his second secretary of war. Even as a cabinet member, Stanton referred to Lincoln as a fool. Lincoln, however, continued treating his detractor with respect. When told of Stanton's insults, Lincoln brushed the matter off, saying, "Did he call me that? Well, I reckon it must be true then, for Stanton is generally right." The Great Emancipator's respect finally won out: Their relationship became increasingly mutual. And when Lincoln died, the grief-stricken Stanton spoke of the president as "the greatest ruler of men the world has ever seen."

Fortunately, we listeners are not faced with the need to express such resolute respect as President Lincoln, William Ury, and many others have had to summon up. But a listener's respect for the speaker must permeate his approach to conversation. It's a low-key way of making a meaningful impact. Jane Dutton, professor of business administration and professor of psychology at the University of Michigan, finds that:

> Small acts of respectful engagement infuse a relationship with greater energy while at the same time sending signals and modelling behavior that gets picked up by others.[3]

LISTEN RESPECTFULLY WHEN
RECEIVING REMEDIAL FEEDBACK

It is challenging to listen open-mindedly when you are on the receiving end of corrective feedback. Here are some ways to embody respect when on the receiving end of remedial feedback:

- Reflect the speaker's views, opinions, and suggestions—whether her position is similar to, different from, or contradicts your own.
- React nondefensively to criticism of you, your behavior, your performance, or your comments. Remind yourself of psychologist George Miller's maxim:

> In order to understand what another person is saying you must assume it is true and try to imagine what it might be true of.[4]

- If it is a negative comment about your idea, statement, behavior, or performance, you can respond by reflecting the comment and saying something like:

Thanks for your input. Any other reactions?

- And, when fitting, apply the suggested improvement as soon as possible.
- When you find yourself internally disagreeing with the speaker's statement, consider saying:

  ▶ Tell me more about your point of view.

  ▶ Help me understand your thoughts about this.

- And listen intently to the response.

LISTEN RESPECTFULLY TO CRITICAL OR DISCOURTEOUS COMMENTS

Even in highly emotional conversations, the respectful listener hears the other person out. Here's a constructive way of responding to critical or discourteous comments. Make no change from the way you were responding to the person when everything was going well. Continue to do the following:

- **Distance:** Keep the same distance from the speaker that you normally do when conversing with someone.
- **Eye contact:** Continue the same type of eye contact that you had before the negative comments were made.
- **Facial expression:** Show interest in what you're being told. Avoid grimacing or appearing worried or disgusted.
- **Tone of voice:** Use the same tone of voice you usually use.
- **Word choice:** Refrain from using judgmental or derogatory words.
- **Use constructive self-talk:** To help you do the above, tell yourself things like:

  ▶ This person is using language and behavior that he's learned to use over the years. I don't want *his* behavior to dictate how *I* behave.

The remaining days and years of your relationship will be much more harmonious when you demonstrate respect for the other person even when he has been talking disrespectfully and angrily to you. Of course, if this is frequent behavior, you may choose to confront it or, as a last resort, interact with the person as seldom as possible.

Empathy

Empathy is the second of the trio of facilitative qualities that enhance listening. Many people think *empathy* and *sympathy* are fairly similar responses to another person's discomfort or hardship. However, it is important to recognize that *the two words have very dissimilar meanings*.

THE DIFFERENCE BETWEEN EMPATHY AND SYMPATHY

Empathy is a term that stems from the Greek word *empatheia*, which means "feeling into." With empathy, you accurately take in the facts and feelings the other person is experiencing and reflect them back to the person. Empathy is facilitative; it supports and strengthens the other person. It promotes clearer thinking. And it aids problem solving, whereas sympathy tends to be problem prolonging.

Sympathy is feeling compassion or sorrow for the hardship another person is feeling. When you sympathize, you may have regret for his difficulty, but that's about it. Sympathy keeps the sympathizer in her own shoes and keeps the other person's problems at a distance. And sympathy places the sympathizer in a superior position to the other person.

Empathy is something we're born with; it is embedded in our being. We possess it in varying degrees, however, and each of us can further develop it. Improving one's listening skills enhances one's empathy significantly.

When people feel empathically understood, their mental and emotional capabilities are invigorated. Empathy fosters a stronger interpersonal relationship between the listener and the speaker.

Empathic responses are appropriate when listening to successful and joyful times, as well as when listening to someone talk about their difficult feelings and experiences.

MIRROR NEURONS AND MIRROR SYSTEMS

A number of neuroscientists believe there is an inclination in our neuro-biology that biases us toward empathy.[5] Many think that *empathy in animals* is facilitated by *mirror neurons* and that *empathy in humans* is enabled by a more complex *mirroring system*. A growing number of critics, however, argue that the mirror neuron advocates have not convincingly established that there's a mirror system in humans underlying our empathy.[6] In short, there is strenuous disagreement among scientists about *how* humans experience empathy. But *it's widely agreed that empathy is a key factor in relationship building and maintenance, as well as a powerful contributor to the cooperation that is a major factor in our becoming the most successful species on the planet.*

WHAT EMPATHY CONTRIBUTES

Empathy is the primary tool we have for understanding others. Psychoanalyst Heinz Kohut described it this way:

> Empathy, the accepting, confirming, and understanding human echo evoked by the self, is a psychological nutrient without which human life, as we know and cherish it, could not be sustained.

Many social scientists consider empathy to be the *most important quality* for success in life. A University of Texas researcher found that empathy "distinguishes the most tactful advisors, the most diplomatic officials, the most effective negotiators, the most electable politicians, the most productive salespersons, the most successful teachers, and the most insightful therapists." Bestselling business author Stephen Covey wrote that empathic interaction is one of the "seven habits of highly effective people." And psychologist Daniel Goleman considers empathy to be at the heart of emotional intelligence.

The Benedictine Invitation describes the empathic way of being with another as listening "with the ears of the heart." Empathy is our interpersonal radar. It serves as a lubricant that smooths interactions and enhances relationships. It's one of the key qualities for relating well to others. And it is a must-have quality for good listeners.

It's well-known that empathy contributes enormously to one's effectiveness in fields like therapy and education. However, empathy also makes a powerful positive impact in every field in which individuals work together to achieve common goals. Even in the intensely competitive sport of professional basketball, empathy can make a noteworthy contribution. In his book, *Sacred Hoops: Spiritual Lessons of a Hardwood Warrior,* coach Phil Jackson writes that empathy was a powerful performance enhancer in his successful effort to integrate outstanding individual basketball players into a cohesive world championship team:

> In my work as a coach, I've discovered that approaching problems of this kind from a compassionate perspective, trying to empathize with a player and look at the situation from his point of view, can have a transformative effect on the team. Not only does it reduce the player's anxiety and make him feel as if someone understands what he is going through, it also inspires the other players to respond in kind and be more conscious of each other's needs.[7]

EMPATHIZE EVEN WITH THE DIFFICULT PERSONS IN YOUR LIFE

Empathizing with a very difficult person may at first seem to be incredibly challenging, and you can probably think of situations where it would seem to be impossible. Empathy has, however, proven to be not only possible but also a highly effective skill in many conflict-ridden situations. David Burns, MD, says: "Empathy is the ultimate anger antidote."[8]

Surprisingly, empathy is the tactic of choice of innumerable police departments across the country, thanks in part to the work of psychologist and former police officer George Thompson who taught cops how to relate empathically to murderers and other dangerous criminals. In his book, *Verbal Judo,* Thompson wrote, "[T]he single most powerful concept in the English language" is *"empathy."* He added:

> Here is the bottom line of all communication, Empathy absorbs tension. . . . This is the communication warrior's real service: staying calm in the midst of conflict, deflecting verbal abuse, and offering empathy in the face of antagonism. If you cannot empathize with people, you don't stand a chance of getting them to listen to you. . . .
>
> If you take a moment to think as another might be thinking, then speak with his perspective in mind, you can gain immediate rapport. Ill-fitting as his shoes may be, walk a few steps in them. Only then can you provide real understanding. . . . Only then can you help that person see the consequences of what he is doing. . . . Only then can you help him make enlightened decisions.[9]

Verbal Judo describes one incredibly dangerous situation after another that Thompson or other police officers successfully resolved by empathizing with their adversaries.

The international dispute between nation-states is another conflict-ridden arena where empathy is desperately needed but where it is seldom employed. Robert McNamara, drawing on his experience as the longest serving U. S. secretary of defense, asserted:

> What is becoming clear . . . based on the detailed study of the Cuban missile crisis and the Viet Nam War, is that empathy is an absolute fundamental element in determining success or failure in foreign policymaking. If it is present, as it was *at the end* of the Cuban missile crisis . . . war can be avoided, peace established, understanding achieved. If it is absent . . . outcomes are possible that are far worse than even so-called "worse-case" analyses predict.

Defense Secretary McNamara concluded:

> Rule No. 1 in international conflict management is, "Empathize with your enemy."[10]

If empathy is the tool of choice for police dealing with armed criminals and national leaders at the brink of war, it's undoubtedly a useful tool for dealing with the difficult people in your life.

EMPATHY FOR OTHERS IS GOOD FOR YOU

Empathy is something we give to others; we listen sensitively to their plight or opportunity and hope to bring some solace or increase their joy. It's now known, however, that empathy is also an important contributor to the empathizer's well-being. Social science research reveals that the more you care about other people, the more likely you are to be healthy and happy. Empathy helps us create new relationships and deepen friendships, which is especially important today when it's reported that one person out of four suffers from loneliness. Also, empathy expands our mental outlook so that we have a deeper and broader outlook on life.

Genuineness

Genuineness is the third facilitative quality that undergirds good listening. When a listener's respect and empathy are supported by genuineness, the listening spirit is powerfully present in a conversation.

WHAT GENUINENESS IS

We all have a general sense of what genuineness means—being natural, open, and honest with others. It is presenting yourself as you really are—not as you think you should act. It is being "dependably real" in that what you say and do closely matches what you think and feel. This quality of genuineness is sometimes encapsulated in the phrase, "What you see is what you get."

Here are two aspects of genuineness that contribute greatly to one's proficiency as a listener.

1. AVOID TAKING ON A TEACHER ROLE

Of course, some role behavior is constructive. For instance, teachers have a vocational role to play—broadly speaking—to encourage pupil learning. Many a teacher performs that role while being genuinely herself. However, some teachers adapt certain vocal, postural, and gestural "teacher mannerisms." It's obvious to students that the teacher is taking on a "teacher role" rather than being himself. Taking on a role rather than being real greatly undermines a teacher's (or anyone else's effectiveness [other than actors, clowns, and the like]).

Similarly, when interacting with others, some people take on a "listener role." Instead of focusing their attention on grasping what the speaker is trying to communicate, they devote much of their effort on coming across as their stereotype of how a "good listener" would look and respond.

Obviously, genuine listeners don't put on a special "listener persona." Psychologist Robert Carkhuff states:

> At the very minimum, we present no façade that would misrepresent ourselves. We present no mask from a professional or other role.[11]

2. PROCESS WHAT YOU HEAR NONDEFENSIVELY

In your long lifetime of listening, you'll undoubtedly be told more than a few things about yourself or your performance that are unpleasant to hear. People tend to turn a deaf ear to that type of information. But that's the very time when it's especially important to listen up. Many cultures have proverbs that make the point, "You can learn more from the criticisms of your enemies than from the compliments of your friends." Clearly, it makes sense to listen thoughtfully to both points of view.

Receiving information through defensive filters may spare you some temporary discomfort, but it will only postpone dealing with reality, and that type of delay is almost always costly.

Important as they are, respect and empathy are shallow attributes unless they are undergirded by genuineness. It's the three qualities together—integrated—that constitute the listening spirit.

> Listening is an attitude of the heart, a genuine desire
>
> to be with another which both attracts and heals.
>
> —J. ISHAM

22

Make Great Listening Part of Your Everyday Life

What's well begun, is half done.

—ARISTOTLE, *POLITICS*

PLATO POINTED OUT that, "The beginning is the most important part of the work." And psychologist William James stated that *when developing a new ability, "we must take care to launch ourselves with as strong and decided an initiative as possible."* If you get off to a bad start, you are apt to flounder needlessly and perhaps even give up on your effort to improve. But with a sound beginning, the development of a new ability gets a big boost.

Now that you've developed the basic know-how of good listening (acquired by reading the previous chapters of this book), these seven start-up guidelines will help you to integrate better listening into your daily life:

- Start *now*!
- Be patient with yourself—and with the plateaus and valleys in the learning curve.
- Be prepared to encounter occasional resistance.
- Gain experience with these skills before using them in highly challenging situations.
- Act preventatively to keep most resistance from developing.
- Make and implement a simple action plan.
- Recoup if you blow it.

Start Now!

Knowledge entails understanding what to do; *skill* is the ability to do it. There's a big difference between the two—between reading a how-to book like this and actually acquiring the skills it teaches. The route from know-how to can-do inevitably leads through practice. Psychologist B. F. Skinner insisted that, "To acquire behavior the student must engage in behavior."[1] Acquired knowledge is a deluded comfort if it does not influence behavior. As with any expertise, the skills of listening are acquired by doing them repeatedly.

There's no time as good as the present for putting your newly learned listening skills to work. New skills are vulnerable to extinction if they're not used immediately after they're learned. Evidence from many types of skill development shows that if the learner doesn't start using a newly learned skill within the first week or so, she probably never will. *Using what you've learned about improving your listening skills is literally a "now-or-never" matter.* Sports psychologist Keith Bell states the blunt truth:

> Later is a misnomer. . . . Putting things off for later is not a way of delaying them. It's a way of never getting them done.[2]

Most efforts at self-improvement die on the bridge from knowing to doing. Since you've already invested your time in reading this book, make sure you enjoy the benefits of good listening ASAP. Get started while the know-how from reading is fresh in your mind. Getting off to a good, quick start is a key step in skill development.

Be Patient with Yourself—and with the Plateaus and Valleys in the Learning Curve

When developing a skill like listening, many people naively expect to achieve mastery quickly. However, if you've ever tried to improve your golf swing, tennis serve, or swimming stroke, you know that proficiency doesn't occur overnight. It's been said that:

> Skill mastery is like the process of breaking in new shoes. At first it feels unnatural but, with enough wear, the shoes begin to feel comfortable.[3]

Historian Jacques Barzun noted that, when developing a new ability, "conscious awkward effort precedes unconscious ease."[4] And no-nonsense football coach Vince Lombardi used to tell his players, "If you're not making mistakes, you're not trying hard enough."

Learning a new skill typically advances in an erratic progression—two steps forward and one step back. Psychologists refer to the often encountered periods of stagnation and regression as "plateaus in the curve of learning." Working your way through the plateaus and regressions is part of the price you pay for developing an important new ability.

Psychiatrist Alfred Adler, one of the creators of modern psychology used this analogy:

> What do you do when you learn to swim? You make mistakes do you not? And then what happens? You make other mistakes, and when you have made *all* the mistakes you possibly can without drowning—and some of them many times over—what do you find? That you can swim. Well, life is just the same as learning to swim! Do not be afraid of making mistakes, for there is no other way of learning how to live.[5]

Initially, your reflections will probably be a bit awkward. However, it's important to realize that, although your early reflections may feel awkward and unnatural to you, even at this novice stage you are undoubtedly doing a better job of tuning in to others than you were before you started reading this book. While you are not yet the listener you want to be, you've reduced your use of the missteps of listening and are attending reasonably well. And, although your reflections may not be as brief and on target as they'll be with more practice, they provide an important accuracy check on what's been said. Not bad for starters.

Be Prepared to Encounter Occasional Resistance

Beginners at reflecting are sometimes concerned that others might object to this change in their behavior. That seldom happens. People usually appreciate and gladly make the minor adaptations to the changes in the way they relate to you due to your improved listening.

But once in a rare while, someone might object to your reflecting what they say. In the unlikely event that someone might take issue with the way you are listening to them, it's helpful to:

- Understand why people sometimes resist a person's effort to listen better.
- Act preventively to keep most resistance from developing.

UNDERSTAND WHY PEOPLE SOMETIMES RESIST A PERSON'S EFFORT TO LISTEN BETTER

When resistance to a change in the way one listens does occur, it typically springs from one or more of five factors:

1. The listener may not have taken the steps that will prevent most resistance from occurring. (Resistance prevention steps are described in the next section of this chapter.)
2. If someone objects to your new way of listening, it may be a tip-off that you're not doing a very good job of reflecting. So, upon encountering resistance, check to see whether:

   ▶ You are using your own words and are not just parroting what was said.

   ▶ Your reflections are brief.

   ▶ Your reflections are accurate.

   ▶ Your facial expression, tone of voice, and other nonverbals are in sync with the other person's mood and message.

3. Some people new to reflecting trigger resistance by using reflective listening when it's not appropriate. Reflective listening skills are mainly useful in medium- to high-intensity conversations. *Reflections are rarely appropriate during small talk.* Reflecting can be overkill when people are amiably chitchatting.
4. Another source of resistance to your use of reflective listening could be the history of the relationship. When people's shared experience generates a wariness of each other's actions, any change of behavior is apt to be viewed negatively—even when that change is a sincere effort to improve communication.
5. A final source of resistance stems from the fact that every relationship is, among other things, a social system. Social systems— even small, two-person systems—tend to be conservative and resistant to change. In part, that's due to the fact that in any social system the way people relate is interdependent—a change in one person's behavior is likely to generate a need for change

in the behavior of other members of the system. Picture two people dancing: When one person changes what he or she is doing, the partner must make some adjustments.

But sometimes when a person changes the way he listens, it puts demands on others that they may not want to cope with. Doug's interaction with his team is a case in point. Doug is a very articulate, well liked, and hard charging manager who dominated team meetings with his ideas and plans. After attending a listening skills workshop, he sensed that his team would be more effective if he listened more and encouraged more participation. He told the team the changes he wanted to make in their meetings. Instead of his doing 90 percent of the talking as he'd done in the past, he wanted everyone to contribute. In what we thought was a novel approach, Doug planned to break his habit of doing most of the talking by disciplining himself to speak only after he'd already remained silent for at least three times when he normally would have spoken. At the first team meeting in which the new approach was used, virtually no one spoke. Everyone on the team agreed that the meeting was awful—a total failure. The second meeting was no better. One of us was brought in to facilitate the third meeting. That didn't help. Almost no one spoke. The silences were painful rather than productive: Instead of using the silence productively, people were glancing at the floor and squirming uncomfortably in their chairs.

Fortunately, the debriefing at the end of the meeting was helpful. People explained that they had been generally happy with Doug's decisions and thought he was better at planning and problem solving than they were. They felt inept at the new behavior that was now expected of them. Furthermore, they felt vulnerable about putting forth ideas that might not be accepted by others on the team. In short, the fact that Doug was listening more and not dominating the meetings called for changes in their behavior that they were reluctant to make. At his urging, they agreed to continue with the new approach and evaluate it after four more sessions. The team gradually became accustomed to the more participative style of meeting. Its sessions soon became more productive, and in short order all but one of the team members preferred the new process.

Gain Experience with these Skills Before Employing Them in Highly Challenging Interactions

It's better to have several weeks experience using these skills before using them in high-stress conversations. Hold off for a bit from reflecting in stressful interactions; wait until you have more experience under your belt. Temporarily limit your use of reflective listening to *noninflammatory conversations on topics of some importance* to one or both persons.

With several weeks of use in normal conversations, you should be able to begin employing them in conversations that are a bit more challenging. These listening skills are great for navigating conversational white water, but wait until you have considerable practice with them before using them in emotionally turbulent conversations.

Act Preventatively to Keep
Most Resistance from Developing

It's much easier and less stressful to head off resistance than to cope with it after it has developed. When family members, friends, or people you work with regularly note unexpected and unexplained change in your behavior, they may wonder what's going on. So, before using your new skills, consider telling the people with whom you'll be listening differently that you'll be making some changes.

CAREFULLY SELECT THE PEOPLE WITH WHOM YOU'LL FIRST USE YOUR NEW SKILLS

Ironically, experience has shown that it's generally easier to break in one's use of new listening skills with people who are not especially close to you. It's normal to develop rather habitual ways of relating to family members and friends. If you suddenly begin reflecting what they say, the unexplained change in your behavior may make some folks feel uncomfortable. The same principle applies at work: It's often best to build listening skill experience in relationships that are infrequent and unimportant to your success. Then, when you have gained capability with the skills, begin applying them in your more important personal and work relationships.

TELL THE INDIVIDUALS IN YOUR TARGET POPULATION WHAT YOU'LL BE DOING DIFFERENTLY AND WHY

Playwright Lillian Hellman wrote, "People change, and forget to tell each other." Don't make that mistake as you implement your newly developed listening skills. Since any change of behavior on your part has a potential impact on those who are close to you or work with you, it's both wise and considerate to discuss any forthcoming behavioral change with them. Let them know you are working at becoming a better listener. Here's an example of what you might say to a coworker:

> One of my developmental goals for the rest to the year is to become a more accurate listener. That may sound easy, but I'm finding it to be quite a challenge. I get so caught up in the topic we're discussing that I don't pay enough attention to what others are saying. To help me concentrate on what people are telling me, I'll occasionally summarize what was said. Then, if I've misunderstood, the other person can help me get back on track.
>
> I hope you'll put up with these efforts for a few weeks while I get better at this.
>
> Also, I'd appreciate your opinion on whether my listening has improved. After a couple of weeks, I'd like to ask for your feedback on the changes you notice. What do you say? Will you bear with me on this for a few weeks?

Make and Implement a Simple Action Plan

Now is the time to get started incorporating reflective listening into your communication repertoire. Follow this simple action plan, and you'll be off to a strong start.

1. Select a *few* people with whom you will begin using your reflecting skills. Perhaps schedule one person a day or every other day and assess:

   ► What went well that you'll keep doing.

   ► What you'd like to do better—more of/less of—or do differently.

   ► Incorporate some of the learnings from these interactions into your planning for future conversations.

2. Discuss with each of them your intention to listen better.
3. Ask each person if he would be willing to give you feedback in a few weeks' time.

Recoup If You Blow It

No one is at his best all the time. Even the finest communicators that we've known have had their off conversations. The rest of us are even more likely to break into the talking role at the speaker's first pause, slip back into using missteps, or forget to reflect when that's clearly the appropriate response. Fortunately, you can recover and still have a positive interaction.

When you suddenly realize that you've been listening with your "old ears," you can say something like:

> I'm sorry, I started talking. I now realize that you may have had more to say. Would you mind repeating the last part and continue with anything else you were going to say?

Of course, you better pay attention and get what you're being told this time around.

Sometimes several hours will have elapsed before you realize that you muffed an important opportunity to listen. Even then, it's often possible to recoup. Perhaps as you are driving home from work, you find yourself feeling uncomfortable about the way you handled a conversation earlier in the day—when you pursued your agenda, but, in retrospect, you realize that the other person probably had the greater need to talk but didn't because you pushed on with your agenda.

Rather than think of it as a lost opportunity, consider that you can have a "recovery conversation." Seek the person out the next day or as soon as possible and say something like the following:

> I've been thinking about our conversation yesterday. I don't feel comfortable with the way I handled it. I'm trying to be a better listener. It's not easy for me and sometimes I blow it. I hope you'll hang in there with me.

We've raised a lot of red flags in this chapter to prepare you for problems you could possibly encounter as you start using the listening skills you've learned. But rest easy. It's like when you buy a prescription drug and all the possible difficulties that could occur from the use of the drug are listed. Seldom do any of the possibilities actually occur.

With the improved listening ability that comes from applying the skills you're learning, you can look forward to improved relationships and being an enhanced asset to every group you're part of.

> A little knowledge that acts
>
> is worth infinitely more
>
> than much knowledge that is idle.[6]
>
> —KAHLIL GIBRAN

Epilogue

Knowing is not enough;

We must apply.

Willing is not enough;

We must do.

—JOHANN WOLFGANG VON GOETHE

APPENDIX

Skilled Listening Transforms Inmates' Lives in the World's Most Violent Women's Prison

From serving life to a life of service.
— MOTTO OF THE PRISON OF PEACE

*Since these listening skills function well here,
they'll undoubtedly work in your situation.*

Many people think of listening as a soft skill—nice for the easy moments in conversation but not suitable for the rough and tumble times that often bedevil daily life in the "real world." So, it's not surprising that in listening skills workshops a rather frequent objection to learning and using listening skills is that this ability might be useful in some situations *but* not with the difficult people in their lives—not with their non-attentive boss, not with their recalcitrant employee, not with their stubborn spouse, not with their headstrong teenager, etc.

However, these listening skills passed an "acid test" with flying colors. This appendix:

- Describes a communication *environment* more alien to the listening skills taught in this book than 99 to 100 percent of the environments where readers of this book are likely to implement the skills.
- Notes how a group of women, each of whom murdered someone or committed some other heinous crime for which they were incarcerated for life, learned the skills taught here, applied them resolutely, and taught the skills to many other inmates. The motto they created summarizes the transformation they achieved: "From prison for life to Prison of Peace."

- The program which began in 2010 is still going strong in 2017 and continues expanding its services and influence on other prisons in the United States, Europe, and Australia.

All the speakers and listeners mentioned in the following workshop evaluations were convicted murderers or felons serving life sentences in California's Valley State Prison for Women which has been called *"the most violent maximum security prison for women in the world."* They learned these listening skills as well as a few other conflict resolution abilities and successfully applied them in what you'll soon see was an incredibly hostile environment. Since these listening skills have been effective with the population in this incredibly challenging setting, they certainly can be effective when employed in the far less challenging situations you'll undoubtedly find yourself in.

The Prison

For virtually all its history, the Valley State Prison for Women has been acutely overcrowded. For example, in April 2007 the prison received inmates from another prison swelling the inmate population. The "court appointed overseer of prison medical care" said that VSPW's medical system might "collapse entirely" due to the extra prisoners.

In March 2012, the facility's population was 141.5 percent of its design capacity. And to make matters worse, the prison was—and currently is—deplorably understaffed. Furthermore, most of the staff members dealing directly with the inmates are not suitable for such work: international guidelines for staffing women's prisons state that guards, physicians, and others who interact regularly with inmates in women's prisons should be female. If male attendants or physicians interact with women prisoners, a female staff member must accompany the male staff member when dealing with female prisoners. Amnesty International studied the prison some years ago and reported that despite the international guidelines, the vast majority of those positions at Valley State Prison were filled by males who are seldom, if ever accompanied by female staff. This key staffing requirement has continued to be ignored through the years.

The director of the nonprofit Prison Law Office which investigates inmate mistreatment, Don Spector, says:

There are serious problems there including verbal abuse of prisoners, failure to protect them from other prisoners, contraband,
sexual abuse. . . .

The prison has a recidivism rate (tendency to return to criminal habits
and activities) of 72 percent—vastly higher than in other women's prisons.
So, Valley State Prison is definitely not functioning as a correctional facility. Inmate morale is much lower than in comparable facilities and in an
18 month period in 2014 and 2015, the suicide rate was eight times the
national average for women prisoners.

A Plea for Help

Between 2007 and 2009, a lifer in the prison, Mrs. Russo, sent 49 hand-
written messages requesting help from mediators throughout the state of
California. No one responded to her dogged effort to get a professional
mediator to teach her and her fellow inmates how to live more peacefully
with one another.

Finally, a Response

In August of 2009, Mrs. Russo's fiftieth letter reached the mailbox of Laurel Kaufer, a well-known Southern California lawyer, mediator, and Ridge
Training workshop leader. Laurel said:

> As soon as I read the letter, I was hooked, but I also knew I
> couldn't do it alone. Still standing at the mailbox, I called my friend
> and colleague, Doug Noll. I read the letter to him. He was silent for
> a moment before he said, "I'm in. What's our next step?"

They knew this would be a huge time-consuming task with no compensation and with all the expense money coming out of their own pockets. But
they both had a service-oriented history and resolutely accepted the challenge.

They decided to teach peacemaking skills (the listening skills presented
in this book along with other valuable skills) to these hardened inmates.
A bit later in this appendix you'll see from the inmates' post-training reports that Noll's and Kaufer's intervention was incredibly successful.

Meet the Mediators

Laurel Kaufer is a social engineer, attorney, law professor, and Ridge Communication Skills trainer. She is past chair of the California Bar standing Committee on Dispute Resolution, a Diplomat of the California and National Academy of Distinguished Neutrals, and teaches at the University of California, Santa Barbara. She was named one of Southern California's "Best Lawyers" in the field of Alternate Dispute Resolution by U S News and World Report in 2010 and 2011. She is a past chair of the California State Bar Standing Committee on Dispute Resolution.

Doug Noll is rated among the top 1 percent of attorneys worldwide. After his successful twenty-two-year trial lawyer career, Doug concluded that litigation was a wasteful way to resolve conflicts. So he earned a Master's Degree in Peacemaking and Conflict Studies and has since dedicated his life to mediation and peacemaking. He is on the core faculty of the American Institute of Mediation and is an adjunct professor at San Joaquin College of Law where he teaches Restorative Justice and Peacemaking for Lawyers. For many years his weekly radio show provided a platform for international peacemakers. He has mediated more than 1,500 cases. In his spare time he authored three books, one of them a bestseller.

The Prison of Peace

The resulting training and mediation program that Noll and Kiefer designed and led, together with those who participate in it, is known as the Prison of Peace (POP), a pro bono non-profit project established by Kaufer and Noll in 2010 to reduce violence and promote peaceful conflict resolution among prison inmates. The POP experience that they designed and led transform's inmates lives "From Serving Life to a Life of Service."

That certainly was a formidable challenge. Before working with their first group in 2010, neither Laurel nor Doug had ever stepped inside a prison.

Prison of Peace serves a group of highly marginalized, low income, ethnically diverse women by giving them skills to promote positive change in their environment and reduce the destructive impact of life in prison. Participants learn how to handle their conflict before it escalates to violence, creating a safer, more peaceful environment, and enhancing opportunities for rehabilitation during incarceration.

At the heart of POP is an intense 12 week course that teaches deep listening skills, how to run peace circles, and how to mediate the emotionally charged conflicts that arise daily in the prison community.

Prisoner of Peace's first results exceeded all expectations. Within six weeks of completing Mediation Training, the 12 new Mediators had resolved over 30 disputes within the prison. As prison staff witnessed the positive results, they solicited POP mediators for assistance in managing conflict. Peace circles became so popular that new applications for POP increased to a waiting list of over 150 women. By the end of 2010, its first full year of operation, POP had certified 68 Peacemakers and 32 mediators. In 2011 and 2012, eighteen POP graduates who wanted to become POP trainers each put in over 260 hours of classroom time and conducted three rounds of their own POP workshops. After two years of intensive training the day to day responsibility for teaching and administering this program was turned over to this dedicated group of inmates.

By the end of July 2016, more than 200 women were trained as Peacemakers and more than 75 were trained as mediators. Over 12,000 inmates have participated in a peace circle or mediation.

In recognition of their impressive work, the first fifteen women trained as Peacemakers were awarded the Southern California Mediation Association Cloke/Millen Peacemaker award for 2010.

Judge James Gray of the Superior Court of Orange County California summarized the impact of the Prison of Peace by July 2011:

> Ms. Kaufer and her colleague, attorney Douglas E. Noll established a peace mediation program at that prison [Valley State Prison in Chowchilla Calif.], initially with 15 inmates as students, and it has been successful.
>
> But it wasn't easy. These two mediation professionals found out that Ms. Russo was right. Confrontation and violence were a standard and routine part of almost everyone's existence at the prison.
>
> Nevertheless, they established a program through using simple communication skills based upon listening—really listening. That means that the students were taught to listen to what other people were saying and then to acknowledge what the speaker said by saying it back. The benefit is that this shows other people that they are being heard, which is a huge gratification of their humanity—and also a proven way to reduce tensions.
>
> By using this simple skill, the 15 female inmates were slowly able to reduce conflict and bring some amount of peace to the prison. For example, rather than use pepper spray to break up potentially

violent situations, prison guards started to call in Ms. Kaufer's students to mediate them. It often worked.

Of course, no one can avoid conflict. But the secret is for people in conflicts to understand that they have choices to make about how they will respond and react to them. Conflicts become destructive when people give in to anger, which then thwarts their ability to make good choices about how to respond.

But choosing to listen, understand and confirm the other side's views and feelings often results in addressing the problems peacefully on their merits, instead of having them escalate to violence.[1]

Two Unanticipated Effects

An unexpected effect of the program is that the participants have grown in maturity in many ways that were not directly related to the Prison of Peace intervention. Many are enjoying a greater fullness of life than they have known for years.

In addition to the enormous benefit of living in a climate of reduced conflict and violence, many of them have used the Prison of Peace skills and other learnings to restore relationships with loved ones outside of prison. This has been especially true of many of relationships between mothers and their children. In fact, many of the participants say that this was by far the most important outcome for them—for them to be able to rebuild and greatly enhance relationships with their children. What a boon it is when families reconcile.

A Self-Perpetuating Program

From its inception, the Prison of Peace was designed to be self-perpetuating. After the first few workshops, some of the trainees went through an additional demanding learning process to become skilled at leading listening skills workshops for other inmates. Others qualified to lead mediation sessions with quarreling inmates and at times mediated between a guard and a prisoner. The Prison of Peace subculture that developed is a supportive and growthful contrast to their prison life before the creation of the Prison of Peace.

Laurie and Doug supervise these programs but the successful inmate leadership of much of the training and mediation enables the founders to instigate the program in other prisons.

Doug has also redesigned the program for use in schools and is using it to enhance the performance of teachers and students.

Prison of Peace Listening Skills Workshop Evaluations

As you'll see from reading the following evaluations of a recent listening skills workshop, the impact of the Prison of Peace is not limited to those who attend the workshops. The workshop participants are conduits through which these skills infuse much of the prison environment. Since 84 percent of the participants indicate they will actively share these skills with others, their continuing efforts greatly magnify the impact of the program.

Note: The content of the evaluations is exactly as each inmate wrote it. For confidentiality we deleted signatures to each evaluation. When another prisoner's name was mentioned in an evaluation, a blank line _____ appears instead of participants' name.

As you read, remember that each writer is doing hard time in a maximum security prison for committing murder.

- Prison of Peace has dramatically opened my eyes as to the deep significance of listening. Making me much more compassionate and attentive to others' needs. I've learned how to effectively listen for more positive results. . . . I have learned how to reflect what others are saying; with this tool I have subdued potential conflict even before it began. Reflecting has also helped me to fully understand and comprehend what the other person is saying and respect others' ideas, feelings, and thoughts, thus giving me a broader understanding of the uniqueness of a human's mind and the complexity of it.

- Prison of Peace workshop has taught me some patience in my life which was much needed in my life; ultimately giving me a divine peace within myself.

- Since taking the EPSS workshop and weekly follow-up training with Laurel and Doug, I have attempted to integrate the skills into my daily exchanges. One benefit about life in this environment is that I am afforded ample opportunity to interact with other people.

- In practicing the listening skills, I've noticed the biggest, most obvious change is within me. It takes conscious awareness and daily self-reminders, but I have found that through active and reflective listening, I have become a more active and more present participant in my relationships. I am more attuned to others; more compassionate, caring, and empathic. As a result, I have noticed that my peers seek me out more for advice, companionship, and a listening ear.

- In my training to be a drug and alcohol counselor, these skills are invaluable. I am more confident about sharing my insight on problem solving communication and healthy relationships. These skills will benefit me greatly in my transition back into society as well.

- The web of relationship in humanity is dependent on healthy communication. I am deeply grateful to have the tools to ensure my connection to others is strong and enduring.

- In the short time we have been in this workshop I have learned better listening skills. I talk to a lot of people every day and maybe I have a hard time when it comes to hearing. I knew that I listened to others but now I hear what they are saying. I also like to brainstorm as I feel it gives all parties an opportunity to toss different ideas around and come up with the best solutions.

- I guess I can start with how aware I became when I stopped my mouth and used my ears. I went back to square one by re-reading the training manual. Having a few extra moments of quiet gave me more time to absorb the material.

- I started using the skills the following days and thought I had "somewhat" communication abilities, found out not so sharp as I had thought. In one or two ways I did do the listening then I connected that with what I needed to reflect back. The thing I liked most about the checking was I used my emotion vocabulary and did receive a facial response favorable in expression indication that I truly listened to my participating partner.

- I felt inspired. The workshop put myself back on track, I really enjoyed learning again. I found that these tools go beyond my past experience . . . with practice I can use the skills successfully. The best part, I am enjoying the listening part now.

- This workshop has taught me to be a better listener. Then to reflect what the person is saying. Taking interest in others has shown me how important it is to pay attention and listen to what others are saying, to be more aware of others' emotions. I am learning to be more of a friend by learning to focus on them more. I never knew how important it was to listen. I can now take time to listen and know the results will be greater. Then reflect what they are saying so they know it's important to me also. I have compassion for others so this workshop is helping me so much. I love it. Thank you. I want to be a good steward of my thoughts. What this workshop is teaching me is to walk through, I hope to be able to teach one day. I want to be a great listener.

- Since the initial workshop two weeks ago I have noticed a huge shift in my communication with others. Listening has given me a better idea of how to be compassionate, empathic, and present while interacting with others. I feel less overwhelmed, anxious, and confused.

- I make a very conscious effort to use the skills I've learned and see how changing myself has made others around me begin to try to change as well. Change comes in small increments and takes time to measure the results over time. Yet in just a two week span I feel the shift in the behaviors, mentality, emotion, and how it is expressed.

- I'm thankful and eager to learn more so I can enrich my life further but also be able to reflect my learnings on others, for the greater good of all I come in contact with. Validating and being validated has become as equally important as being respected & shows caring for me.

- In the 2½ weeks we've been taking this class I've learned a lot about myself and the ways I communicate or lack to. I learned that the Explore Step was the biggest problem in all my communication w/ others. The lack of using it or knowing how to use it. I feel in this environment the "You" approach will work well. In the past we have been taught all about "I" as it relates to communication.

- Using these skills for 2½ weeks has greatly improved my way of both listening and communication effectively. I am in a position in my community that demands effective communication & listening. I feel learning and using these tools will be one way of spreading its greatness throughout the institution. I have shared these tools with my Chair & Vice Chair in an organization I Chair & have encouraged them to start at least with _____ and _____ by reflecting with their subcommittee members. This will eliminate a lot of misunderstandings and misconceptions. I am totally "it's all about you" type of person so I am enjoying this learning experience.

- When I first found out I got accepted in to peacemakers, I was ecstatic knowing I was going to be able to add another layer to my new foundation I call "Improved self." I always felt I could carry on a conversation or follow one, and prayed for better skills. I feel like my prayers have been answered. I have been trying to find a way to get my son to talk to me, and nothing has worked, don't get me wrong, we were speaking before I got here. But now I see it's because I've been blaming, shaming, & trying to guilt him into doing what I feel he should. You should get your life together. Last night I wrote him more like this. "I understand you're angry" or "Try taking a step back, reflect on your life and decide where you want to be in 5 years, I can't change the past but you are responsible for your future. (The print on the final sentence was too faint to read.)

- What I've learned from prison of peace so far is how to be a more empathic and genuine listener to others. I've learned to stop necessarily listening to the words an individual uses and listen closely to the emotions and feelings to focus on what is beneath the words.

- I am learning to be a more assertive speaker in communicating my needs and wants and stopping arguments before they are started or blown out of proportion or escalated.

- I am becoming more sensitive to the needs and feelings of others and what I am so grateful for right now is that I will now be able to understand and communicate with my mother far better than I ever have been. This is something that I've been wanting and desiring ever since I had become a teenager.

- This is something I can share with my mother and my sister so that we can all communicate better with each other and squash all misunderstandings. I've been less sensitive to how I've been talked to as well and I truly appreciate being chosen for this opportunity.

- Thank you so much for this.

- Bless you!

- The effect of "Peace Makers" has had on my life in such a short time approx. 2 weeks is amazing.

- I've learned that when you truly become an avid listener the whole dimension of the conversation changes. By reflecting back, verifying and clarifying you are able to reach a better and truer understanding of the underlying issue; whether it be an argument, any confrontation, or coming to terms for a good concise agreement.

- The effect of good communication is not an emotional endeavor and if you have a genuine concern for the well-being of others as well as . . . a will of "Self devoted to the cause of Neighbor." Wow! Selflessness . . . what a concept . . . .

- I love the impact this has had on my life already even before I've even totally grasped the concepts.

- New techniques come easy in the first few weeks of most workshops. They fade like old roses without water if we don't apply them and reapply them until they're second nature.

- So—I'm getting insights about examining my automatic responses or triggers that I believe will stick—not fade. I see this as necessary for my survival. My own commitment is strong so my attitude has affected people around me in two ways! I get more love and I get more hate.

Note: Readers who are interested in hearing the women speak can go to the Prison of Peace website at www.prisonofpeace.org and watch the videos on the Press & Media page.

ENDNOTES

INTRODUCTION

1   S. Scott, *Fierce Conversations: Achieving Success at Work and in Life, One Conversation at a Time* (New York: Viking, 2002), p. 1.

2   In the language of the day (1776), Benjamin Franklin wrote in *Poor Richard's Almanac*, "The Wit of Conversation consists more in finding it in others, than shewing a great deal yourself."

3   H. D. Thoreau, *A Week on the Concord and Merrimack Rivers*, "Wednesday."

4   W. Loban, quoted in A. Wolvin and C. Coakley, *Listening*, 3rd ed. (Dubuque, IA: William C. Brown Company, 1988). On average, people spend more time listening than they do in speaking, in part because many interactions occur in groups.

5   W. Loban, p. 15.

6   "Families Were Admitted to the National Institute of Mental Health and, Like 'Jane Goodall Watching Her Chimps' Psychologists Observed the Communication Processes at Work in the Human Family" in R. Gilbert, M.D., *Extraordinary Relationships: A New Way to Think About Relationships* (New York: Wiley, 1992).

7   C. Rogers, *A Way of Being* (Boston: Houghton Mifflin, 1980), p. 138.

8   The in-depth analysis of a five-minute conversation is by R. Pittinger, C. Hockett, and J. Danehy, *The First Five Minutes* (Ithaca, NY: Martineau, 1960).

9   W. Condon, "Cultural Microrhythms," in M. Davis (ed.), *Interaction Rhythms: Periodicity in Communication Behavior* (New York: Human Sciences Press, 1982), pp. 53–76.

10 Plutarch, *Plutarch's Moralia*, tr. Frank Cole Babbitt (Cambridge, MA: Harvard University Press, 1987), p. 259.

PART I

1   E. Atwater, I Hear You: A Listening Skills Handbook, Revised Ed., (N. Y.: Walker & Co., 1988), p. ix.

CHAPTER 1

1   M. Morris and W. Morris, *Morris Dictionary of Word and Phrase Origins* (New York: Harper & Row, 1977), p. 146.

2   Mark Golan, a Cisco executive, quoted in *Newsweek*, April 28, 2003.

3   J. Kouzes and B. Posner, *The Leadership Challenge: How to Make Extraordinary Things Happen in Organizations* (San Francisco: Jossey-Bass, 2012), pp. 294–295.

4   J. Dutton, *Energize Your Workplace: How to Create and Sustain High-Quality Connections at Work* (San Francisco: Jossey-Bass, 2003), p. 2.

5   S. Culbert, *Mind-Set Management: The Heart of Leadership* (New York: Oxford University Press, 1996), pp. 176–177. In a recent *Bloomberg Businessweek* article, Rebecca Greenfield wrote, "Organizations have an interest in promoting work friendships, because they're good for business. Friends motivate each other with social pressure; not performing means letting a friend, not just a colleague, down. Having best friends at work is one of the strongest predictors of a solid team performance, according to Gallup's annual engagement survey" (p. 78).

6   T. Rath, *Vital Friends* (New York: Gallup Press, 2006).

7   S. Turkle, *Reclaiming Conversation: The Power of Talk in a Digital Age* (New York: Penguin, 2015), pp. 250–51.

8   S. Turkle, p. 287.

9   S. Turkle, pp. 271–272.

10   J. Collins, *Good to Great* (New York: HarperBusiness, 2001), p. 62.

11   J. Collins, p. 63.

12   D. Dana, *Conflict Resolution* (New York: McGraw Hill Education, 2001).

13   *Businessweek*, November 17–23, 2014.

14   O. Harari, "The Lab Test: A Tale of Quality," *Management Review* 82, no. 3 (February 1993): pp. 55–59.

15   R. Gould, *Sacked! Why Good People Get Fired and How to Avoid It* (New York: Wiley, 1986).

16   N. Christakis and J. Fowler, *Connected: The Surprising Power of Our Social Networks and How They Shape Our Lives—How Your Friends' Friends*

Affect Everything You Feel, Think, and Do (New York: Back Bay Books Reprint Edition, 2011), p. 157.

17 M. Szalavitz and B. Perry, *Born for Love* (New York: William Morrow, Reprint edition, 2011), p. 104.

18 M. Lieberman, *Social: Why Our Brains Are Wired to Connect* (New York: Broadway Books, 2014).

19 J. Powell, *Why Am I Afraid to Tell You Who I Am?* (Niles, IL: Argus, 1969), p. 5. (Quotation reformatted by the authors.)

20 S. Covey, *Principle-Centered Leadership* (New York: Summit Books, 1991), p. 45.

21 J. Tamm and R. Luyet, *Collaborative Relationships: Five Essential Skills to Overcome Defensiveness and Build Successful Relationships* (New York: HarperBusiness, 2005), Introduction.

CHAPTER 2

1 G. Thompson, *Verbal Judo: The Gentle Art of Persuasion* (New York: Morrow Paperbacks, 2013).

2 Walter Loban, quoted in A. Wolvin and C. Coakley, *Listening*, 3rd ed. (Dubuque, IA: William C. Brown Company, 1988), p. 15.

3 D. Stone, B. Patton, and S. Heen, *Difficult Conversations: How to Discuss What Matters Most* (New York: Penguin, 1999), p. 202.

4 D. Goleman, *Social Intelligence: The New Science of Human Relationships* (New York: Bantam Reprint Ed., 2007), p. 88.

5 B. Ferrari, *Power Listening: Mastering the Most Critical Business Skill of All* (New York: Portfolio/Penguin, 2012).

6 B. Ferrari, p. xi. Emphasis is the authors'.

7 H. Levinson and S. Rosenthal, *CEO* (New York: Basic Books, 1984), pp. 212–213. Emphasis is the authors'.

8 Quoted in A. Kahane, p. 77.

9 A. Wolvin and C. G. Coakley, *Listening*, 5th ed. (Chicago: Brown & Benchmark, 1996), p. 22.

10 T. Hast, *Powerful Listening. Powerful Influence. Work Better. Live Better. Love Better.: by Mastering the Art of Skillful Listening* (CreateSpace Independent Publishing Platform 2013), p. 31.

CHAPTER 3

1   Psalms 115: 6 and 135:17. Jesus is reported to have said, "Thou hearest
    in thy one ear but the other thou hast closed." This quotation from the
    Apocryphal New Testament is mentioned in B. Branscomb, *The Teachings
    of Jesus: A Textbook for College and Individual Use* (New York: Abingdon,
    1931), p. 23.

2   L. Steil, J. Summerfield, and G. de Mare, *Listening: It Can Change Your
    Life—A Handbook for Scientists and Engineers* (New York: John Wiley,
    1983), pp. 203–205. See also L. Barker and K. Watson, *Listen Up: How
    to Improve Relationships, Reduce Stress, and Be More Productive by Using
    the Power of Listening* (New York: St. Martin's Press, 2000), pp. 58–60.
    Consultant Dorothy Leeds asked people in her seminars to evaluate their
    listening ability and only 5 to 10 percent thought of themselves as good
    listeners. The rest judged themselves to be fair or poor, "with a surprising
    number in the poor category." *The Seven Powers of Questions: Secrets to
    Successful Communication in Life and Work* (New York: Perigee, 2000),
    p. 148.

3   C. Osgood, *Osgood on Speaking: How to Think on Your Feet Without
    Falling on Your Face* (New York: William Morrow, 1988), pp. 45–46.
    Osgood comments, "One third! In the game of baseball .333 might be a
    good batting average, but in the game of communication it does not seem
    too impressive." In their listening training programs, two communication
    scholars show a twenty-second video segment about an emergency hospital
    situation. Before showing the video, they tell participants to "imagine that
    this is a life-and-death situation where high-level listening is critical." Then
    participants are asked ten simple questions about what they have seen and
    heard. People rarely answer more than four questions correctly. L. Barker
    and K. Watson, p. 4. They typically missed the meaning of the message 60
    percent of the time!

4   Pioneering research on listening comprehension by Professor Harry Jones
    of Columbia University is described in E. Bormann, W. Howell,
    R. Nichols, and G. Shapiro, *Interpersonal Communication in the Modern
    Organization* (Englewood Cliffs, NJ: Prentice-Hall, 1969), pp. 184–185.
    Similar research at the University of Minnesota, Florida State University,
    Michigan State University, and elsewhere found that "[i]mmediately after
    the average person has listened to someone talk, he remembers only about
    half of what he heard—*no matter how carefully he thought he had listened.*"
    R. Nichols and L. Stevens, *Are You Listening?* (New York: McGraw-Hill,
    1957), pp. 5–6. Researchers also found that within two weeks, the average
    listener remembers only about a quarter of what was said. On the basis
    of studies like these, many experts on listening assert that the average
    person listens at only a 25 percent level of effectiveness. "Forty to eighty

percent of medical information provided by health care practitioners is forgotten immediately," according to researcher Roy Kessels, Ph.D., of Utrecht University in the Netherlands. Quoted in Marc Silver, *Breast Cancer Husband: How to Help Your Wife (and Yourself) During Diagnosis, Treatment, and Beyond* (Emmaus, PA: Rodale, 2004).

5   L. Steil, J. Summerfield, and G. de Mare, p. 3.

6   R. Ailes, *You Are the Message* (New York: Currency; Reissue Edition, 1998), pp. 43–44.

7   Ineffective listening has been a major factor in an appalling number of airplane disasters. See S. Cushing, *Fatal Words: Communication Clashes and Aircraft Crashes* (Chicago: University of Chicago Press, 1993).

8   S. Finkelstein, *Why Smart Executives Fail and What You Can Learn from Their Mistakes* (New York: Portfolio, 2003), pp. 1, 9, 213. A recent issue of *Businessweek* editorialized, "People skills and cross cultural teamwork is what MBAs need" (April 18, 2005, p. 112).

9   S. Finkelstein. The accounts of not listening to customers, suppliers, and employees are scattered throughout the book, but a glance at pages 74, 170–175, and 225–227 indicates how destructive a CEO's refusal to listen can be to an organization's profitability and even to its survival.

10 J. Salopek, "Is Anyone Listening?" *Training & Development* (September 1999): 58–59. See also A. Carnevale et al., "Workplace Basics: The Skills Employers Want." *Training and Development Journal* 42 (October 1988): 22–30; T. Harris and T. Tomlison, "Career-Bound Communication: A Needs Analysis." *Central States Speech Journal* 34 (Winter 1983): 260–267, and J. Henry and S. Raymond, *Basic Skills in the U.S. Workforce* (New York: Center for Public Resources, 1982), pp. ii–iii, 14.

11 M. McCormack, *What They Don't Teach You at Harvard Business School* (New York: Bantam, 1984), p. 8.

12 J. Salopek. The specific figure was 28 percent.

13 A. Robertson, *Listen for Success: A Guide to Effective Listening* (New York: Irwin, 1994), p. vi. *Effective* training is definitely needed. Robertson further reports that "70 percent of the managers in those companies are perceived to be only fair listeners."

14 M. McCall, Jr., and M. Lombardo, "What Makes a Top Executive?" *Psychology Today* (February 1983): 31.

15 C. Notarius and H. Markman, *We Can Work It Out: Making Sense of Marital Conflict (New York: Putnam, 1993), p. 124.*

16 L. Steil, J. Summerfield, and G. de Mare, pp. 203–205. Supporting this

data is a survey by Dr. Michael Purdy, which found that people listen more intently at work than in social or family situations. "Listening and Consciousness: Research in Progress," presented at the International Listening Association conference, in St. Paul, Minnesota, March 1982.

17 T. S. Eliot, *The Cocktail Party* (New York: Harcourt Brace Jovanovich, 1950), p. 140. Oxford historian, Theodore Zeldin says that in France, where the matter has been studied, "[t]here is almost as much loneliness among the married as among the unmarried." T. Zeldin, *An Intimate History of Humanity* (New York: Harper Perennial, 1995), p. 60.

18 *Ladies Home Journal,* September 1998, p. 146.

19 C. Mithers, "When You Talk, Does He Listen?" *Mademoiselle,* 86 (March 1980), p. 201.

20 A summary of this massive research is reported in D. Aspy and F. Roebuck, "From Humane Ideas to Humane Technology and Back Again Many Times." *Education* Winter 1974, pp. 163–171. See also D. Aspy, *Toward a Technology for Humanizing Education* (Champaign, IL: Research Press. 1972).

21 D. Aspy, pp. 15, 22.

22 R. Nichols and L. Stevens, pp. 12–13.

23 A criterion-based study by Haggbloom et.al. found Carl Rogers to be the second most eminent psychological clinician of the twentieth century. Sigmund Freud was considered the most eminent.

CHAPTER 4

1 P. Lencioni, *The Five Dysfunctions of a Team* (San Francisco: Jossey-Bass, 2002).

2 J. Rogers. Quoted in *Listening,* 5th ed. (Chicago: Brown & Benchmark, 1996), p. 23.

3 R. Bolton and D. Grover Bolton, *People Styles at Work and Beyond: Making Bad Relationships Good and Good Relationships Better* (New York: Amacom, 2009).

4 R. Bainton, *Here I Stand: A Life of Martin Luther* (Nashville, TN: Abingdon Press: 1960), p. 302.

5 W. Shakespeare, *A Midsummer Night's Dream,* Act I, Scene I, Line 132. Carl Jung, one of the founders of modern psychology, said, "Seldom, or perhaps never, does a marriage develop into an individual relationship smoothly and without crisis."

6   J. C. Maxwell, *Relationship 101* (New York: Thomas Nelson, 2004), p. 71.

7   Joi M. Sears, "Millennials as Moms and Dads, Compared to Previous Generations." Youthtime, February 24, 2016, http://www.youth-time.eu/ slideshow-analytics/millennials-as-moms-and-dads-compared-to-previous-generations.

PART II

1   S. Covey, *The Seven Habits of Highly Successful People* (New York: Simon & Schuster, 1989), p. 237.

CHAPTER 5

1   P. Harkins, *Powerful Conversations: How High Impact Leaders Communicate* (New York: McGraw Hill Education, 1999), p. xiii.

2   Plato, *Dialogues*. In the Introduction to S. I. Hayakawa's, *The Use and Misuse of Language* (Greenwich, CT: Premier Book of Fawcett Publications, 1943, 1962, p. 23), the Russian-born American mathematical psychologist Anatol Rapoport noted:

> All existing cultures are based partly on true-to-fact orientations and partly on false-to-fact orientations. A tribe may have highly efficient fishing and canoe-building techniques, but its notions of health and disease may be organized into a body of superstition, which renders it helpless in an epidemic. Our own culture has attained a high level of true-to-fact orientation with respect to technology and hygiene, but our social organization is such that technology threatens to blast us out of existence.

3   R. Feynman, "The Value of Science" in R. Feynman and R. Leighton, *Classic Feynman: All the Adventures of a Curious Character* (New York: W. W. Norton & Co., 2005), p. 487.

4   A. Treisman and G. Geffen, "Selective attention: Perception or response?" *Quarterly Journal of Experimental Psychology* 19 (1): pp. 1–17.

5   C. Webb, *How to Have a Good Day* (New York: Crown Business, 2016), p. 18.

6   H. Mosak and M. Maniacci, *A Primer of Adlerian Psychology: The Analytic-Behavioral-Cognitive Psychology of Alfred Adler* (New York: Routledge, 1999), p. 31.

7   S. Chase, *The Tyranny of Words* (New York: Harcourt Brace Jovanovich, 1938, 1966), pp. 352–353.

8   D. Tannen, *That's Not What I Meant!: How Conversational Style Makes or Breaks Relationships* (New York: Harper, 1983), p. 24.

9   T. S. Eliot, "Burnt Norton" pt. 5 in *Four Quartets* (1936). In a similar vein, another British poet, A. E. Houseman, wrote: "A year or two ago . . . I received from America a request that I would define poetry. I replied that I could no more define poetry than a terrier can define a rat, but I thought we both recognized the object by the symptoms which it provoked in us." *The Name and Nature of Poetry* (New York: Macmillan, 1933).

10   The literary critic, Raymond Williams, found several hundred usages for the word "culture!" R. Sennett, p. 7.

11   According to general semanticist and former U.S. Senator S. I. Hayakawa, one of the premises upon which modern linguistic thought is based is that *"no word ever has exactly the same meaning twice." Language in Thought and Action*, 4th ed. (New York: Harcourt Brace Jovanovich, 1978), p. 54. Italics in the original.

12   I. Lee, p. 68.

13   I. Lee, p. 3.

14   S. Chase, p. 348.

15   R. Gould, *Sacked! Why Good People Get Fired and How to Avoid It* (New York: Wiley, 1986), p. 44. Gould comments, "[E]ven though a manager may not come right out and tell someone that his or her job is on the line, there are usually numerous indications of serious dissatisfaction with the person's behavior or performance. An impartial observer might have difficulty believing that the subordinate could not see it coming— all the signals pointed in that direction." In *Family Therapy Techniques*, Salvador Minuchin and H. Charles Fishman describe a therapy session in which the counselor repeated the same five-word message about seventy-five times over the course of three hours before the client finally got it! (Cambridge, MA: Harvard University Press, 1981), p. 119.

16   M. J. Adler, *How to Speak, How to Listen* (New York: Touchstone, 1997), p. 91.

17   D. Tannen, *You Just Don't Understand: Women and Men in Conversation* (New York: Ballantine, 1990), p. 37. According to an old military tradition, Edgar Allen Poe was expelled from West Point in 1831 for "gross neglect of duty" because he appeared naked at a public parade. Parade dress instructions called for "white belts and gloves, under arms." Poe took this literally and arrived with his rifle over his bare shoulder, wearing a belt and gloves. And nothing else.

18   Quoted in M. E. Douglass and D. N. Douglass, *Manage Your Time,*

Manage Your Work, Manage Yourself (New York: Amacom, 1980), p. 143.

19   D. Westell, "Misinterpretations Hurt Transit," *Globe & Mail*, May 3, 1991, p. 4. Hard as it is to believe that the corporation's executives *and* lawyers could have made such a blunder, the report is from Canada's largest circulation newspaper with a weekly readership of 950,000 (in 2011). Furthermore, the *Globe & Mail* is regarded as Canada's "Newspaper of Record." So we assume this incredible event occurred as reported.

CHAPTER 6

1   T. Gordon, *Parent Effectiveness Training: The Proven Program for Raising Responsible Children* (New York: Three Rivers Press, 2000), p. 53.

2   S. Covey, *The Seven Habits of Highly Effective People* (New York: Simon & Schuster, 1989).

3   A number of psychologists identified major communication missteps that have sometimes been termed "roadblocks" or "barriers." C. Rogers, *Client-Centered Therapy: Its Current Practice, Implications and Theory* (Boston: Houghton Mifflin, 1951); T. Gordon, *Leader Effectiveness Training: The No-Lose Way to Release the Productive Potential of People* (New York: Wyden Books, 1977); H. Ginott, *Between Parent and Child: New Solutions to Old Problems* (New York: Macmillan, 1965); P. Donoghue and M. Siegel, *Are You Really Listening: Keys to Successful Communication* (Notre Dame, IN: Sorin Books, 2005); and J. Gibb, "Defensive Communication," *Journal of Communication* 11, no. 3 (September 1961): pp.141–148.

4   T. Packer, "Finding a New Way to Listen" in M. Brady, ed., *The Wisdom of Listening* (Boston: Wisdom Publications, 2003), p. 238.

5   The Book of Job (written in 2100–1800 BCE), possibly the oldest book in the Bible, depicts a good man of fine health, great wealth, and attentive children. Suddenly everything changes: He loses his health and wealth, and his sons and daughters are killed in a natural disaster. Job's friends come to comfort him. After a period of listening to his intense grief, they began talking to him. However, the words that flowed from their mouths were strong examples of what this chapter terms "missteps." Job understandably responds, "Miserable comforters are you all." Book of Job 16:2.

6   E. Schein, *Process Consultation: It's Role in Organization Development*, Volume I (Reading, MA: Addison-Wesley, 1988), p. 26. Researchers found that the average amount of time physicians spend listening prior to interrupting a patient is a mere seventeen seconds. Ironically, when patients are permitted to speak until they finish, they generally stop talking

in about forty-five seconds, and the level of satisfaction is higher for both the patient and the physician. R. Shafir, *The Zen of Listening: Mindful Communication in an Age of Distraction* (Wheaton, IL: Quest Books, 2003), p. 152.

7   A. Wolvin and C. G. Coakley, *Listening*, 5th ed. (Chicago: Brown & Benchmark, 1996), p. 285.

8   P. Swets, *The Art of Talking So That People Will Listen* (Englewood Cliffs, NJ: Prentice-Hall, 1983), p. 41.

9   S. Minuchin, *Family Healing: Tales of Hope and Renewal from Family Therapy* (New York: Free Press, 1993), p. 64.

10 S. Culbert, *Mindset Management: The Heart of Leadership* (New York: Oxford University Press, 1996), p. 45.

11 C. Rogers, *On Becoming a Person* (Boston: Houghton Mifflin, 1961), p. 330.

12 J. Gottman, *Why Marriages Succeed or Fail and How You Can Make Yours Last* (New York: Simon & Schuster, 1995).

13 Reported in "Self-Esteem," an audio cassette tape, by Jack Canfield, 1984.

14 Reported in D. Tannen, *I Only Say This Because I Love You: Talking to Your Parents, Partner, Sibs, and Kids When You're All Adults* (New York: Ballantine Books, 2001), p. 201.

15 F. Wolff and N. Marsnik, *Perceptive Listening*, 2nd ed. (New York: Harcourt Brace Jovanovich College Publishers, 1992), p. 102. Emphasis is the authors'.

16 T. H. White, *In Search of History: A Personal Adventure* (New York: Warner Brothers, 1990), p. 498.

17 Cited by Professor J. Sterling Livingston of Harvard Business School, *Harvard Business Review* January–February 1971.

18 B. Franklin, *The Autobiography of Benjamin Franklin & Selections from His Writings* (New York: Random House, 1944), p. 225. Emphasis is the authors'.

CHAPTER 7

1   M. Maultsby, Jr., *Rational Behavior Therapy* (Appleton, WI: Rational Self Help Aids, 1990), p. 45.

2   S. Minuchin, *Family Healing: Strategies for Hope and Understanding* (New York: The Free Press, 1998), p. 226.

CHAPTER 8

1   A. Alda, in R. Maurer, *Why Don't You Want What I Want?* (Austin, TX: Bard Press, 2002).

2   M. S. Peck, *The Road Less Travelled: A New Psychology of Love, Traditional Values, and Spiritual Growth* (New York: Simon & Schuster, 1978), pp. 127–128.

3   G. Miller, "Thirteen Maxims for the Mind" quoted in P. Elbow, *Embracing Contraries: Explorations in Learning and Teaching*, (New York: Oxford University Press, 1986), p. 254.

4   D. Halberstam, *The Best and the Brightest* (New York: Penguin, 1983), pp. 126–127.

5   I. Janis, *Victims of Groupthink: A Psychological Study of Foreign-Policy Decisions and Fiascoes* (Boston: Houghton Mifflin, 1972), p. 138.

6   D. Halberstam, p. 164.

CHAPTER 10

1   S. Turkle, *Reclaiming Conversation: The Power of Talk in a Digital Age* (New York: Penguin, 2015), p. 44.

2   J. Gottman and C. Notarius, *A Couple's Guide to Communication* (Ottawa, Canada: Research Press, 1979), p. 149.

3   E. Atwater, *I Hear You: Listening Skills to Make You a Better Manager* (New York: Walker and Company, 1992), p. 21. This summarizes material in A. Ivey and J. Hinkle's unpublished manuscript, "The Transactional Classroom," University of Massachusetts, 1970.

4   J. Loehr, *Mental Toughness Training for Sports: Achieving Athletic Excellence* (New York: Stephen Greene Press, 1986), p. 181.

5   S. Minuchin and M. Nichols, *Family Healing: Tales of Hope and Renewal from Family Therapy* (New York: The Free Press, 1993), p. 83.

6   L. Chang, "What Is Phubbing and Is It Ruining Your Relationship?" *Digital Trends*, October 3, 2015.

7   M. Buber, *I and Thou*, tr. Ronald Gregor Smith (Edinburg: T. and T. Clark, 1937).

8   S. Turkle, p. 213. One researcher on multitasking wondered, "Why do people think they're so good at something that doesn't exist?"

9   E. Fromm, *Man for Himself: An Inquiry into the Psychology of Ethics* (New York: Fawcett, 1949), p.107.

10 P. Marsh, ed. *Eye to Eye: How People Interact* (Top Field, MA: Salem House, 1991).

11 M. Argyle, *Bodily Communication* (New York: International Universities Press, 1975), p. 229.

12 M. La France and C. Mayo, "Racial Differences in Gaze Behavior During Conversations: Two Systematic Observational Studies," *Journal of Personality and Social Psychology* 33 (1976): pp. 547–552. More examples of cultural and subcultural differences in attending behavior are noted in T. Thomlison, "Intercultural Listening" in M. Purdy and D. Borisoff, eds., *Listening in Everyday Life: A Personal and Professional Approach*, 2nd ed. (New York: University Press of America, 1997).

13 K. Horney quoted in R. Chessick, *The Technique and Practice of Listening in Intensive Psychotherapy* (Northvale, N J: Jason Aaronson, 1989), p. 46.

14 M. Goldsmith with M. Reiter, *What Got You Here Won't Get You There: How Successful People Become Even More Successful!* (New York: Hyperion, 2007), p. 149.

15 Technically speaking, a listener cannot totally avoid influencing the speaker's message. J. Greenspoon, "The Reinforcing Effects of Two Spoken Sounds on Two Responses." *American Journal of Psychology*, 1955, 68: pp. 409–416. However, as noted in Chapter 7, good listening influences a speaker by *enhancing* his effectiveness.

CHAPTER 11

1 W. Bennis and B. Nanus, *Leaders: Strategies for Taking Charge* (New York: Harper & Row, 1985), p. 96.

2 C. Webb, *How to Have a Good Day: Harness the Power of Behavioral Science to Transform Your Working Life*, (New York: Crown Business, 2016).

3 D. J. Boorstin, *The Creators: A History of Heroes of the Imagination* (New York: Vintage Books, 1963), p. 37.

4 D. Halberstam, *The Best and the Brightest* (New York: Penguin, 1986), p. 514.

5 J. Barber, ed., *Good Question: The Art of Asking Questions to Bring About Positive Change* (Great Britain, BookShaker.com, 2005), p. 238.

6 J. Drake, *Interviewing for Managers* (New York: Amacom, 1972), p. 76.

7 D. Leeds, *The 7 Powers of Questions: Secrets of Successful Communication in Life and at Work* (New York: Perigee, 2000), p. 101.

8   S. I. Hayakawa, "How to Attend a Conference." *ETC: A Review of General Semantics* 13, no. 1 (Autumn 1955): pp. 5–9.

9   W. Ury, *Getting Past No: Negotiating with Difficult People*, (New York: Bantam, 1991), pp. 70–71. Mike Wallace, formerly of the TV program, *60 Minutes*, liked to "ask a good question and let the answer hang there for two or three or four seconds more as though you are expecting more. You know what? They . . . give you more." J. Barber, p. 71.

10   D. McCullough and Jean Strauss, "The Unexpected Harry Truman" in W. Zinsser, ed., Extraordinary Lives: The Art and Craft of American Biography (Darby, PA: Dianne Publishing Company, 1986), p. 47.

11   A. Fontaine and W. Glavin, *The Art of Writing Nonfiction* (Syracuse, NY: Syracuse University Press, 1987), p. 48.

CHAPTER 12

1   P. Bottome, *Alfred Adler, A Biography*. (New York: G. P. Putnam's Sons, 1939), p. 69.

2   T. Fadem, *The Art of Asking: Ask Better Questions, Get Better Answers* (Upper Saddle River, NJ: Prentice Hall, 2009), p. 15.

3   D. Leeds, *Smart Questions: The Essential Strategy for Successful Managers* (New York: Berkley Books, 1987), p. 41.

4   *Businessweek*, May 3, 1999, pp. 142–143.

CHAPTER 13

1   S. Culbert, *Mind-Set Management: The Heart of Leadership* (New York: Oxford University Press, 1996).

2   M. S. Peck *The Road Less Travelled* (New York: Touchstone, Anniversary edition, 2003), p. 86.

3   B. Farber, *Making People Talk* (New York: Morrow, 1987), p. 98.

4   G. Goodman and G. Esterly, *The Talk Book* (Emmaus, PA: Rodale Press, 1988).

CHAPTER 14

1   M. Rosenberg, *Nonviolent Communication: A Language of Life*, 3rd ed. (Encinitas. CA: PuddleDancer Press, 2015), p. 96.

2   C. Rogers, *Carl Rogers on Personal Power* (New York: Delacorte, Press, 1977), pp. 38–39. Over time, Rogers came to be "more and more allergic to the term" (reflecting). "Although I am partially responsible for the use of the term," Rogers wrote, "I have, over the years, become very unhappy with it." He was reacting to the fact that this kind of listening was sometimes taught as a "wooden technique" rather than as a sensitive and genuine effort to empathize with another person. Some of Rogers's respected colleagues, like Harvard's John Schlien, agreed with these concerns but for practical reasons decided to continue using the term. C. Rogers, "Reflections of Feelings and Transference." *Person-Centered Review* 1, no. 4 (November 1986): p. 375. We're sympathetic to Rogers's point of view but continue to use the term "reflecting" because we're not aware of anyone coming up with a preferable substitute.

3   M. Rosenberg, p. 100.

CHAPTER 15

1   M. Twain, Introduction to *Mark Twain's Speeches*, ed. Albert Bigelow.

2   G. Goodman and G. Easterly, *The Talk Book: The Intimate Science of Communicating in Close Relationships* (Emmaus, PA: Rodale Press, 1988), pp. 147–148.

3   N. Kline, *Time to Think: Listening to Ignite the Human Mind* (London: Ward Lock, 1999), p. 51.

4   Z. Ziglar, *Courtship After Marriage* (Nashville, TN: Thomas Nelson, 1990), p. 123.

5   D. Leeds, *Smart Questions: A New Strategy for Successful Managers* (New York: McGraw-Hill, 1987), pp. 113–114.

6   Plutarch, *Plutarch's Moralia*, tr. F. C. Babbitt (Cambridge, MA: Harvard University Press, 1927), pp. 213–215.

7   T. Reik, *Listening with the Third Ear* (New York: Pyramid Books, 1948), pp. 124–126. Italics are the authors'.

8   W. Isaacs, *Dialogue and the Art of Thinking Together: A Pioneering Approach to Communicating in Business and in Life* (New York: Currency, 1999), p. 174.

CHAPTER 16

1   T. Lewis, *A General Theory of Love* (New York: Vintage Reprint Edition, 2001), p. 36.

2   R. W. Levinson, "Human Emotion: A Functional View," in P. Ekman and R. Davidson, eds, *The Nature of Emotion: Fundamental Questions* (New York: Oxford University Press, 1994), p. 123.

3   We find it interesting that *"feelings,"* as a word for emotions, made a late entry into the English language—in 1771. M. von Franz and J. Hillman, *Lectures on Jung's Typology* (Switzerland: Spring Publications, 1971), p. 78.

4   Here's how the noted behavioral neurologist Antonio Damasio, summed up the problem of defining *"emotion."* "Deciding what constitutes an emotion is not an easy task, and once you survey the whole range of possible phenomena, one does wonder if any sensible definition of emotion can be formulated, and if a single term remains useful to describe all these states. Others have struggled with the same problem and concluded that it is hopeless."

5   Antonio Damasio concurs. His experimental neuropsychological research shows that "certain aspects of the process of emotion and feeling are indispensable to rationality." *Descartes' Error: Emotion, Reason, and the Human Brain* (New York: Penguin Books, 2005), pp. xii–xiii and chap. 4. The brilliant French encyclopedist, Denis Diderot, anticipated this finding with his colorful statement: "There is a bit of the testicle at the bottom of our most sublime reasonings." D. Diderot, *Letter to Falconnet*, July 1767, cited in A. Comte-Sponville, *A Small Treatise on the Great Virtues*, tr. by C. Temerson (New York: Metropolitan Books, 2001), p.184.

6   W. Howell, *The Empathic Communicator* (Belmont, CA: Wadsworth, 1982), p. 105.

7   J. Wareham, *Secrets of a Corporate Headhunter* (New York: Athenaeum, 1980), p. 83. Italics in the original.

8   Proverbs 17:22, *The Holy Bible: Revised Standard Edition.*

9   D. Goleman, *Destructive Emotions: A Scientific Dialogue with the Dalai Lama* (New York: Bantam, 2004), p. 96.

10 G. E. Vaillant, *Triumphs of Experience: The Men of the Harvard Grant Study* (Cambridge, MA: London: Belknap Press of Harvard University Press, 2012), p. 126.

CHAPTER 17

1   M. Karlins in the Foreword in J. Navarro and M. Karlins, eds., *What Every BODY is Saying: An Ex-FBI Agent's Guide to Speed-Reading People* (New York: William Morrow, 2008).

2　D. Goleman, *Emotional Intelligence* (New York: Bantam, 1995), p. 97.

3　D. Dinkmeyer and L. Losoncy, *The Encouragement Book: Being a Positive Person* (New York: Simon & Schuster, 1992), p. 181.

4　A. L. McGinnis, *The Friendship Factor: How to Get Closer to the People You Care For* (Quezon City, Philippines: Kadena Press, 1991), p. 116.

5　St. Jerome, Letter 54.

6　Dr. Paul Ekman developed an hour-long DVD-based training program designed to teach people to read facial expressions better and distinguish real feelings from faked feelings. Ekman's interactive self-administered training program costs about $50. It can be ordered from his website (www.paulekman.com). As you've probably experienced, even without this type of training, you can gain valuable information about another person's feelings through facial expressions.

7　E. Hall, *The Silent Language* (Garden City, NY: Doubleday, 1959).

8　H. Ginott, *Between Parent and Child* (New York: Scribner, 1965), p. 34.

9　H. Ginott, p. 34.

CHAPTER 19

1　E. Jones, *The Life and Work of Sigmund Freud: Edited and Abridged in One Volume by Lionel Trilling and Steven Marcus* (New York: Basic Books, 1961), p. 253.

2　G. Egan, *The Skilled Helper: A Model for Systematic Helping and Interpersonal Relating* (Monterey, CA: Brooks Cole, 1975) p. 138.

3　Edgar Schein, who spent much of his career observing conversations and meetings. *Process Consultation: Its Role in Organizational Development, Volume I* (Reading, MA: Addison-Wesley, 1988), p. 67.

4　E. Nightingale, *Earl Nightingale's Greatest Discovery* (New York: Dodd, Mead, 1987), p. 146.

CHAPTER 21

1　R. Fisher and D. Shapiro, *Beyond Reason: Using Emotions as You Negotiate* (New York: Penguin, 2006), p. 32.

2　W. Ury, *The Power of a Positive No: Save the Deal, Save the Relationship, and Still Say No* (New York: Bantam, 2007), pp. 81, 83.

3 J. Dutton, *Energize Your Workplace: How to Create and Sustain High-Quality Connections at Work* (San Francisco: Jossey-Bass, 2003), p. 22.

4 G. Miller, "Thirteen Maxims for the Mind," quoted in P. Elbow, *Embracing Contraries: Explorations in Learning and Teaching* (New York: Oxford University Press, 1986), p. 254.

5 Many, like noted primatologist and ethologist Franz de Waal, believe animals have a similar capacity. Although your authors aren't scientists, we think de Waal makes a convincing case.

6 M. D. Lieberman, *Social: Why Our Brains Are Wired to Connect* (New York: Crown, 2013), p. 139.

7 P. Jackson and H. Delehanty, *Sacred Hoops: Spiritual Lessons of a Hardwood Warrior* (New York: Hachette, 1995), p. 53.

8 D. Burns, MD, *Feeling Good: The New Mood Therapy* (New York: Harper Reprint Edition, 2008), p. 166.

9 G. Thompson with J. Jenkins, *Verbal Judo: The Gentle Art of Persuasion* (New York: William Morrow, 2013).

10 J. Blight and J. Lang, *The Fog of War: Lessons from the Life of Robert S. McNamara* (Lanham, MD: Rowman & Littlefield, 2005).

11 R. Carkhuff, *The Art of Problem Solving: A Guide for Teachers, Counselors, and Administrators* (Amherst, MA: Human Development Press, 1973).

CHAPTER 22

1 J. G. Holland and B. F. Skinner, *The Analysis of Behavior: A Program of Self-Instruction* (New York: McGraw Hill College, 1961, p. 389. Quoted in C. Rogers, *Freedom to Learn*, Charles E. Merrill, 1969), p. 140.

2 K. Bell, *The Nuts and Bolts of Psychology for Swimmers* (Austin, TX: Keel Publishers, 1980), pp. 38–39.

3 M. Silberman assisted by Carol Auerbach, *Active Training: A Handbook of Techniques, Designs, Case Examples and Tips* (New York: Wiley, 2015), p. 6.

4 J. Barzun, *A Stroll with William James* (Chicago: University of Chicago Press, 1984), p. 76.

5 P. Bottome, *Alfred Adler: A Biography*, (New York: G. P. Putnam's Sons, 1939), p. 17. Freud and Jung were the other major founding fathers of psychology.

6   K. Gibran, *The Voice of the Master*, pt. 2, Ch. 8 (1960; reprint in *A Second Treasury of Kahlil Gibran*, tr. by Anthony Ferris, 1962).

APPENDIX

1   Judge Jim Gray, "It's a Gray Area: Making peace, even when in prison." Internet article.

INDEX